Meaning and Method
in Comparative Theology

Meaning and Method in Comparative Theology

Catherine Cornille

WILEY Blackwell

Registered Offices
111 River Street, Hoboken, NJ 07030, USA
John Wiley & Sons Ltd, The Atrium, Southern Gate, Chichester, West Sussex, PO19 8SQ, UK

Editorial Office
The Atrium, Southern Gate, Chichester, West Sussex, PO19 8SQ, UK

For details of our global editorial offices, customer services, and more information about Wiley products visit us at www.wiley.com.

Wiley also publishes its books in a variety of electronic formats and by print-on-demand. Some content that appears in standard print versions of this book may not be available in other formats.

Library of Congress Cataloging-in-Publication Data
Names: Cornille, C. (Catherine), author.
Title: Meaning and method in comparative theology / Catherine Cornille.
Description: First edition. | Hoboken : Wiley, 2019. | Includes
    bibliographical references and index. |
Identifiers: LCCN 2018056440 (print) | LCCN 2019005559 (ebook) | ISBN
    9781119535157 (AdobePDF) | ISBN 9781119535249 (ePub) | ISBN 9781119535225 (pbk)
Subjects: LCSH: Religion–Comparative studies. | Religion–Methodology.
Classification: LCC BL41 (ebook) | LCC BL41 .C625 2019 (print) | DDC
    202.01–dc23
LC record available at https://lccn.loc.gov/2018056440

Cover Design: Wiley
Cover Image: © CARACOLLA/Shutterstock

Set in 10/12pt Warnock by SPi Global, Pondicherry, India
Printed in Singapore by C.O.S. Printers Pte Ltd

10 9 8 7 6 5 4 3 2 1

For Wilfried Cornille, my father

Contents

Acknowledgments

The young discipline of comparative theology is taking shape through the combined effort of many scholars and students whose pioneering work has inspired and informed the theoretical models and methodological reflections presented in this book. Among the trailblazers of this academic field, I wish to thank in particular Francis Clooney, David Burrell, James Fredericks, Paul Knitter, Daniel Madigan, John Keenan, Klaus von Stosch and Joseph O'Leary, whose friendship and support, and fearless exploration of new ways of doing theology, have sustained and inspired me.

This book has grown out of years of teaching and introducing graduate students to the complex field of comparative theology. I want to thank the many students whose questions and comments have helped to shape and sharpen my thinking on the subject. Thanks in particular to my colleagues and students in comparative theology who participated in the year-long doctoral colloquium focusing on draft chapters of the book: John Makransky, Ruth Langer, James Morris, David Mozina, Natana DeLong-Bas, Michael VanZandt-Collins, Bethany Slater, Hans Harmakaputra, Katie Mylroie, Sam Zhia, Won-Jae Hur, and David Mayaan. Their critical and constructive feedback, arising not only from Christian, but also from Buddhist, Jewish, and Muslim approaches to comparative theology has been invaluable. The lively discussions during the seminars strengthen my hope that this book will stimulate critical reflection on some of the fundamental methodological questions in comparative theology and draw in theologians from any religious tradition engaged with the teachings and practices of any other tradition. A special thanks to David Mayaan for his careful and thoughtful editorial work. I am grateful also to Marianne Moyaert and Thierry-Marie Courau for reading selected chapters of the book and for their helpful comments.

Finally, I wish to thank my husband, Jeffrey Bloechl, and my children, Tessa, Nicholas and Julia, for filling my life with joy and meaning.

Introduction

Comparative theology forms an integral part of every religious and theological tradition. Throughout history, religions have developed their beliefs, practices, and overall sense of identity through a process of borrowing, refuting, and reinterpreting elements from other religious traditions. Any new religion builds on the materials of prior religions through a play of adoption and rejection that remains profoundly indebted to the other. And in the course of history, religions continue to consciously or unconsciously absorb ideas and practices of other religions even as they clash with one another or coexist in the same cultural sphere. As such, the reality of religious growth and change through engaging the teachings and practices of other religions is as old as the history of religions.

What is new about the modern discipline of comparative theology is the conscious, open, and systematic engagement of other religions in the process of theological development. While religious borrowing traditionally happened unwittingly or without revealing its source, comparative theology openly acknowledges and credits other religions as a possible repository for constructive theological insight and inspiration. This attitude of humility and generosity toward other religions is the result of both historical and theological developments, and of the remarkable scholarly advances in the study of religions in the course of the past century.

A synthesis of religious studies and theology, comparative theology draws from the methods of both disciplines. From the history and the comparative study of religions, it has inherited not only a vast amount of scholarly material, but also an understanding of the complexity and diversity of religious tradition and of the need to focus on particular texts, teachings or practices. It has also gained a keen awareness of the challenges and instability of applying "what the one thing shows me to the case of two things"[1] and of the fact that comparing religions is, as Kimberley Patton puts it, "like juggling torches; either we mishandle them and they will burn and wither us, or else our faces will begin to glow."[2] Comparative theologians are thus expected to engage in an in-depth study of another religion, of its languages and history in order to understand a particular religious text in its own historical and cultural context and in order to perform relevant and fruitful comparisons. Like theology, on the other hand, comparative theology is oriented to gaining not only greater understanding of a particular religious phenomenon, but of the ultimate reality and truth itself. It is thus an explicitly normative discipline that involves the comparison of religions from a faith perspective and/or for the purpose of advancing theological understanding.

Though the term theology may be seen to suggest a focus on teachings, texts, and purely speculative or philosophical understanding, comparative theology may be applied to ritual practices, ethical principles, spiritual practices, and institutional and artistic forms.[3] The absorption of elements from other religions on a popular level indeed generally occurs in the area of ritual practices, leaving speculative theology to the level of second order reflection. And artists are often at the forefront of comparative theological activity, expressing through sculptures, paintings or architecture a vision of reality which includes inspiration from various religious traditions and which may in turn become the basis for further reflection. To be sure, sacred texts form a relatively stable and accessible component of religious traditions, and often contain a blueprint or record of other forms of religious expression. They also tend to be more hermeneutically flexible and thus open to different interpretations within and across religious traditions. While it is thus not surprising that comparative theology often focuses on texts, it may involve any dimension of religions.

Though a relatively new discipline, comparative theology has taken different forms. Not only is there a natural diversity depending on the religions involved and the topics addressed, but even within one and the same religion, theologians have developed different conceptions of the nature and goal of the discipline. This is already reflected in the various definitions of comparative theology. While some emphasize the tradition-based or confessional origin and goal of comparative theology, others present it as a transreligious or meta-confessional discipline. David Tracy defines comparative theology as "any explicitly intellectual interpretation of a religious tradition that affords a central place to the fact of religious pluralism in the tradition's self-interpretation."[4] This broad definition attempts to avoid the particularity of the term "theology" while also including internal religious reflection on the very fact of religious plurality (often called "theology of religions"). Focusing more specifically on the actual process of comparison, Francis Clooney defines comparative theology as:

> acts of faith seeking understanding which are rooted in a particular faith tradition but which, from that foundation, venture into learning from one or more other faith traditions. This learning is done for the sake of fresh theological insights that are indebted to the newly encountered tradition/s as well as the home tradition.[5]

This classical definition emphasizes the confessional nature of comparative theology while pointing to the possibility for theological change and growth through learning from other religious traditions. The constructive dimension is also in evidence in James Fredericks's definition of comparative theology as "not only a revisionist but also a constructive project in which theologians interpret the meaning and truth of one tradition by making critical correlations with the classics of another religious tradition."[6]

While these definitions thus approach comparative theology from within the self-understanding of a particular religion, others seek to move beyond the boundaries of any particular religion. John Thatamanil describes comparative theology as engaging "specific texts, motifs and claims of particular traditions not only to understand better these traditions but also to *determine* the truth of theological matters through conversation and collaboration."[7] Whereas confessional comparative theologians might seek to *elucidate* the truth of their own traditions, religious truth is here considered more open-ended, to be *determined* in the process of comparative theological engagement. Thatamanil still emphasizes the relationship between theological reflection and practice when he states that "Comparative theology in its constructive dimension seeks to do what theology has done always and everywhere: guide and orient faithful practice, especially when practice assumes forms heretofore unseen."[8] Here, however, faithful practice may or may not be understood in terms of traditional religious communities.

Keith Ward draws a sharp contrast between confessional theology as "the exploration of a given revelation by one who wholly accepts that revelation and lives by it" and comparative theology as "theology not as a form of apologetics for a particular faith but as an intellectual discipline which enquires into ideas of the ultimate value and goal of human life, as they have been perceived and expressed in a variety of religious traditions."[9] Here, comparative theology thus draws from the teachings of various religious traditions without privileging or assuming the perspective of any one in particular. Perry Schmidt-Leukel speaks of interreligious theology as a process of reflecting on one's own tradition "in order to see what possible contribution might be made to the issues on the agenda of a global interreligious inquiry." He believes that "theology, instead of being an essentially denominational enterprise, will become increasingly interreligious."[10] In the same universalizing vein, Ram-Prasad Chakravarthi similarly conceives of comparative theology as "a global discourse beyond cultural hegemonies."[11] Though these comparative theologians still acknowledge a home tradition, and draw from the material of various religions, they thus seek to move beyond the confines of any particular tradition. Chapter 1 elaborates on this basic distinction between confessional and meta-confessional approaches to comparative theology.

There is an ongoing debate – at least among Christian comparative theologians – about the relationship between comparative theology and theology of religions, the latter referring to the religious conceptions of the status of other religions. While some argue that comparative theology should be conducted without prejudices as to the presence of truth in other religions, others insist that the very engagement with other religions already reflects an implicit theology of religions.[12] In Chapter 2, I will discuss various religious views of the status of other religions and their direct impact on the ways in which comparative theology is conducted.

Though comparative theology, like comparative religion, presupposes in-depth study of the other religion and an effort to understand the religious other on its own terms, it also is particularly attuned to the historical and cultural shaping of all understanding across religious and cultural borders, and to the hermeneutical shifts that occur when teachings from one tradition are brought into the framework of another. Chapter 3 discusses some of the particularities of comparative theological hermeneutics, and addresses the critiques of religious hegemony or domestication often leveled against comparative theology.

The ultimate goal of comparative theology involves "deep learning across religious borders."[13] This learning, however, may take different forms, ranging from the rediscovery of certain forgotten or neglected elements of one's own tradition, through the appropriation of relatively new teachings and practices, to the reaffirmation of one's own teachings or practices in light of the other. In Chapter 4, I identify and discuss six possible types of comparative theological learning.

Though a solitary and demanding theological pursuit, comparative theology, like all theology, is ultimately in the service of the truth and of the faith and understanding of others. This raises various questions, discussed in Chapter 5, regarding the relationship between comparative and confessional theology. What is the place of comparative theology among the other traditional disciplines of theology? How might the insights of comparative theologians become part of a broader process of theological discernment and reception? A fairly new discipline within theology, comparative theology still faces a number of methodological and procedural challenges which need to be addressed not only within the community of comparative theologians but also with other theologians and with the communities that are ultimately the beneficiaries of comparative theological efforts.

The book draws mainly on examples from Christian comparative theologians. This inevitably raises the question whether comparative theology is a distinctly Christian discipline and whether the methodological issues raised have any bearing on other religious traditions. It is true that the modern discipline of comparative theology has developed mainly in the context of Western and Christian academic theology. There are various reasons for this. Considering the number of Christian universities where theological teaching and research are being promoted and institutionally supported, it is not surprising that it is here that new avenues for theological reflection are being explored. It is also here that the discipline of religious studies has taken flight, with departments of theology in some cases becoming departments of religious studies, and the boundaries between the two disciplines at times fading or leading to new approaches to theology. The establishment of scholarly groups, PhD programs and academic positions in departments of theology has led to a further acceleration of this field of study within Christian institutions of learning.

But these practical circumstances do not address the more fundamental question of whether comparative theology is a uniquely Christian theological discipline. This question has been answered in different ways. Though Marianne Moyaert admits that it may be in theory possible to engage in comparative theology from within different religions traditions, she suggests that, at least in its current state, it is "Catholic/Christian through and through." She believes that this has to do with its textual focus and argues that "comparative theology would fare well through critical reflection on its own genealogy and how some of its Christian biases may limit this project when it comes to transfer to other traditions."[14] Though Klaus von Stosch admits that comparative theology is "grounded in the Western academic tradition" and that its focus is mainly on the rational understanding of the faith,[15] he sees no reason why Muslims should not "want and be able to participate in the project of comparative theology."[16] Reinhold Bernhardt states more unequivocally that comparative theology "is to be regarded as a method which can be applied to every religion. The method remains the same while the frame can change."[17]

Theologians from various religious traditions have indeed been actively engaged in comparative theology. The Buddhist scholar John Makransky, for example, has drawn from Christian social teaching in developing a more communal Buddhist understanding of liberation.[18] Amy-Jill Levine and Marc Brettler edited a Jewish commentary on the New Testament.[19] Anantanand

Rambachan and Ram-Prasad Chakravarthi both explicitly use the methods of comparative theology to develop Hindu Thought.[20] And Reza Shah-Kazemi has engaged in comparative theological dialogue from a Muslim perspective with both Buddhism and Christianity.[21] And a host of examples can be given of conscious or unconscious, spontaneous and deliberate forms of interreligious borrowing and learning. The systematic and constructive engagement with other religions is thus by no means a prerogative of the Christian tradition.

Insofar as comparative theologians situate themselves within a particular religious tradition, they will need to draw from their own religion the rationale and motivation for engaging constructively with other religious traditions. As Paul Griffiths points out,

> different communities of practice will have different methods of proceeding here. Muslims or Hindus or Buddhists who work as deep readers of alien texts or practices with a view to seeing what can be learned from them about the LORD have different constraints upon what they do and what they hope to learn from doing it than do Christian theologians in general, or Catholic theologians in particular.[22]

The reasons for learning from other religions as well as the types of learning may thus differ from one religion to the next. But most of the methodological questions and approaches discussed in this book apply to comparative theologians from any religious tradition. Even though the institutional structures may differ from one religion to the next, as well as within religions, the challenges of injecting comparative theology into the mainstream religious discourse and practice, and of reaching a broader community of faith are pertinent to all comparative theologians, regardless of their religious background and commitments.

Notes

1. Jonathan Z. Smith, "In Comparison a Magic Dwells," in *Imagining Religion: From Babylon to Jonestown* (Chicago: University of Chicago Press, 1982), 35.
2. Kimberley Patton, "Juggling Torches: Why We Still Need Comparative Religion," in *A Magic Still Dwells*, ed. K. Patton and B. Ray (Berkeley: University of California Press, 2000), 168.
3. See Marianne Moyaert and Joris Geldhof, eds., *Ritual Participation and Interreligious Dialogue* (London: Bloomsbury, 2015).
4. David Tracy, "Comparative Theology," in *Encyclopedia of Religion*, 2nd rev. ed., ed. L. Jones (Detroit: Macmillan Reference, 2005), 13: 9126.
5. Francis Clooney, *Comparative Theology: Deep Learning across Religious Borders* (Oxford: Wiley-Blackwell, 2010), 10.

6. James Fredericks, "Introduction," in *The New Comparative Theology*, ed. F. Clooney (New York: T&T Clark, 2010), x–xi.

7. John Thatamanil, *The Immanent Divine: God, Creation, and the Human Predicament* (Minneapolis: Fortress Press, 2006), 3, emphasis added.

8. Thatamanil, *The Immanent Divine*, 7.

9. Keith Ward, *Religion and Revelation* (Oxford: Clarendon Press, 1994), 40.

10. Perry Schmidt-Leukel, *Religious Pluralism and Interreligious Theology* (Maryknoll: Orbis Books, 2017), 8.

11. Ram-Prasad Chakravarthi, *Divine Self, Human Self: The Philosophy of Being in Two Gītā Commentaries* (London: Bloomsbury, 2013), xiii.

12. For a critical reflection on this debate, see Kristin Beise Kiblinger, "Relating Theology of Religions and Comparative Theology," in *The New Comparative Theology*, ed. F. Clooney (New York: T&T Clark, 2010), 21–42.

13. This is the subtitle of Francis Clooney's *Comparative Theology: Deep Learning across Religious Borders*, which he himself attributes to my colleague and Buddhist comparative theologian John Makransky.

14. Marianne Moyaert, "Response to Klaus von Stosch," *Studies in Interreligious Dialogue 24* (2014): 69.

15. Though Klaus von Stosch does not deny that people from other religions may practice their own form of comparative theology, he states that "it is especially suited to catholicity in the original sense of the term as well as to Catholic Christianity in particular." Klaus von Stosch, "Is Comparative Theology Catholic?" *Studies in Interreligious Dialogue 24* (2014): 59. He mentions in particular the Christian command to love one's neighbor, its conception of its own comprehensiveness and universality, its age-old openness to non-theological sources of knowledge (*loci alieni*) as resources for theological reflection, and its awareness of the contingency of its theological categories and insights.

16. Klaus von Stosch, "Understanding and Appreciation: A Reply to Marianne Moyaert," *Studies in Interreligious Dialogue 24* (2014): 75.

17. Reinhold Bernhardt, "Comparative Theology: Between Theology and Religious Studies," *Religions 3* (2012): 971.

18. See John Makransky, "A Buddhist Critique of, and Learning from, Christian Liberation Theology," *Theological Studies 75*, no. 3 (2014): 635–57.

19. Amy-Jill Levine and Marc Brettler, eds., *The Jewish Annotated New Testament: New Revised Standard Version Bible Translation (JANT)* (New York: Oxford University Press, 2011).

20. Anantanand Rambachan, A *Hindu Theology of Liberation* (New York: SUNY Press, 2014); Chakravarthi, *Divine Self, Human Self*.

21. Reza Shah-Kazemi, *Common Ground between Islam and Buddhism* (Louisville, KY: Fons Vitae, 2010); and "Light upon Light? The Qur'an and the Gospel of John," in *Interreligious Hermeneutics*, ed. C. Cornille and C. Conway (Eugene: Wipf & Stock, 2010), 116–48.

22. Paul Griffiths, "What Are Catholic Theologians Doing When They Do Comparative Theology?" *Studies in Interreligious Dialogue 24* (2014): 42.

1

Types of Comparative Theology

In the centuries since its first use – which has been traced back to 1700[1] – the term "comparative theology" has been used in various ways, or applied to different types of engagement with religious plurality. It has been put forth as a counterpart to apologetic approaches to other religions, as proto-comparative religion, as a means to develop a universal or world theology, and as a new form of constructive systematic theology. It may involve any two or more religions and any schools or denominations within larger traditions. There is thus a natural proliferation of different types and expressions of comparative theology.

In one of the early systematic discussions of the modern field of comparative theology, David Tracy developed a basic distinction between comparative theology as "a comparative enterprise within the secular study of the history of religions in which different 'theologies' from different traditions are being compared" and comparative theology as "a more strictly theological enterprise (sometimes named 'world theology' or 'global theology') which ordinarily studies not one tradition alone but two or more, compared on theological grounds."[2] Though the difference between the secular or historical and the normative or theological approaches to the discipline seems clear, there is in the actual practice of comparative theology often less of a marked differentiation between the two. Historians of religions have come to duly recognize their own normative biases, while comparative theologians at times refrain from explicit normative statements or conclusions.

There are, nevertheless, still important differences between historical and theological approaches to the comparison of religions. These differences are manifest in both the starting point and the goal of the comparativist. While the comparative theologian and the scholar of comparative religion alike may declare their particular historical and religious or other identity and location,

Meaning and Method in Comparative Theology, First Edition. Catherine Cornille.
© 2020 John Wiley & Sons Ltd. Published 2020 by John Wiley & Sons Ltd.

scholars in the history and comparative study of religions generally disclose their personal biases in order to minimize their impact. In contrast, comparative theologians fully embrace their religious presuppositions as constitutive of their work. Though recognizing the continuity between comparative theology and comparative religion, Reid Locklin and Hugh Nicholson highlight this important difference:

> Comparative theology can therefore be regarded less as an alternative to comparative religion, running alongside the latter in a parallel track, than as one of a range of critically self-conscious approaches to the study of religion after "religion," albeit with at least one important difference: whereas the recognition of normative commitment remains a methodological problem for most scholars in religious studies even today, it belongs to the very nature of the comparative theological project.[3]

In addition to its starting point, comparative theology is also distinguished from the comparative study of religion by its goal. While the scholar of comparative religion may be driven primarily by intellectual curiosity and the desire to understand a particular phenomenon in light of a larger whole, the comparative theologian seeks to deepen and advance theological truth. The ultimate goal of comparative theology thus involves comparison not for its own sake or only for the sake of greater scholarly insight, but for the purpose of enriching and enhancing the self-understanding of a particular religion, or theological truth more broadly conceived. While comparative religion is oriented to a deeper understanding of the nature of religion or the meaning of a particular religious idea or phenomenon, comparative theology is more interested in their meaningfulness or validity. It is this normative question which ultimately separates comparative theology from comparative religion.

Within the field of comparative theology itself, different types or approaches to comparative theology have developed rooted in varying conceptions of theology and of theological truth. While some view theology as a reflection on the faith and practice of a particular community, others view it more generically as a discourse on the gods, or as the study of divine realities. And while some conceive of theological truth as based on a body of revealed or received teachings and practices, others do not limit theological truth to any particular religion. I mark the difference between these two approaches by distinguishing between confessional and meta-confessional comparative theology. The term confessional is here thus used to denote a tradition-specific type of comparative theology. It may be practiced from within any religion and it is oriented to advancing the self-understanding of that particular tradition. Meta-confessional comparative theology, on the other hand, uses the teachings of different religious traditions to pursue a more encompassing or universal truth. The difference between confessional and meta-confessional comparative theology is at times only a matter of degree. Meta-confessional comparative theologians are often still shaped primarily by a particular religious tradition, and confessional comparative theologians often test and push the boundaries of the revealed teachings of a particular religion. But the two approaches still use slightly different methods that also warrant different nomenclatures.

Both confessional and meta-confessional comparative theology themselves arose from the checkered history of the comparative study of religions, and remain grounded in some of its basic methodological principles. The term comparative theology was originally used to designate an attempt at a more neutral and scientific approach of religious differences and as a counterpart to the apologetic and normative approaches to other religions. Adding to the confusion about terms is the occasional discrepancy between the stated and the actually apparent goals of the work of some comparative theologians. Whereas early forms of comparative theology claimed to offer a neutral and scientific comparison of religions while being in reality profoundly biased, more recent forms readily admit their normative and religious presuppositions without always drawing out the normative conclusions of their work. In basic terms, comparative theology involves comparing theologies from a normative starting point and/or with a normative goal.

1.1 Comparing Theologies

The origins of comparative theology and the comparative study of religions are intimately intertwined. Early attempts to develop a more historical and descriptive approach to other religions often used the term comparative theology to distinguish it from the explicitly normative and apologetic approaches to other religions. As Louis Jordan points out in his early history of comparative religion (1905), there was some debate among scholars about what to call the new science of religion. Historians of religions such as Friedrich Max Müller and James Freeman Clarke favored the term comparative theology, but since "the designation in question would cover only a part of the field which has to be surveyed" and since "it would limit inquiry to the purely dogmatic teaching of the several Faiths that chanced to be compared," it was decided that the designation comparative religion was "decidedly to be preferred to that of Comparative Theology."[4] Within this framework, comparative theology was thus to be seen as "only a department of Comparative Religion."[5] Clarke spoke of the "science of Comparative Theology" and stated that "It may be called a science, since it consists in the study of the facts of human history, and their relation to each other," adding that "It does not dogmatize: it observes."[6] He also took aim at Christian apologetics and its tendency to denigrate religious others, writing, "Comparative Theology, pursuing its impartial course as a positive science, will avoid the error into which most of the Christian apologists of the last century fell, in speaking of ethnic or heathen religions."[7]

Nevertheless, these early attempts at a neutral and scientific comparison of theologies were themselves infused with overt apologetic aims. When, in the middle of the nineteenth century, James Freeman Clarke wrote *Ten Great Religions: An Essay in Comparative Theology*[8] his intent was thus to offer a scientific and historical introduction to the different religions. His approach to different religions was based on the evolutionary theories of his time, and he complemented the historical, descriptive or "analytical" parts of his work with a "synthetic" part which:

> considers the adaptation of each system to every other, to determine its place, use and value in reference to universal or absolute religion. It must, therefore, examine the different religions to find wherein each is complete or defective, true or false; how each may supply the defects of the other, or prepare the way for a better; how each religion acts on the race which receives it, is adapted to that race, and to the region of the earth which it inhabits … It shows that both the positive and the negative side of a religion make it a preparation for a higher religion, and that the universal religion must root itself in the decaying soil of partial religions.[9]

Clarke ends each chapter with a comparison with Christianity, and states that whereas earlier apologists had attempted to "prove Christianity to be true," his approach would "show it to be true."[10] Clarke's work was thus from beginning to end informed by Christian faith and by the desire to demonstrate objectively the superiority of Christianity.

Max Müller's approach to the science of religion similarly contained a mixture of normative and non-normative notions. Though he is recognized as the father of the comparative study of religions, some of his views are unabashedly theological, and some of his comments might be seen as a blueprint for comparative theology. Like Clarke, he believed that the comparative study of religion would "give a new life to Christianity itself."[11] His interest in other religions was based on clearly religious foundations. "Every religion," he stated, "even the most imperfect and degraded, has something that ought to be sacred to us, for there is in all religions a secret yearning after the true, though unknown God."[12] And his description of the process of learning not only about but also from other religions captures the heart of comparative theology: "If we can teach something to the Brahmans in reading with them their sacred hymns, they too can teach us something in reading with us the Gospel of Christ."[13]

In *The Invention of World Religions*, Tomoko Masuzawa thus rightly takes issue with the pretensions of objectivity or neutrality of the pioneers of the comparative study of religions.[14] Drawing from examples of a number of nineteenth-century comparativists (Frederick Denison Maurice, James Freeman Clarke, John Caird, Charles Hardwick, John Wordsworth, and Frank Field Ellingwood), she points out that "what today's historians might consider an illicit collusion of interests – between the scientific and the evangelical – was unapologetically championed by numerous nineteenth-century comparativists."[15] Though twentieth-century historians of religion and scholars of comparative religion have attempted to approach the discipline from a more neutral or objective perspective, many, from Friedrich Heiler and Gerardus van der Leeuw to Joachim Wach and Mircea Eliade, have also been accused of being covert theologians, as their presuppositions, categories, and conclusions were thought to be inflected by religious presuppositions.[16] The work of Eliade has been widely scrutinized for its traces of Eastern Orthodox Christian theological motifs,[17] and Jonathan Smith laments that Eliade's integration of morphological and historical methods happened "at an extraordinary cost – by encompassing both within an onto-theological hierarchy."[18] Even the very attempts "to demarcate the science of religion from recognized forms of theological discourse" have been judged to "appear as moments within the larger liberal theological project of liberating the discourse on religion from dogmatism and exclusivism."[19] As such, most of the early history of the comparative study of religion might effectively be read as the history of comparative theology. Both disciplines ultimately emerged on different sides of the checkered attempts to engage the reality of religious diversity in a scholarly manner.

It may be somewhat misleading to trace the origins of the new comparative theology directly to the older use of the term, since its intention was to develop a scientific comparison of religions. However, in contrasting the old and the new usages of the term comparative theology, some of the distinctive features of comparative theology clearly come to the fore. While the comparative study of religions continues to pursue the goals of scholarly neutrality and scientific understanding, comparative theology has come to acknowledge and fully embrace its normative starting point and goal. The distinctiveness of what has come to be called the "new" comparative theology involves "an honest acknowledgment of its own normative commitments and interests as the principal means – paradoxically – of avoiding the kind of distortion and bias of its nineteenth-century predecessor."[20] Nicholson identifies three ways in which the new comparative theology differs from its old "namesake": its resistance to generalization, its attempt to understand the other religion on its own terms, and the acknowledgment of its own normative commitments. In contrast with the new comparative theology, Francis Clooney also states that "the older comparative theology seems, on the one hand, too comfortably immune to the complicated implications of what is learned, and on the other hand, too diffident about how a faith bravely vulnerable to scholarship might truly profit from the deep study of another tradition."[21]

Though the explicit normative starting point and/or goal of comparative theology distinguishes it from the comparative study of religions, and from the historical and scientific comparison of theologies, comparative theology is still steeped in the methods and materials of the comparative study of religions. One of the primary principles of comparative religions as well as of comparative theology involves generating accurate historical understanding of the other religion in its internal diversity and development. Though comparative theologians are keenly aware of the inevitable biases coloring their understanding of the other, they still attempt to enter into the self-understanding of the other and affirm its distinctiveness. In *Divine Mother, Blessed Mother*, Francis Clooney states that "We do well to learn to read along with readers in the traditions, so that our own persisting ways of reading can be assessed and critiqued in light of the interests and interpretations of these respected traditional readers."[22] And in his Christian commentary on the Three Holy Mantras of the Śrīvaiṣṇava Hindus, *The Truth, the Way, the Life*, he delves deeply into important Hindu commentaries on the text before advancing his own Christian resonances and reflections.[23]

Like historians of religion and scholars of comparative religion, comparative theologians have come to narrow the focus of their comparison. While earlier comparative work sought to draw insight from the comparison of massive amounts of material on a variety of different topics, comparative scholarship today focuses on discrete phenomena in a limited number of traditions. In *Religion in Essence and Manifestation* (originally published in 1933), Gerardus van der Leeuw attempted to cover most of the important religious topics in all of the religions known by him,[24] and in *The Myth of the Eternal Return*, Mircea Eliade similarly drew from a vast number of oral as well as scriptural traditions to develop his theory on the role of cosmogonic myths in the history of religions.[25] By contrast, in her work in the comparative study of religions, Wendy Doniger dedicates an entire volume to the theme of "splitting" or creating a double in Greek and Hindu myths,[26] while Kimberley Patton engages in comparative work in order to make sense of images on Attic Greek vases of gods offering libations.[27] Similarly, Francis Clooney's work in comparative theology focuses on specific themes in the work of particular

Christian and Hindu texts, such as the theme of surrender in the works of the Christian Francis of Sales and in the text of the Hindu Vedānta Deśika, or on a limited number of devotional texts dedicated to feminine expressions of the divine in *Divine Mother, Blessed Mother.*[28] In discussing human nature and the relationship between the transcendent and immanent realities in Christianity and Hinduism, John Thatamanil focuses in particular on Paul Tillich and Shankara, and Michelle Voss Roberts limits herself to Mechthild of Magdeburg and Lalleśwarī of Kashmir in teasing out the theme of fluidity in the relationship between the human and the divine.[29]

This focused approach to comparative theology is a way to overcome generalities. With regard to his comparison of the Virgin Mary and Hindu Goddesses, Clooney states: "Experiments in careful and comparative reading also help us to avoid essentializing the problem and solution, as if there is any unitary problem such as patriarchy or any unitary meaning for words such as 'goddess' or 'human' or even 'mother.'"[30] It also allows the theologian or the comparativist to gain reasonable control of the material and to preserve a certain scholarly accountability and respectability. One of the challenges for all comparative work is that of mastering two religious traditions and avoiding superficiality or amateurishness. The focus on a relatively limited body of materials in two traditions goes a long way toward addressing these concerns. However, comparative theologians, like scholars of comparative religion, still need to account for the meaning of particular texts, teachings, and practices in the broader tradition and in its own reception history. The drawback of focusing on ever more detailed or narrow aspects of particular religions in comparative work may be its diminished relevance or impact, and the difficulty of inserting the work within broader intellectual or theological discussions.[31]

As is the case with the comparative study of religions, comparative theology proceeds by way of generating a *tertium comparationis*,[32] or what Robert Neville and Wesley Wildman have called "vague comparative category" as the basis for comparison.[33] It represents a bridge between the traditions which allows both similarities and differences to appear. It may be derived from one or the other tradition, but is then abstracted or neutralized in order to form a generalized category applicable to different traditions. As such, while "bat mitzvah" represents a distinctly Jewish category, "girl's puberty rite of passage" might represent the comparative category, and while "the dark night of the soul" might be a Christian concept, "mystical drought" might be the more generalized concept. Much has been made in the field of comparative religion about the nature and the bias of these vague categories.[34] Since they are generally derived from a particular tradition, they might be seen to color the perception of the other religion by imposing a particular alien focus or distorting the material. Neville and Wildman therefore caution that "a vague comparative category ought to be vulnerable to correction through the discovery that aspects of the ideas being compared by means of it do not fit within its scope."[35] In his discussion in *Beyond Compare: St. Francis de Sales and Śrī Vedānta Deśika on Loving Surrender to God*, Francis Clooney states that the expression "loving surrender" "is found explicitly in neither text."[36] It is a theme that permeates both texts and that is expressed through images and analogues.

The religious origin or bias of certain comparative categories may represent less of a methodological challenge for comparative theology than for the comparative study of religion. In the former it is generally acknowledged that the comparative quest arises from a particular religious tradition and with particular theological interest. Comparative theologians must of course also develop comparative categories that allow them to probe the proper analogues in another tradition. But comparative theology does not engage in comparison for its own sake, or only for the sake of greater scholarly understanding, but in order to gain deeper understanding of a topic of religious interest to the theologian. The difference with the comparative study of religions may not always be obvious or pronounced. After all, the commitment of the scholar of comparative religions to engage in a prolonged comparative effort is also often based on a profound personal interest in the material. Yet comparative theologians might also feel called to tackle some of the broader theological questions of their respective traditions. It is thus not surprising that the *tertium comparationis* in comparative theology is often shaped and informed by the tradition of the comparative theologian.

While comparative theologians may use vague comparative categories as a bridge into other religions, some focus theological reflection on the vague categories themselves. Thus, in the Comparative Religious Ideas project, comparative theologians Robert Neville and Wesley Wildman attempt to develop more overarching theories on the very categories of "ultimate reality," "the human condition," and "religious truth," based on the materials harnessed from different religious traditions.[37] This approach may be seen to exhibit more affinity with classical comparative religion or with philosophy of religion.[38] The beliefs and insights of the various religious traditions are used as preliminary to the philosophical work, which is arguably ultimately the focus and goal. Neville indeed defines comparative theology "in terms of its subject matter, not in terms of the antecedent theological commitment of the comparativists."[39]

Comparative theology, like the comparative study of religions, focuses on both the similarities and the differences between the objects compared. Whereas in the case of comparative religion, similarities may shed new interpretive light on the nature and function of a particular phenomenon, in the case of comparative theology, it may cure a religion of its sense of uniqueness, while also reinforcing the truth or validity of a particular religious idea or practice. As Clooney puts it, the purpose of comparative theology is for theologians to become "professionally aware that the details of their own theological traditions are more often than not shared with the theologies of other religious traditions."[40] Differences, on the other hand, shed light on the particularity of certain religions, which may also serve purely intellectual or normative interests. From a normative perspective, they may lead to a reappraisal of the distinctive truth of one's own tradition, or to a process of learning something new from the other religion. Though comparing theologies and texts with a focus on similarities and differences may seem clear-cut, Clooney points out that the difficulty of this type of comparative theology lies in knowing "what to do with these similarities and differences once they are identified, how to decide which ones matter more, and how to determine which are the significant questions raised by them."[41] In his own work, Clooney focuses mainly on drawing attention to the similarities and differences. After a close and detailed comparison of the Virgin Mary and Hindu goddesses, for example, he notes a series of similarities in that "they are all honored as persons with bodies, as mothers, as defined in relation to the males in their lives but also as possessed of their own power, and as willing to get involved in human affairs in particular ways that male divinities do not rival."[42] The comparison, however, also sheds new light on the particular status of Mary as not-God:

> As not-God, Mary is entirely here, all the more powerfully present. She combines the material and spiritual in a way most analogous to the portrayals of the divine feminine in our three Hindu hymns. The "not" in "not-God" is productive in the construction of Mary as a focus of veneration, as the miraculous person in whom the divine is suddenly present.[43]

These comparative insights may be understood in either historical or comparative theological terms. Clooney himself does not tend to draw normative or comparative theological conclusions from his comparative work. He certainly does not suggest that Christians should worship Hindu goddesses, nor does he seek to argue or conclude from his study of Hindu and Christian conceptions of God that "Jesus is God and Siva is not God."[44] But neither does he elaborate on the implications of his comparative insights for Christian theology. This he leaves to his readers or to other theologians.

Clooney's approach to comparative theology may thus be typified as a comparison of theologies. It provides an immense service to comparative theology in that it models an expert and patient study, and a careful and detailed comparison of ideas and texts. However, since Clooney does explicitly identify himself as a Catholic theologian in all of his books, his work may thus also be considered as an example of confessional comparative theology.

The difference between comparative theology and the comparative study of religions is at times thin, or not always clear-cut. In the Comparative Religious Ideas project, Neville and Wildman emphasize the "primacy of *cognition* in comparing religious ideas"[45] and they ground their approach in careful methodological considerations which include a systematic effort to "avoid imposing biases"[46] on the comparative categories themselves and on their application. All of this indeed represents sage advice for both comparative theology and the comparative study of religions. However, if comparative theology is defined "not by the theological commitments of the comparativist but by the subject matter, religious or theological ideas and how they are well studied,"[47] then there is little to distinguish comparative theology from the comparative study of religions. Nevertheless, Neville himself also wants his comparative theology "to aim at theological truth."[48] His work may thus also be considered as an example of meta-confessional comparative theology.

1.2   Confessional Comparative Theology

Confessional comparative theology involves a process of engaging in constructive theological reflection with other religions from within the religious framework of a particular religious tradition. This tradition provides the impetus, the theological questions or problems to be probed, and the guiding norms for discerning truth in other religions. It also represents the ultimate goal and arbiter of the comparative theological work. Theology is here thus understood as reflection on the faith and practice of a particular religious community, and comparative theology is done at the service of that community.

The confessional approach to comparative theology manifests itself in four principal ways: in the avowedly religious identity of the comparative theologian, in the choice of topics, the criteria of discernment, and the stated goal of the comparative theological exercise. We will examine each of these in turn. Thus, when Francis Clooney compares St. Francis de Sales and Śrī Vedānta Deśika on loving surrender to God, or the biblical Song of Songs with the Tamil Holy Word of Mouth on divine absence and longing, readers presume and accept the fact that he approaches these texts as a member of the Society of Jesus and as a Roman Catholic theologian. Especially in his earlier works, Clooney is very explicit about his own religious and intellectual starting point and location. In *Theology after Vedānta*, he states: "Theology, to characterize it in a non-technical fashion, is distinct from the study of religion (with which it overlaps in many of its procedures) because theology is an inquiry carried on by believers who allow their belief to remain an explicit and influential factor in their research, analysis and writing."[49] Though he immersed himself as much as possible in the traditions and texts he was studying, Clooney states in *Seeing through Texts*:

> I was always quite open about the fact that while I came with a determination to be more than a spectator and was seeking earnestly to step back from my presuppositions about what I was hearing and seeing, I nevertheless remained always a Jesuit, a Roman Catholic priest who was also helping out on Sunday mornings in a large urban parish.[50]

In *Hindu God, Christian God*, he acknowledges that "I write from within the Christian tradition and from a Christian perspective."[51] This firm commitment and grounding continues into his most recent work, *His Hiding Place Is Darkness*, where he proclaims: "To love deeply and affirm deep truths in a world where many loves flourish in the particular, we need first of all to be grounded in the specificity and particularity of our own enduring love – for this author, in Jesus Christ."[52] In confessing their religious starting point, confessional comparative theologians seek to fully utilize it in various stages of the comparative exercise.

This religious starting point of the comparative theologian plays a role in the first place in the choice of texts and topics to be compared. All comparative theology involves some degree of arbitrariness. Not only are there numerous religious traditions, but each religion has a multitude of texts, teachings, practices, and artistic expressions which might become the object of comparison. For a confessional comparative theologian, the choice of another religion will likely have to do with a combination of exposure and appeal. Comparative theologians may be drawn to a particular element in another tradition by their personal religious quest, by more theoretical questions, or by way of the social and historical importance of a particular idea or practice. But in the case of confessional comparative theology, each of these will be shaped by the religious background of the theologian.

James Fredericks describes the process of choosing a focus for comparison as happening "dialectically":

> Comparison begins with the critical study of another religion, sometimes by means of the reading of classic texts, sometimes by means of personal dialogue with the practitioners of the other religious paths, and optimally by taking both

routes. The conversation with the other tradition eventually becomes a conversation within the home tradition in which its classic texts, art, rituals, ascetic practices, etc. are reinterpreted in light of the other tradition. The critical correlations established in the work of comparison can be positive or negative – sometimes the correlation will be a recognition of similarity, sometimes of difference.[53]

Comparison usually begins with the recognition of striking similarities with the theologian's home tradition. It is the awareness of similarities between the role of Amida in Pure Land Buddhism and Jesus Christ in Christianity that led several Christian theologians (Karl Barth, Henri de Lubac, John Cobb) to engage in comparative theological reflection on its meaning for Christian faith.[54] And David Burrell's work on the relationship between medieval Jewish, Christian, and Muslim thinkers is also inspired by the similarities in their notions of creation and freedom.[55]

Most of Francis Clooney's comparative theological work is based on some form of "recognition" of close parallels to Christian theological themes in Hindu texts and a subsequent focus on an analogous Christian text for the purpose of comparison.[56] Thus, in *Beyond Compare*, he notes: "After reading Deśika's *Essence*, I considered a number of possible analogues in my own tradition and found in the *Treatise* a Catholic text that promised to read well with and in light of the *Essence*."[57] It is thus often the experience of being touched or inspired by elements from another tradition that leads to a search for analogues or regrounding in the home tradition. In the end, however, Clooney, like other confessional comparative theologians, frames the comparative endeavor from within his own tradition. "Not only have I begun my chapters with Christian theologians," he states, "but I frame the questions and discover the answers that fit nicely into the categories and expectations of the Christian theological tradition."[58]

The series Christian Commentaries on Non-Christian Sacred Texts illustrates the dialectical process involved in the choice of material for comparative theological engagement.[59] The authors are drawn to a particular text partly due to their religious background and predispositions. But the text from the other tradition in turn brings them back to their own tradition and to a recovery or reinterpretation of their own texts or ideas in light of the other. In his Christian commentary on the Hindu *Nārada Sūtras*, Daniel Sheridan speaks of the sacred texts of other religions as "catalysts" which

can help to grasp afresh our own tradition and to make it our own in a way adequate to the demands and challenges of the modern culture that we live in. The catalyst will function to reinvigorate our imaginations and our enthusiasm, to re-stimulate our jaded perception of the beauty of God so that we may respond with our whole heart, soul, mind and strength to the lovable and personal reality of God.[60]

As is evident in the Christian commentaries on the Bhagavad Gītā, one and the same text may draw comparisons with any number of Christian texts and thinkers, from the *Spiritual Exercises* of St. Ignatius to the *Book of Common Prayer*, and from the Patristic theologian Evagrius Ponticus to the modern mystic Simone Weil. The very diversity of possible texts and topics for fruitful comparative theological reflection may raise the specter of arbitrariness but also suggests the endless potential of comparative theology.

The choice of material for comparative theology may also arise from pressing theological questions and challenges in the home tradition. The confrontation with certain existential or theological problems may lead to inquiry into how the same questions have been dealt with in another tradition, and what one may learn from this. The Buddhist thinker Masao Abe, for example, was mainly interested in Christianity in order to learn from the ways in which this tradition had tackled the questions of secularization or "the problem of religion and irreligion."[61] And Christian comparative theologians such as Henri Le Saux, Raimon Panikkar, John Keenan, Joseph O'Leary, John Thatamanil, and Michelle Voss Roberts have all turned to Hinduism or Buddhism to deal with some of the intractable problems of Christian dualistic metaphysics.[62] Besides these large theological questions, comparative theologians may also look to other traditions to address concrete social and ethical questions such as economic injustice or ecological devastation.[63] Thus, Laurenti Magesa and other African Christian theologians have drawn from the communitarian approach of traditional African religions to garner a greater sense of solidarity and sufficiency in Christian approaches to economic development and ecological awareness.[64]

In his work on the problem of moral struggle in Christianity and Buddhism through a comparative theological engagement of Bonaventure and Buddhaghosa, David Clairmont argues that "every potentially transformative inter-religious encounter is based, at least to some degree, on mutual acknowledgment of personal weakness and struggle (both moral and intellectual), and as such presupposes that religious traditions carry through time, in multiform exemplars and sustained arguments, tentative answers to fundamental human questions which few if any individual religious persons ever fully answer or embody."[65] It is thus an experience of moral failure or powerlessness that here drives the comparative theological exercise. Among the various reasons for engaging in comparative work (facilitative, persuasive, dialectical, and reconstructive), Clairmont focuses in particular on the "transformative rationale" which "seeks through its work to bring religious communities to more acute sensitivities to their own past moral failures and future possibilities, precisely through the process of comparison that emphasizes mutual moral transformation within strong religious difference."[66] The transformation here envisaged has less to do with new constructive ethical proposals or with religious change, but rather with a return to one's "own tradition with new approaches to reading its resources gathered through the comparative study, balancing attention to real and irreconcilable diversity of life with a hope that visions of what is good and fitting for human life are not ultimately incommensurable."[67]

In these confessional approaches to comparative theology, the home tradition thus represents the starting point or the point of reference in engaging the other religion. It determines not only the focus for comparison but also the relative importance of certain similarities and differences. Though the other tradition is treated with openness and respect, each tradition thus approaches the other with its own theological questions.

A second characteristic of a confessional approach to comparative theology is the use of criteria of discernment derived from one's own religious tradition. For believers or members of a particular religion, all truth is ultimately derived from the core texts, teachings, and practices of that tradition. Hence, these will inevitably play a role in judging the truth or validity of other religions.

Though the general principle of relying on religion-specific criteria in confessional comparative theology may be clear and evident, the actual identification and application of such criteria is more complicated. Every religion is based on a whole range of normative truth claims that are expressed in narrative, precepts, and doctrines, and it is not always easy to determine a clear hierarchy of norms, or which principles or criteria apply to a particular instance of discernment. The normative criteria of a tradition may moreover themselves shift and develop through time, as the interpretation of certain texts may change in response to historical and social developments.

The complexity of identifying clear criteria of discernment within any religious tradition is evident in the volume *Criteria of Discernment in Interreligious Dialogue*, where theologians from different religions reflect on their own religious principles and processes of discernment.[68] Theologians from the same tradition may emphasize different general criteria, while certain criteria may at times overlap in different religions. In his discussion of criteria of moral discernment in the Jewish tradition, David Elcott also points to the general "messiness of moral deliberation."[69] Though the prohibition against idolatry and the Decalogue represents a constant and central criterion in the Jewish tradition, he doubts that there are any other criteria which would be accepted as normative in all contemporary varieties of Judaism. In reflecting on Christian criteria of discernment, Reinhold Bernhardt states that he finds these principles "not in the first instance in propositional beliefs about Jesus Christ but in the foundational attitudes Jesus Christ proclaimed to be essential for the God-relationship and that thus have become essential for Christian faith at the existential level."[70] He identifies in particular transcendence, freedom, agape, and responsibility. Gavin D'Costa, for his part, focuses more on Jesus's unconditional love and self-sacrifice as a criterion for assessing the truth of another religion or religious practice.[71] Perry Schmidt-Leukel also uses this criterion of self-negating love for recognizing validity and truth in the Mahāyāna Buddhist notion of the Bodhisattva (and vice versa, for Buddhists to recognize elements of truth in the person and example of Jesus Christ).[72] Besides texts and founding figures, comparative theologians may also turn to the example of saints or leaders as guides in the process of interreligious discernment.[73]

In addition to the criteria themselves, it is not always clear how and by whom the process of discernment is to take place, or who becomes the ultimate arbiter of truth. Some traditions may refer to a highest teaching authority or else the reception of the community as the final authority. But any integration of new ideas or practices within a particular tradition is generally a slow process and the result of various factors. In the case of confessional comparative theology, discernment may at least start with comparative theologians belonging to the same tradition,[74] and lead to a broader dialogue with other theologians and with the religious community at large.

Even though the idea of the normativity of one's own tradition does not provide a clear and ready answer to the questions of interreligious discernment, it is the intention to judge the other tradition not on the basis of one's own personal or subjective views, but in accord with the given teachings of a tradition that characterizes the confessional approach to comparative theology. The use of religion-specific criteria of truth does not necessarily presuppose belief in the uniqueness and superiority of these criteria above those of any other religious tradition. A good number of criteria of discernment are in fact shared by numerous religious traditions. And resorting to the revealed norms of a particular tradition may be regarded as an expression of humble recognition that from a position of faith one cannot but understand and assess the teachings and practices of another from within the contours of one's own tradition. Additionally, it may be regarded as an expression of respect for the other insofar as only the use of criteria derived from one religion with its own history of revelation and collective discernment would be equal to the task of discerning truth in another.

The third distinctive characteristic of confessional comparative theology relates to its goal, which involves contributing to theological reflection within a particular religious tradition. Confessional comparative theology seeks to deepen, enrich, enhance, or critique the teachings and practices of a given religion without questioning or going beyond its basic beliefs and religious presuppositions. This, of course, sets certain limits to the possibilities of comparative theology. It does not entertain religious questions or practices that have no relevance for the religion seeking to learn from the comparative exercise. And it does not consider the possibility of discovering truth that would fundamentally exceed or clash with the contours of that tradition. But in focusing on a particular tradition, it aims at ultimately enriching the lives of all those who belong to that religion. In the process of attempting to enrich a particular religious tradition, the confessional comparative theologian thus remains mindful of the particular community of believers for whom he or she develops his or her theological thinking. In his comparative theological engagement with Hindu conceptions of God, Clooney maintains that he seeks "to develop plausible views on God's existence, character, embodiment, and revelation in a way that is recognizable to Christians and able to be affirmed by Christians."[75] Elsewhere, he also emphasizes that comparative theology "needs to remain in living connection with the tradition and faith experience of particular communities, which must be convinced that a comparativist's work is actually theological … Accordingly, we have to continue using tradition-specific theological language in setting up and working out our comparisons, as we 'read from' and 'write for' communities with specific theological cultures."[76] And with regard to his particular focus on moral struggle, Clairmont states that "one who adopts a theological perspective in a comparative conversation is committed to keeping the person who believes in the wisdom of a tradition, despite her or his doubts and inability to live by that tradition's moral judgments, at the center of comparative investigation."[77] Though this does not mean that all comparative theological thinking has to be immediately understood by or translated for people in the pew, it does mean that they are never far from the theologian's mind and remain as ultimate recipients of the comparative theological effort.

Essential to confessional comparative theology is thus its sense of accountability to a larger theological and religious community. Though the work of comparative theology is often solitary, involving demanding scholarly engagement with the other tradition, it is open to critical reflection by scholars from the other tradition, by fellow comparative theologians, and by the broader theological and religious community. This communal approach to comparative theology may be more easily achieved in some traditions than in others. Some religions may have more developed institutional structures which allow for the theological vetting of ideas, and which support theological experimentation. But institutions may also be more conservative and resistant to change. Comparative theologians may themselves also become torn between religions, or develop some degree of hybrid religious identity which may come to lessen concern with the orthodoxy or orthopraxis of any particular religion. Confessional comparative theology thus requires mutual commitment and openness on the part of the theologian as well as the tradition it seeks to serve.

The question of the confessional identity of the theologian and the confessional boundaries of a tradition presents itself of course differently from one tradition to the next. Each religion has its own approach to initiation and sets its own parameters of membership and belonging. While some may be well-defined and stringent, others may be more vague and flexible, and while some religions attach great importance to orthodoxy, others might be more focused on orthopraxis. As such, the negotiation of confessional boundaries may differ significantly for comparative theologians from different religious traditions.

1.3 Meta-Confessional Comparative Theology

While comparative theology may be firmly anchored in a particular tradition, it may also be approached as essentially unconstrained by the doctrinal or ritual constraints of any particular tradition. This type of comparative theology has been called interreligious theology,[78] transreligious theology,[79] or interstitial theology.[80] I here use the term meta-confessional theology to point to both the continuity and discontinuity with confessional theology. It still uses the theological insights of different religions or confessional traditions in order to attain to religious truth that is not limited to any one religion. For J. R. Hustwit, transreligious theology indeed "involves a theologian encountering the other and, rather than applying the fruits of that encounter to her own tradition, proceeds in a process of collaborative inquiry that transgresses the boundaries of what can be accommodated by the tradition. Coherence with any particular tradition is not strictly necessary."[81]

Proponents of this type of comparative theology often draw inspiration from Wilfred Cantwell Smith, the famous historian of religions and founder of the Harvard Center for the Study of World Religions. In his *Towards a World Theology*, he seeks to develop what he calls a "Theology of Comparative Religion" in which "the material on the basis of which a theological interpretation shall be proffered, of the world, man, the truth, and of salvation – of God and His dealings with His world – is to be the material that the study of the history of religion provides."[82] By drawing a distinction between a universal experience of "faith" and particular "cumulative traditions,"[83] he sought to develop a "theology of the faith of man" which "when constructed, should be acceptable to, even cogent for, all humankind."[84]

This meta-confessional approach to comparative theology has found a home in the "theology without walls" scholarly group and forum and in the *Open Theology* journal. Jerry Martin, one of its pioneers, presents transreligious theology or theology without walls as an alternative to comparative theology. While the latter "looks beyond their traditions, but keeps intact sufficient elements to provide compasses and rudders," he sees transreligious theology as a way "to go further and to consider the total spiritual resources of humankind, every source of revelation and enlightenment and insight anew, without dragging our traditional anchors behind us."[85] Wesley Wildman also agrees that, though transreligious theology has its roots in confessional comparative theology, it should be clearly distinguished from the confessional orientation of the latter.[86] Though he recognizes the necessity of religious traditions to nourish transreligious theology at this stage, he also envisions a state beyond such dependency when "its parasitic relationship with positive religious traditions falls away." He describes that type of theology as a "postreligious theology, or nonreligious theology – that is, theology that makes intellectual sense with no specific religious tradition at its root and remains socially viable with no living religious institution for support."[87] Wildman is especially concerned with the place of theology in the secular academy and with the need to divest it from any sectarian basis or biases while still allowing for the "highest level thinking about ultimate reality and the human condition."[88] Thatamanil defines transreligious theology as "the quest for interreligious wisdom," and as "constructive theology done in conversation with and drawing from the resources of more than one tradition."[89] Unlike confessional comparative theology, transreligious theology does not "make a neat and singular point of origin or mode of religious belonging normative for transreligious theology."[90] Perry Schmidt-Leukel uses the term interreligious theology and defines it as "that type of doing theology that reflects on the major issues of human life by drawing on insights from more than one religious tradition."[91] The goal of such theological exercise is again not so much the furthering of any particular theological tradition, but the development of a "World Theology," a "Global Theology," or a "Universal Theology."[92]

The main difference between confessional and meta-confessional comparative theology thus lies in its conception of religious truth. Whereas confessional comparative theology accedes to the conception of truth developed in a particular religion, meta-confessional comparative theology starts from a more open-ended and undefined conception of religious truth as not limited to the normative teachings of any one religion, and thus requiring "conversation and collaboration" between religions.[93] Thatamanil here adheres to Gordon Kaufman's dynamic and dialogical understanding of truth as always "in the process of becoming" and as "emerging (quite unexpectedly) in the course of conversation."[94] Meta-confessional comparative theologians thus consider their approach to truth to be more universal or encompassing than that of confessional comparative theology. Robert Neville argues that "commitments to certain ideas as true, for us comparative theologians, should come at the end of the inquiry, not the beginning."[95] Rather than "faith seeking understanding," he thus views his approach to comparative theology as "understanding seeking faith."[96] Meta-confessional comparative theology thus moves toward a philosophical, rather than a traditional, theological understanding of truth. Neville acknowledges that "my theology is a systematic philosophical theology that I turn back on the comparative base to line up new comparative perspectives to investigate."[97] In a similar vein, Raimon Panikkar speaks of his approach as "imparative philosophy" involving an "open philosophical attitude ready to learn from whatever philosophical corner of the world, but without claiming to compare philosophies from an objective, neutral and transcendent vantage point."[98] His "diatopical hermeneutics" also moves away from identification with one specific tradition toward an attempt to speak a more universal language: "I am attempting to speak a language that will make sense for the followers of more than one philosophical tradition – a risky task perhaps, but necessary if one is to do justice to a cross-cultural investigation."[99]

While confessional comparative theologians are consciously grounded in a particular religious tradition, meta-confessional comparative theologians often identify with more than one religious tradition. The phenomenon of religious hybridity, multiple religious belonging or spiritual fluidity has become more widespread in society at large as individuals have ready access to the teachings and practices of many religious traditions.[100] Theologians steeped in the study of one or more other religious traditions may also find themselves torn between religions, or drawing from the teachings of different religions without privileging any one, in the process of forming their own theological views. While some experience this as a source of conflict and even torture,[101] others celebrate it as a source of freedom to develop their own religious views without submitting to the confines of any one tradition. Religious hybridity is thus characterized by the freedom to move back and forth between the teachings, practices, and normative criteria of different religions.

With regard to the choice of topics for comparative theological engagement, meta-confessional comparative theology tends to focus on theological questions common to various religious traditions, or on broad religious topics. For example, Robert Neville's volumes thus focus on *Ultimate Realities,*

The Human Condition, and *Religious Truth*, while Keith Ward's work in comparative theology centers on revelation, creation, human nature, community, and human fulfillment.[102] John Thatamanil's book *The Immanent Divine* also has the subtitle *God, Creation and the Human Predicament*, and the topics proposed in the Theology without Walls forum were presented under such general topics as "the meaning of life, the role of narrative, love, death, eschatology, prayer and meditation, or the theological relevance of one's own life experiences."[103] Each of these topics is discussed drawing from the teachings of various religions and without privileging any in particular.[104]

The criteria for determining or discerning the truth of particular teachings or the validity of certain practices are here derived not from one particular tradition, but from various traditions, depending on the topic at hand, or else on criteria extrinsic to all religions. As a Buddhist-Christian, Paul Knitter states that for him Christianity represents the norm when it comes to questions of social justice and engagement, while Buddhism has become the norm with regard to questions of spirituality.[105] Wesley Wildman, for his part, argues that science might become the starting point for a transreligious theology, testing religious hypotheses and claims and providing the basis to adjudicate the greater validity or plausibility of the teachings of one religion over the other.[106] Perry Schmidt-Leukel still views himself primarily as a Christian theologian and he regards "Jesus as a normative exemplar of what a genuine mediation of divine presence is like."[107] However, he immediately qualifies this by allowing for "the possibility of other savior figures of equal status … who may also reveal something of God that is normative."[108] There is thus no conformity among meta-confessional comparative theologians regarding criteria of truth. Though sympathetic to the overall project of transreligious theology, J. R. Hustwit remarks that the absence of given criteria for intelligibility represents the greatest challenge for meta-confessional comparative theology, since "no matter how many experts agree, or how elegantly a theological hypothesis coheres, in the end, truth claims can never be verified with finality. I suspect that the best we can do are 'better' and 'worse' judgments, cobbled together from various indirect and worldview-contingent truth criteria."[109] He suggests elsewhere that criteria of truth may here derive simply from the inner coherence of the theological insights, or else from "the relative consensus of a community of experts."[110] He does not specify, however, how such a community might be constituted.

Meta-confessional comparative theology is addressed not only to members of a particular religion but also to individuals who find themselves outside, beyond, or between religious traditions. John Thatamanil, for example, speaks of the relevance of this work for those who belong within the category of "spiritual but not religious" or "nones."[111] Perry Schmidt-Leukel also speaks of interreligious theology as the expression "at an extremely high level of intellectual sophistication" of what takes place on a more popular level among individuals with multireligious identities. "People with different degrees of multireligious identities," he states, "represent on a micro level a development which on the macro level of our global society indicates the overall future of theology."[112] Tinu Ruparell develops his "interstitial theology" as "a form of cross-cultural philosophy which seeks to consciously hybridize elements of disparate traditions to better articulate the religious location of many people living in pluralistic societies."[113] He envisions this type of comparative theology to lead to what he calls a "recombinant religious tradition," the validity and truth of which would be tested on pragmatic grounds:

> If sufficient people settle this liminal land, the newly formed recombinant tradition will have been found to be viable. Interstitial theology thus asks pragmatic questions: does the new tradition "speak" to people, does it fill their needs, reflect their unique place between traditions? A viable tradition will retain ties to its parents yet exhibit the open-endedness and novelty which will be its hallmarks, but being pragmatically justified, the viability of a recombinant tradition can only be ascertained after the fact.[114]

Since meta-confessional or interreligious comparative theology situates itself consciously outside or beyond traditional theological and institutional structures, its impact is more difficult to measure. It may indeed lead to new communities, based on a synthesis between particular religions. Clooney also states that comparative theology may call into existence "liminal communities" which will be rooted in multiple communities and draw people who also remain committed to one or the other primary community. He also suggests that "As the number of persons living this complicated intellectual and spiritual life grows larger, the fixed boundaries separating religions become all the less plausible, not due simply to demographics or social change, but now also because the theological insights arising in comparative study will push the boundaries."[115]

One of the challenges for meta-confessional comparative theology, however, remains the tension between its universal claims and the absence of actual communities of theologians or practitioners who might be the arbiters and recipients of comparative theological insights. In aiming to be more universal, meta-confessional comparative theology paradoxically tends to become more idiosyncratic. It may speak to a certain number of individuals, but there is no ready mechanism to adjudicate between one and the other comparative theological synthesis. Though claiming to go beyond any particular theological tradition, meta-confessional comparative theology may still play an important critical role with regard to confessional theologies in that it may, as Hans Gustafson puts it, "nudge religious and interreligious theology and dialogue out of their usual secure comfort zones and possibly oversimplified view of religious identities and pull them into the liberative and imaginative growth-filled spaces of transreligious theology."[116]

1.4   Between Confessional and Meta-Confessional Comparative Theology

Though confessional and meta-confessional comparative theology represent two different conceptions of the meaning and goal of comparative theology, there is in actual practice also some continuity between the two. Meta-confessional comparative theologians who aim or claim to go beyond the borders of any religion tend to still be shaped predominantly by the conceptual or symbolic framework of a particular religion, whether consciously or not. And confessional comparative theologians at times push the boundaries of their respective traditions so far that they challenge or test the self-understanding of particular religions. The notion of universality moreover applies to both confessional and meta-confessional comparative theology, as confessional comparative theology generally considers its particular teachings and practices to be universally true and valid.[117]

Though pursuing a truth that is not limited to the revealed teachings of any one tradition, the worldview, symbol system, and values of meta-confessional comparative theology are often still indebted primarily to one or the other tradition. Some comparative theologians might also move back and forth between theological and more philosophical approaches to truth. A case in point is Raimon Panikkar. While his early work is clearly confessional, engaging Hinduism from a normative Christian position, his later work becomes less incarnational or Christocentric and focuses more on a conception of reality beyond or encompassing the particularities of all religions.[118] He comes to refer to theology as "the handmaid of philosophy"[119] and stretches Christian terms or develops his own neologisms (the cosmotheandric experience, christophany) that may be interpreted in more abstract and inclusive ways. While using Christian symbols and texts, he thus knowingly interprets them in ways that transcend traditional Christian meanings. Though never rejecting his Christian identity, Panikkar speaks paradoxically of his "refusal – as a Christian – to belong to a simple religious sect that has existed on its own for only two thousand years."[120]

Other comparative theologians might claim identification with more than one religion, but still seek to orient their work toward consideration by one religion in particular. Though moving back and forth between Buddhist and

Christian categories and criteria, Paul Knitter still states in *Without Buddha I Could Not Be a Christian* that he is writing for his "fellow Christians" and that the questions of orthodoxy that are raised in the book are "directed to the Christian community, not the Buddhist."[121] While John Thatamanil seems to be in search of a "consensus" between Hindu and Christian conceptions of the relationship between immanence and transcendence,[122] he also emphasizes the importance for comparative theologians to have and engage a home community:

> Ultimately only sustained conversation between theologians and their home communities will determine whether the fruit of any particular venture in comparative theology will be received by those communities as contributing to their collective flourishing. Comparative theologians cannot afford to be solo operators. They are obliged to articulate why their proposals ought to be received by their home communities even if globally valid a priori criteria are unavailable.[123]

Conversely, confessional comparative theologians may at times find themselves temporarily in between traditions and without firm mooring in one or another religion. Even though Clooney emphasizes the importance of a primary commitment in comparative theological work, he also suggests, especially in his later work, that this type of theology may come to unsettle that commitment and that in-depth knowledge of another tradition leaves the comparative theologian "if she is successful, at a border between two worlds, in a space distinguished by a seeming multiplication of loyalties."[124] He speaks in this regard of a "cultivated hybridity" which may lead to the creation of a "liminal religious community that seeks to understand faith that is complexified by comparative learning."[125] He thus openly reflects on the possibility of a loss of a primary or dominant commitment for those involved in comparative theology:

> We are then left in a vulnerable, fruitful learning state, engaging these powerful works on multiple levels and, paradoxically, learning more while mastering less; we have more teachers and fewer masters. It may appear that by this practice we acquire a surfeit of scriptures, yet have no Scripture; multiple languages and words and images, yet no tested, effective manner of speaking; a wealth of theological insights, yet no sure doctrine; not one but two rich religious traditions from which to benefit, and yet – because we know too much – no single, normative tradition that commands our attention.[126]

Throughout *His Hiding Place Is Darkness*, Clooney gives expression to the tension involved in immersing oneself fully in another tradition and imagining ourselves "falling, mostly by choice, into the somewhat obscure and unstable space lying between traditions"[127] and the desire or need "to find our way back into Christian theology."[128] He plays with the notion of divine presence and absence that is the theme of the texts compared in this book to express his sense of loyalty to two different traditions:

> In the unfinished drama of our times, we are always stepping away from the certainties of faith, even if we return a moment later, steadfast again until the beloved departs again. When we expect one love to put aside all others but come to see that the intensity of one love does not diminish the intensity of another, then we stand onto admittedly uncharted ground.[129]

Though there is no doubt that Clooney remained established within the Christian tradition, he voices the experiences of other confessional comparative theologians who become personally implicated and enriched by their study of another religion. The very engagement in comparative theology generally arises from a fascination and identification with certain teachings or practices of another religion and a desire to integrate something of these in one's own. Michaël Amaladoss likens in-depth dialogue with another religion with a state of liminality, or with individuals who "exist on the border between two communities and their symbolic universes, feeling at ease within both, and thus experience religious solidarity with each of the two communities."[130] While for confessional comparative theologians, this liminal state is temporary or transitional, it may become a more permanent reality for meta-confessional comparative theologians.

Some comparative theologians may use criteria of truth that are only tangentially related to one or the other tradition. In her work, Michelle Voss Robert alludes to the importance of the "normative gesture" in comparative theology.[131] It is not always clear, however, whether that normativity is grounded in a particular religion or whether it transcends the religions compared. Her book *Dualities* compares the writings of Christian mystic Mechthild of Magdeburg and the Kashmir Shaiva theologian Lalleśwarī, who are both considered outsiders within their own religious traditions. Through a careful reading of these theologians, she surfaces the metaphor of fluidity as an important theme in both religious thinkers. Voss Roberts uses it as a resource to develop a feminist theology which draws on both traditions to break through the traditional dualisms and develop a more intimate and fluid relationship between the divine and human bodies, between human beings and between humans and nature. Though the criterion for discerning truth in the Christian and Hindu texts is not clearly derived from one or the other tradition, the starting point and goal of her work is still the Christian theological tradition: "The interplay of the texts and lives of Mechthild and Lalleśwarī has drawn us more deeply into a fluid dynamic that deserves greater prominence in Christian theology."[132] Similarly, in her book *Tastes of the Divine*, Voss Roberts attempts to develop a "holistic theology of the emotions," and she challenges traditional Christian theology by demonstrating the spiritual richness and depth of the Hindu theory and expression of the *rasas*: "Although there is nothing predictable about this interplay, I have suggested that Christian readers might enhance their peaceful contemplation, reinforce their heartfelt love of God, or find fuel for their prophetic zeal as they immerse themselves in Hindu texts."[133] There are thus different ways in which individual comparative theologians might conceive of their confessional or meta-confessional religious identity (as criteria and/or as target) and the way in which it plays out in their comparative theological work.

The point of demarcation between confessional and meta-confessional comparative theology is at times determined not by the intention of the comparative theologian, but by the religious or confessional tradition itself. While a comparative theologian may hope to contribute to theological reflection within a particular tradition, some traditions may be averse to all comparative theological work, or to the work of a particular comparative theologian. In rejecting certain comparative theological insights or conclusions, a tradition thus places them automatically within the realm of meta-confessional comparative theology. The confessional nature of comparative theology thus also depends on the receptivity of a particular tradition, its theologians, believers, and guardians of orthodoxy or orthopraxis.

Robert Neville suggests that, in the case of Christianity, the difference between confessional and meta-confessional comparative theology may lie in the particular denomination of the comparative theologian, Roman Catholic comparative theologians being more invested in "contributing to this Roman Catholic theological firmament on the principle that locating here is how to be a good Catholic Christian," while Protestants maintain a more critical attitude toward their tradition, believing that "true religion … has to do with direct relationship between individuals and God."[134] The difference between religions and denominations and their respective institutional and theological structures may indeed play a role in the sense of identity and purpose of comparative theologians. Some traditions may have clearer avenues for theological engagement and discernment than others. Similarly, some religions or denominations may be more open to critical and constructive theological work than others, or have more clearly defined theological boundaries than others. The interaction between comparative theologians and their home traditions thus undoubtedly differs from one tradition to the next. But the main distinguishing element between confessional and meta-confessional comparative theology lies in its sense of accountability to a practicing community and its connection with a community of theologians or religious thinkers who reflect on the broader theological questions and the meaning of such practice.

Though there are significant differences between confessional and meta-confessional comparative theology that could justify a completely different nomenclature, there are also sufficient similarities and continuities between the two approaches to the discipline to view them as variations of the same fundamental theological enterprise. Both approaches share the acknowledgment and constructive engagement of the reality of religious plurality in the pursuit of theological truth. There are, moreover, more subtle variations in the way comparative theology is conducted, depending on the epistemological status attributed to other religions. This will be the focus of Chapter 2.

Notes

1. Francis Clooney has identified the first English use of the term comparative theology in 1700 in a work by James Garden, *Comparative Theology: Or the True and Solid Grounds of Pure and Peaceable Theology*. Here, the search is for a common ground between religions which would do away with violence over less important elements of religions. Francis Clooney, *Comparative Theology: Deep Learning across Religious Borders* (Oxford: Wiley-Blackwell, 2010), 31.
2. David Tracy, "Comparative Theology," in *Encyclopedia of Religion*, 2nd rev. ed., ed. L. Jones (Detroit: Macmillan Reference, 2005), 13: 9126.
3. Reid Locklin and Hugh Nicholson, "The Return of Comparative Theology," *Journal of the American Academy of Religion 78*, no. 2 (2010): 490.
4. Louis Henry Jordan, *Comparative Religion* (Atlanta: Scholars Press, 1905), 27.
5. Jordan, *Comparative Religion*, 27.
6. James Freeman Clarke, *Ten Great Religions: An Essay in Comparative Theology* (Boston: Houghton, Mifflin, 1889), 3.
7. Clarke, *Ten Great Religions*, 4.
8. The text was originally published in the journal *The Atlantic* in 1868 and in book form in 1871.
9. Clarke, *Ten Great Religions*, 2.
10. Clarke, *Ten Great Religions*, 15.
11. In Max Müller, *Chips from a German Workshop* (New York: Scribner, Armstrong, 1874), xix.
12. Müller, *Chips from a German Workshop*, xxx.
13. Müller, *Chips from a German Workshop*, xxv.
14. Tomoko Masuzawa, *The Invention of World Religions* (Chicago: University of Chicago Press, 2005), 72–105.

15. Masuzawa, *The Invention of World Religions*, 100.

16. See the articles in Christian Wedemeyer and Wendy Doniger, *Hermeneutics, Politics and the History of Religions: The Contested Legacies of Joachim Wach and Mircea Eliade* (Chicago: University of Chicago Press, 2010).

17. See, for example, Bryan Rennie, "The Influence of Eastern Orthodox Christian Theology on Mircea Eliade's Understanding of Religion," in *Hermeneutics, Politics and the History of Religions*, ed. C. Wedemeyer and W. Doniger (Oxford: Oxford University Press, 2010), 197–214.

18. Jonathan Z. Smith, *Relating Religion: Essays in the Study of Religion* (Chicago: University of Chicago Press, 2004), 96.

19. Hugh Nicholson, *Comparative Theology and the Problem of Religious Rivalry* (Oxford: Oxford University Press, 2011), 26.

20. Hugh Nicholson, "The New Comparative Theology and Theological Hegemonism," in *The New Comparative Theology*, ed. F. Clooney (New York: T&T Clark, 2010), 59.

21. Clooney, *Comparative Theology*, 35.

22. Francis Clooney, *Divine Mother, Blessed Mother: Hindu Goddesses and the Virgin Mary* (Oxford: Oxford University Press, 2005), 8.

23. Francis Clooney, *The Truth, the Way, the Life: Christian Commentary on the Three Holy Mantras of the Śrīvaiṣṇava Hindus* (Leuven: Peeters, 2008).

24. Gerardus van der Leeuw, *Religion in Essence and Manifestation*, trans. J. E. Turner (New York: Harper & Row, 1963). The book covers 106 general topics, subdivided into the general topics of "The Object of Religion," "The Subject of Religion," "Object and Subject in Their Reciprocal Operation," "The World," and "Forms."

25. Mircea Eliade, *The Myth of the Eternal Return: Or, Cosmos and History* (Princeton: Princeton University Press, 1954).

26. Wendy Doniger, *Splitting the Difference* (Chicago: University of Chicago Press, 1999).

27. Kimberley Patton, *Religion of the Gods: Ritual, Paradox and Reflexivity* (Oxford: Oxford University Press, 2009); see also Kimberley Patton, "Juggling Torches: Why We Still Need Comparative Religion," in *A Magic Still Dwells*, ed. K. Patton and B. Ray (Berkeley: University of California Press, 2000), 157ff.

28. Francis Clooney, *Beyond Compare: St. Francis de Sales and Śrī Vedānta Deśika on Loving Surrender to God* (Washington: Georgetown University Press, 2008); Clooney, *Divine Mother, Blessed Mother*.

29. John Thatamanil, *The Immanent Divine: God, Creation, and the Human Predicament* (Minneapolis: Fortress Press, 2006); Michelle Voss Roberts, *Dualities: A Theology of Difference* (Louisville: Westminster John Knox Press, 2010).

30. Clooney, *Divine Mother, Blessed Mother*, 231.

31. For all of its shortcomings, the work of Mircea Eliade is still part of broader debates about the nature of religion.

32. See Philippe Bornet, "Comparison as a Necessary Evil: Examples from Indian and Jewish Worlds," in *Interreligious Comparisons in Religious Studies and Theology*, ed. P. Schmidt-Leukel and A. Nehring (London: Bloomsbury, 2016), 74–77.

33. The notion of the "vague comparative category" and its particular properties is developed in some detail in Robert Neville, ed., *Ultimate Realities: A Volume in the Comparative Religious Ideas Project* (Albany: SUNY Press, 2001), 191–208.

34. Bornet, "Comparison as a Necessary Evil," 72–94.

35. Neville, *Ultimate Realities*, 205.

36. Clooney, *Beyond Compare*, 23.

37. The three volumes of the Comparative Religious Ideas Project, edited by Robert Neville, were published in 2001 by SUNY Press in Albany. They are entitled *The Human Condition*, *Ultimate Realities*, and *Religious Truth*.

38. Paul Hedges also notes this in *Comparative Theology: A Critical and Methodological Perspective* (Leiden: Brill, 2017), 14.

39. Robert Neville, "On Comparative Theology: Theology of Religions or a Trans-Religious Discipline," Annual Comparative Theology Lecture at the Harvard Center for the Study of World Religions, March 2017 (forthcoming in the *Brill Companion to Comparative Theology*, ed. W. Valkenberg).

40. Francis Clooney, *Hindu God, Christian God: How Reason Helps Break Down the Boundaries between Religions* (Oxford: Oxford University Press, 2001), 9.

41. Clooney, *Hindu God, Christian God*, 167.

42. Clooney, *Hindu God, Christian God*, 227.

43. Clooney, *Divine Mother, Blessed Mother*, 229.

44. Clooney, *Hindu God, Christian God*, 179. However, Clooney admits that "theological decisions of that sort can in principle be made – and made persuasively – if someone is willing to do the work involved." In the introduction to the same book, Clooney also states: "Although I do not attempt to decide here the truth of particular claims about the nature of reality, God, and the interaction of God with humans, this volume aims to restore a proper context in which professions of truth can become intellectually credible, and a well-informed apologetics can be plausible and useful" (11).

45. Neville, *Ultimate Realities*, 188; emphasis added.

46. Neville, *Ultimate Realities*, 213.

47. Neville, "On Comparative Theology," 11.

48. Neville, "On Comparative Theology," 16.

49. Francis Clooney, *Theology after Vedānta: An Experiment in Comparative Theology* (Albany: SUNY Press, 1993), 4.

50. Francis Clooney, *Seeing through Texts: Doing Theology among the Śrīvaiṣṇavas of South India* (Albany: SUNY Press, 1996), 46.

51. Clooney, *Hindu God, Christian God*, 21.

52. Francis Clooney, *His Hiding Place Is Darkness: A Hindu-Catholic Theopoetics of Divine Absence* (Stanford: Stanford University Press, 2014), x.

53. James Fredericks, "Introduction," in *The New Comparative Theology*, ed. F. Clooney (London: T&T Clark, 2010), xi.

54. Karl Barth, *Church Dogmatics*, vol. *1*: The Doctrine of the Word of God, part 2 (London: T&T Clark, 1961), para. 17; Henri de Lubac, Amida (Paris: Seuil, 1955); John Cobb, *Beyond Dialogue: Toward a Mutual Transformation of Christianity and Buddhism* (Philadelphia: Fortress Press, 1982).

55. Cf. David Burrell, *Freedom and Creation in Three Traditions* (Notre Dame: University of Notre Dame Press, 1993); David Burrell, *Towards a Jewish-Christian-Muslim Theology* (Oxford: Wiley-Blackwell, 2011).

56. Patterns of theological reasoning in *Hindu God, Christian God*, the importance and role of the feminine divine in *Divine Mother, Blessed Mother*, the centrality of loving surrender to God in *Beyond Compare*, and the dynamic of the presence and absence of God in *His Hiding Place Is Darkness*.

57. Clooney, *Beyond Compare*, 14. Similarly in his latest work, it is the ritual texts of the Mimamsa tradition of Hinduism that is the starting point for comparison with Christian ritual and legal texts.

58. Clooney, *Beyond Compare*, 181.

59. Volumes in the series, published by Peeters, are Catherine Cornille, ed., *Song Divine: Christian Commentaries on the Bhagavad Gītā* (2006); Daniel Sheridan, *Loving God: Kṛṣṇa and Christ: A Christian Commentary on the Nārada Sūtras* (2007); Clooney, *The Truth, the Way, the Life*; Leo Lefebure and Peter Feldmeier, *The Path of Wisdom: A Christian Commentary on the Dhammapada* (2011); Reid Locklin, *Liturgy of Liberation: A Christian Commentary on Shankara's Upadeśasāhasrī* (2011); John Keenan and Linda Keenan, *I Am / No Self: A Christian Commentary on the Heart Sutra* (2011); Joseph O'Leary, *Buddhist Nonduality, Paschal Paradox: A Christian Commentary on The Teaching of Vimalakīrti* (2017); Daniel Joslyn-Siemiatkoski, *The More Torah, the More Life: A Christian Commentary on Mishnah Avot* (2018); Perry Schmidt-Leukel, *Buddha Mind – Christ Mind: A Christian Commentary on the Bodhicaryāvatāra* (2019).

60. Sheridan, *Loving God*, 6–7.

61. Masao Abe, "Buddhism and Christianity as a Problem of Today," *Japanese Religions 3*, no. 2 (1963): 15.

62. John Keenan, *The Meaning of Christ* (Maryknoll: Orbis Books, 1989); John Keenan, *The Emptied Christ of Philippians* (Eugene: Wipf & Stock, 2015); Joseph O'Leary, *Religious Pluralism and Christian Truth* (Edinburgh: Edinburgh University Press, 1996) down to his latest, *Buddhist Nonduality, Christian Paradox*.

63. See, for example, Paul Knitter, *One Earth, Many Religions* (Maryknoll: Orbis Books, 1995); Catherine Cornille and Glen Willis, eds., *The World Market and Interreligious Dialogue* (Eugene: Wipf & Stock, 2011).

64. Laurenti Magesa, "African Indigenous Spirituality, Ecology and the Human Right to Integral Development," in *The World Market and Interreligious Dialogue*, ed. C. Cornille and G. Willis (Eugene: Wipf & Stock, 2011), 164–89.

65. David Clairmont, *Moral Struggle and Religious Ethics: On the Person as Classic in Comparative Theological Contexts* (Oxford: Wiley-Blackwell, 2011), 2.

66. Clairmont, *Moral Struggle and Religious Ethics*, 193.

67. Clairmont, *Moral Struggle and Religious Ethics*, 194.

68. Catherine Cornille, ed., *Criteria of Discernment in Interreligious Dialogue* (Eugene: Wipf & Stock, 2009).

69. David Elcott, "Meeting the Other: Judaism, Pluralism and Truth," in *Criteria of Discernment in Interreligious Dialogue*, ed. C. Cornille (Eugene: Wipf & Stock, 2009), 39.

70. Reinhold Bernhardt, "Coordinates for Interreligious Discernment from a Protestant View," in *Criteria of Discernment in Interreligious Dialogue*, ed. C. Cornille (Eugene: Wipf & Stock, 2009), 56.

71. Gavin D'Costa, "Roman Catholic Reflections on Discerning God in Interreligious Dialogue: Challenges and Promising Avenues," in *Criteria of Discernment in Interreligious Dialogue*, ed. C. Cornille (Eugene: Wipf & Stock, 2009), 69–86.

72. Perry Schmidt-Leukel, "Christ as Bodhisattva: A Case of Reciprocal Illumination," in *Interreligious Comparisons in Religious Studies and Theology*, ed. P. Schmidt-Leukel and A. Nehring (London: Bloomsbury, 2016), 204–19.

73. Buddhist theologian Judith Simmer-Brown focuses on the Dalai Lama, who judges other religions according to "their capacity to promote harmony and peace for both individuals and the world, and to produce warm-hearted human beings." Judith Simmer-Brown, "Without Bias – The Dalai Lama in Dialogue," in *Criteria of Discernment in Interreligious Dialogue*, ed. C. Cornille (Eugene: Wipf & Stock, 2009), 253.

74. This typically happens through scholarly societies and journals such as the *Journal of Hindu-Christian Studies* or *Buddhist-Christian Studies*, and equivalent scholarly groups as part of the American Academy of Religion.

75. Clooney, *Hindu God, Christian God*, 27.

76. Clooney, *Comparative Theology*, 114.

77. Clairmont, *Moral Struggle and Religious Ethics*, 195.

78. See, for example, Perry Schmidt-Leukel, *Religious Pluralism and Interreligious Theology* (Maryknoll: Orbis Books, 2017).

79. See, for example, J. R. Hustwit, "Myself, Only Moreso: Conditions for the Possibility of Transreligious Theology," *Open Theology 2* (2016).

80. See, for example, Tinu Ruparell, "Inter-Religious Dialogue and Interstitial Theology," in *The Wiley-Blackwell Companion to Inter-Religious Dialogue*, ed. C. Cornille (Oxford: Wiley-Blackwell, 2013), 117–32.

81. Hustwit, "Myself, Only Moreso," 236.

82. Wilfred Cantwell Smith, *Towards a World Theology* (Philadelphia: Westminster Press, 1981), 126.

83. In his famous distinction he defines faith as "an inner religious experience or the involvement of a particular person; the impingement on him of the transcendent, putative or real," and cumulative traditions as "the entire mass of overt objective data that constitutes the historical deposit, as it were, of the past religious life of the community in question." Wilfred Cantwell Smith, *The Meaning and End of Religion* (New York: Macmillan, 1964), 16–17, 36.

84. Smith, *Towards a World Theology*, 126.

85. Jerry Martin, "Introduction to the Topical Issue 'Is Transreligious Theology Possible?'" *Open Theology 2* (2016): 261.

86. Wesley Wildman, "Theology without Walls: The Future of Transreligious Theology," *Open Theology 2* (2016): 243.

87. Wildman, "Theology without Walls," 247.

88. Wildman, "Theology without Walls," 247.

89. John Thatamanil, "Transreligious Theology as the Quest for Interreligious Wisdom," *Open Theology 2* (2016): 354.

90. Thatamanil, "Transreligious Theology," 355.

91. Schmidt-Leukel, *Religious Pluralism and Interreligious Theology*, 113.

92. These are terms that meta-confessional comparative theologians borrow directly or indirectly from Wilfred Cantwell Smith's *Towards a World Theology*.

93. Thatamanil, *The Immanent Divine*, 3.

94. Thatamanil here quotes from Gordon Kaufman, *God, Mystery, Diversity: Christian Theology in a Pluralistic World* (Minneapolis: Fortress Press, 1996), 199.

95. Neville, "On Comparative Theology," 18.

96. Neville, "On Comparative Theology," 20.

97. Neville, "On Comparative Theology," 19.

98. Raimundo (Raimon) Panikkar, "What Is Comparative Philosophy Comparing?" in *Interpreting across Boundaries*, ed. G. Larson and E. Deutsch (Princeton: Princeton University Press, 1988), 127.

99. Raimundo (Raimon) Panikkar, *Myth, Faith and Hermeneutics* (New York: Paulist Press, 1979), 381.

100. I have elsewhere distinguished different types of multiple religious belonging: involuntary versus voluntary, temporary versus permanent, and equal versus unequal belonging to more than one tradition. See Catherine Cornille, "Multiple Religious Belonging and Interreligious Dialogue," in *Understanding Inter-Religious Relations*, ed. D. Thomas, D. Cheetham, and D. Pratt (Oxford: Oxford University Press, 2013), 324–40; Catherine Cornille, "Strategies of Negotiation in Buddhist-Christian Dual Belonging," in *Buddhist-Christian Dual Belonging: Affirmations, Objections, Explorations*, ed. G. D'Costa and R. Thompson (Farnham: Ashgate, 2016), 143–60.

101. I have commented at length on the tortured experiences of multiple belonging of the French Benedictine monk and Hindu sannyasin Henri Le Saux/Abhishiktānanda in Jeffrey Bloechl and Catherine Cornille, *Christian Identity between Secularity and Plurality* (Bangalore: Dharmaram, 2015), 107–35.

102. Keith Ward, *Religion and Revelation: A Theology of Revelation in the World's Religions* (Oxford: Clarendon Press, 1994); Keith Ward, *Religion and Creation* (Oxford: Clarendon Press, 1996); Keith Ward, *Religion and Human Nature* (Oxford: Oxford University Press, 1999); Keith Ward, *Religion and Community* (Oxford: Oxford University Press, 2000).

103. These were the topics proposed for forum discussions during the 2017 American Academy of Religion meeting.

104. Keith Ward's books do pay greater attention to the Christian view on these topics and to what it may learn from other religions.

105. Paul Knitter, "Comparative Theology Is Not 'Business-as-Usual Theology,'" *Buddhist-Christian Studies 35* (2015): 185–91.

106. Wildman proposed this approach to normativity in the area of Transreligious Theology or Theology without Walls at the American Academy of Religion meeting in 2016.

107. Perry Schmidt-Leukel, *Transformation by Integration: How Inter-faith Encounter Changes Christianity* (London: SCM Press, 2009), 158.

108. Here Schmidt-Leukel quotes Roger Haight, *Jesus, Symbol of God* (Maryknoll: Orbis Books, 1992), 281.

109. Hustwit, "Myself, Only Moreso," 241.

110. J. R. Hustwit, *Interreligious Hermeneutics and the Pursuit of Truth* (Lanham: Lexington Books, 2014), 115.

111. Thatamanil, "Transreligious Theology," 362. "Nones" describes a category of those who have no particular religious affiliation and who may be "spiritual but not religious." Thatamanil distances his approach from the "market-driven hybrid spiritualities now so much in vogue" by developing an in-depth study of the two traditions and thinkers which may come to "critically evaluate" such spiritualities.

112. Schmidt-Leukel, *Religious Pluralism and Interreligious Theology*, 11.

113. Tinu Ruparell, "Inter-Religious Dialogue as Interstitial Theology," in *The Wiley-Blackwell Companion to Inter-Religious Dialogue*, ed. C. Cornille (Oxford, Wiley-Blackwell, 2013), 121.

114. Ruparell, "Inter-Religious Dialogue," 129.

115. Clooney, *Comparative Theology*, 161–62.

116. Hans Gustafson, "Is Transreligious Theology Unavoidable in Interreligious Theology and Dialogue," *Open Theology 2* (2016): 259.

117. This is, of course, particularly true for universalistic religions such as Buddhism, Christianity, and Islam, which is not the case for tribal religions or traditions such as Judaism and Hinduism whose teachings and practices are considered to be applicable primarily to those who belong to these traditions by birth.

118. Erik Ranstrom traces this development in Panikkar's thought in his doctoral dissertation, "The Unknown Body of Christ: Towards a Retrieval of the Early Panikkar's Christology of Religions," Boston College, 2014.

119. Raimon Panikkar, *Christophany* (Maryknoll: Orbis Books, 2004), 143.

120. Panikkar, *Christophany*, 168. His work never did receive either approval or condemnation from the teaching hierarchy of the Catholic Church.

121. Paul Knitter, *Without Buddha I Could Not Be a Christian* (Oxford: Oneworld, 2009), xiv.

122. Thatamanil, *The Immanent Divine*, 26.

123. Thatamanil, *The Immanent Divine*, 172.

124. Clooney, *Comparative Theology*, 158.

125. Clooney, *Comparative Theology*, 160–62.

126. Clooney, *Beyond Compare*, 209.

127. Clooney, *His Hiding Place Is Darkness*, xi.

128. Clooney, *His Hiding Place Is Darkness*, 114.

129. Clooney, *His Hiding Place Is Darkness*, 121.

130. Michaël Amaladoss, "La double appartenance religieuse," in *Vivre de plusieurs religions. Promesse ou illusion?* ed. D. Gira and J. Scheuer (Paris: l'Atelier, 2000), 52.
131. Voss Roberts, *Dualities*, 4.
132. Voss Roberts, *Dualities*, 159.
133. Michelle Voss Roberts, *Tastes of the Divine: Hindu and Christian Theologies of Emotion* (New York: Fordham University Press, 2014), 191.
134. Neville, "On Comparative Theology," 7.

2

The Status of Other Religions in Comparative Theology

Constructive theological engagement with other religious traditions does not come naturally to most religious traditions. The possibility of comparative theology requires considerable hermeneutical and theological effort, and reconsideration of the status of one's own religion as well as that of other religions. Insofar as comparative theology presupposes a capacity for change and growth, it requires some degree of humility with regard to one's own claims to ultimate truth or efficacy.[1] Such humility may be derived from apophatic teachings, from a dynamic orientation toward a future fulfillment or completion, from awareness of historical changes and cultural adaptations, or from the actual discovery of distinctive truth in other religions or more generally in cultures at large. It also presupposes a concept of religion or theology that would allow the theologian to single out particular phenomena or modes of living, experiencing, and thinking as particularly suited for constructive theological engagement. As the very category of religion has come under pressure from postcolonial critiques, comparative theologians must determine which beliefs and practices are regarded as religious and why.[2] But beyond this, comparative theology presupposes an implicit or explicit conception of the presence and the status of truth in other religions in general or in a particular religion.[3] The denial of any truth in other religions would severely limit, if not preclude, any constructive engagement with them, while the recognition of truth in other religions would make such engagement not only possible but necessary. Between the radical denial and the full recognition of distinctive truth in other religions, there are, however, an array of nuanced positions one may adopt from within any religion with regard to the epistemological status of other religions.

The discussion with regard to the epistemological status of other religions has been conducted mainly in the area of theology called theology of religions.[4] There has been an ongoing and outsized debate in Christian comparative

Meaning and Method in Comparative Theology, First Edition. Catherine Cornille.
© 2020 John Wiley & Sons Ltd. Published 2020 by John Wiley & Sons Ltd.

theology about the relationship between theology of religions and comparative theology, or about the need for a priori conceptions of the religious other for engaging in constructive dialogue. James Fredericks has argued in various publications that the quest for a theology of religions "should be set aside for the time being" and that comparative theology should be regarded as an alternative to theology of religions.[5] Such a moratorium, he believes, would allow for greater attention to the particularity of other religions, avoid domesticating the religious other, preclude a priori judgments of the other, and permit genuine change through engagement with the other.[6] Fredericks thus suggests engaging the religious other without any prejudices as to their epistemological status, or to the possibility or limits of learning from them. John Berthrong and Francis Clooney also reject the need or desirability of any a priori theological stance regarding the status of other religions, arguing that "today's comparative theology is more tentative, for it works with the view that before any normative theological statements can be made, there is need for an extended engagement with the texts and/or praxis of those other religions."[7]

There are, of course, merits to this position. Each encounter with another religion may elicit its own epistemological judgment, and the engagement with other religions itself often changes a theology of religions. Moreover, Christian theology of religions has often focused on the salvific rather than the epistemological status of other religions. While the two are indeed interconnected, there is no need to determine the soteriological efficacy of another religion in order to constructively engage its teachings and practices.[8] Religions may acknowledge elements of truth in other religions without recognizing the whole of the religion as true or salvific, however conceived.

However, there is a direct connection between religious conceptions of the truth of other religions and the way comparative theology is conducted. Such epistemological preconceptions shape the motivation and the contours of comparative theological engagement. In distinguishing the various religious attitudes toward other religions, the classical paradigms of theology of religions may still serve a useful heuristic function.

Exclusivism then denotes the denial of relevant truth outside of the own tradition, inclusivism the recognition of truth in other religions based on the normativity of one's own tradition, and pluralism the recognition of truth in other religions irrespective of one's own religious normativity. Each of these basic heuristic possibilities may contain internal variations. Exclusivism, for example, might involve the denial of all truth outside of one's own tradition or the denial of the possibility of deciding on the truth claims of different religions, veering toward particularism. Inclusivism might recognize the existence of truth only in what is similar in other religions (closed inclusivism) or in what is not in contradiction with the norms of one's own tradition (open inclusivism), and pluralism might involve the rejection of the use of any religion-specific criteria in judging the truth of other religions, or the rejection of the very notion of a bounded religion (postcolonialism). It is true that the epistemological presuppositions of a comparative theologian are not always made explicit. Furthermore, the conception of the truth of the other religion is at times shaped by or shifted through engagement with the other religion. But there is a clear correlation between the ways in which comparative theology is conducted and various theological views of the status of truth of other religions. This will become evident in the following discussion of particular examples of Christian comparative theology which relates their varying approaches to comparative theology to the particular theology of religions to which they are indebted.

Some have suggested that comparative theology is only possible when conducted from within certain paradigms, or with particular views of the truth of the other. While developing his own alternative set of paradigms or models of replacement, fulfillment, and mutuality and acceptance, Paul Knitter associates comparative theology only with the latter model.[9] And Kristin Beise Kiblinger believes that comparative theology fits only within "new forms of inclusivism and pluralism."[10] Though the process and outcome may differ, each of the paradigms allows for some form of comparative theology.

2.1   Exclusivism and Comparative Theology

The term exclusivism is generally used to denote a denial of the salvific function of other religions, or of their efficacy in attaining the highest religious goal. Though this often coincides with a denial of the presence of any truth or any relevant truth in other religions, some theologians may reject the salvific efficacy of other religions while still recognizing the presence of truth, even distinctive truth, in other religions. We shall here focus on the attitude of epistemological exclusivism and its implications for comparative theology.

Exclusivism may be regarded as the default religious position, insofar as most religions present themselves as the ultimate truth or as the sole repository of truth, thus ruling out the presence of relevant truth in other religions. Religious thinkers tend to reflect on questions of truth solely on the basis of their own sources of authority, and the epistemic confidence of believers is nourished by the conclusiveness of their teachings. As long as religions existed in relative isolation from one another, this attitude of exclusivism could be assumed without much need for argumentation. To be sure, religions often built their own views on the claims of others or borrowed elements from other religious traditions. But this borrowing occurred for the most part unconsciously or in the spirit of fulfilling prior and inferior conceptions of truth.

While the attitude of epistemological exclusivism may be regarded as natural, it may also become a more conscious and reactionary theological position, shielding religions and believers from the dangers of religious relativism and the temptations of other religions. Religions or religious thinkers may develop various strategies to immunize or isolate themselves from the possibility of recognizing truth in other religions. They may focus on a limited number of distinctive teachings and elevate these beyond any critical reflection, as is the case in various types of religious fundamentalism. Thus, "Jews can select from the Shulkhan 'Arukh, where one can emphasize certain rules; Muslims from the Shari'a, where one can pick one of the four schools, such as Hanbalism; Roman Catholics from certain papal encyclicals or conciliar doctrines; Protestants, from Christian eschatology, where one can pick either pre- or post-tribulationism."[11] In emphasizing certain selective teachings and clothing them with the status of inerrancy, fundamentalists thus establish a strong sense of epistemic confidence while keeping the truth of other religions at bay.

One of the greatest problems for epistemological exclusivism lies in the presence in other religions of teachings or practices similar to one's own. As Paul Griffiths points out, the radical denial of any truth in other religions is difficult to maintain, since "it commits anyone who holds it to the claim that no alien religious teaching is identical with any teaching of the home tradition."[12] Theologians may develop various strategies to disqualify or neutralize seemingly similar teachings in other religions. From Justin Martyr (100–167) to Ippolito Desideri (1684–1733), the similarities between Christianity and other religions have often been relegated to expressions of demonic plagiarism.[13] In the current context, when similarities between religions have become more evident, and theories of plagiarism less credible or palpable, theologians may resort to a more historical account of the necessary interconnection between teachings and practices within a religious system, and the fact that ostensibly similar teachings are tainted by the overall deficient or erroneous framework in which they are embedded. The Dutch Reformed theologian Hendrik Kraemer thus argued that:

> Every religion is a living, indivisible unity. Every part of it – a dogma, a rite, a myth, an institution, a cult – is so vitally related to the whole that it can never be understood in its real function, significance and tendency, as these occur in the reality of life, without keeping constantly in mind the vast and living unity of existential apprehension in which this part moves and has its being.[14]

The attitude of epistemological exclusivism leaves little openness for comparative theological engagement with other religions. Though it may still generate certain forms of apologetics, its a priori rejection of truth in other religions does not provide much incentive for constructive engagement.

The modern attitude of exclusivism is generally associated in Christianity with the Protestant theologian Karl Barth. He drew a sharp distinction between Christianity as revelation and all other religions. Christianity is to be regarded as the only true religion not on the basis of its own merit, but because "it has pleased God, who alone is the judge in this matter, to affirm it to be the true religion."[15] As historical realities, all religions, Christianity included, are forms of "unbelief" insofar as they attach importance to their own teachings and practices as means of salvation.[16] The truth of Christianity lies thus not in its own merit or superiority as a religion, but in the fact that it recognizes its own sinfulness and salvific incompetence, relying entirely on the grace of God and Jesus Christ as means of salvation. Barth argues that this is itself the fruit of grace, that "when we ground the truth of the Christian religion upon grace, it is not a question of the immanent truth of a religion of grace as such, but the reality of grace itself by which one religion is adopted and distinguished as the true one before all others."[17]

Barth engages in some limited exercise in comparative theology to establish this argument. He displays a more than basic understanding of the traditions of Hinduism and Buddhism that also focus on surrender and grace as the means of salvation.[18] While acknowledging the similarities between evangelical Christianity and the True Pure Land Buddhist and Hindu Bhakti traditions, he focuses mainly on what he considers to be the inadequacies of the Hindu and the Buddhist traditions and the superiority of Christianity. With regard to the Bhakti tradition, he states that "the most uncertain part played by the idea of God, the substitution of surrender and love for faith, and the utter and complete formlessness even of the concept of love show that we are in a quite different world from that of the Japanese religion of grace, and an absolutely different world from that of Evangelical Christianity." But the Pure Land tradition of Buddhism is also found wanting because "In the Yodo religion it is not Amida or faith in him, but this human goal of desire which is the really controlling and determining power."[19] It is through engaging these two traditions that Barth ultimately argues that it is "the name of Jesus Christ, and nothing else" which is the expression of the unique truth of Christianity.[20] Barth's exclusivism is thus itself shaped through apologetic engagement with other religions.

It is a matter of debate whether Barth's relevance for comparative theology might go beyond such exercises in apologetics. Sven Ensminger argues that "Barth's theology is comparative to the extent that he affirms the possibility that God has revealed Godself in Jesus Christ to the entirety of the universe and can use different means of revelation to point to this reality."[21] He points in particular to Barth's theory of lights (*Lichterlehre*), or sources of revelation in history and the world, as well as to his notion of "media of revelation" in similarities or analogies (*Gleichnisse*) with the Christian tradition. However, Ensminger also admits that for Barth, "all of these do not belong to that in which Christians can build their trust in life and death; they are strictly to be distinguished from that which the Church is called to proclaim."[22] Barth also "warns particularly against becoming 'prophets' of particular, unfamiliar ways that God has used as means of revelation."[23] All of this would seem to discourage constructive theological engagement with other religions. Ensminger indeed expresses a common evangelical Christian concern when he states that "the central problem with comparative theology seems to be that it tries to make individual Christian faith dependent on what can be found in other faith communities."[24]

Within the framework of epistemological exclusivism, comparative theology is thus generally limited to religious apologetics. Apologetics forms an integral part of comparative theology. Even though some might like to see comparative theology as an alternative to classical apologetics,[25] its focus on religious truth inevitably involves some degree of argumentation for the superior truth of one or the other, and in the case of exclusivism, one's own religious position. Against the demise of apologetics in interreligious encounters, Paul Griffiths argues that:

> If representative intellectuals belonging to some specific religious community come to judge at a particular time that some or all of their own doctrine-expressing sentences are incompatible with some alien religious claim(s), then they should feel obliged to engage in both positive and negative apologetics vis-à-vis these alien religious claim(s) and their promulgators.[26]

Here, positive apologetics involves "a discourse designed to show that the ordered set of doctrine-expressing sentences constituting a particular religious community's doctrines is cognitively superior, in some important respect(s), to that constituting another religious community's doctrines," while negative apologetics attempts to demonstrate "that a given critique of (any one of) the central truth-claims expressed by an ordered set of doctrine-expressing sentences fails, or that a critique of the set as a whole (as to, say, its consistence or coherence) does the same."[27] In that regard, the work of traditional apologists may continue to play a role in contemporary comparative theology. While their work may at times be based on limited historical knowledge, prejudiced distortions, or flagrant errors about other religions, their lines of argumentation may still prove suggestive for comparative theological thought.

As a mode of comparative theology, modern apologetics presupposes thorough understanding of the other religion. When Griffiths engages in Christian apologetics with regard to the Buddhist understanding of the nature of the person, he brings all of his expertise as a scholar of Buddhism to bear on the argument.[28] Paul Williams's Christian apologetic for a personal understanding of God has similarly become part of a broader comparative theological discussion because of his profound personal and scholarly understanding of Buddhism.[29] To be sure, comparative theological apologetics should not be regarded as a neutral or objective argument for the superiority of one belief or practice over another. It is still based on a faith perspective, and on an attempt to argue for the coherence of a particular faith by critiquing alternative views. However, as Francis Clooney also points out, "if theologians make their criticisms in an informed and professional manner and are knowledgeable about the theological understandings of revelation and religion held by the traditions they criticize, any ensuing arguments will surely be richer, more intelligent, and more helpful to all involved."[30]

Epistemological exclusivism is of course not unique to Christian theology. In *Hindu God, Christian God*, Clooney discusses the similarities between Barth's type of theological reasoning and that of the Hindu Mīmāṃsa theologian Kumārila Bhaṭṭa, or the Arul Nandi. He argues that, with regard to their conception of the exclusive truth of their own revelation and their conception of the relationship between religion and revelation, they are in fact "kindred spirits."[31] They "share a readiness to draw from their theologies of revelation in order to make judgments, benign or harsh, about competing religious communities."[32] Beyond pointing to the similar structures of exclusivism in the two traditions, Clooney also believes that this "theologizing about the other opens them to dialogue with the other."[33] In spite of judging religions by revelation, he argues that theologians making such judgments are still "reasonably obliged to speak with articulate believers in those traditions … [who] can dispute the point and argue against it persuasively."[34] Comparative theological apologetics indeed still involves a degree of accountability not only to one's own tradition but also to the other.

2.2 Particularism and Comparative Theology

Particularism has gradually emerged as a distinctive paradigm in theology of religions. It differs from exclusivism, inclusivism, and pluralism through its strong emphasis on the perspectival nature of truth and understanding. It may be regarded as a type of inclusivism, understood from a sharp awareness of the particularity of all religious perspectives. It is based on a cultural-linguistic approach to religion which is generally associated with the postliberal theology of George Lindbeck. Religions are regarded as "comprehensive interpretive schemes, usually embodied in myths or narratives and heavily ritualized, which structure human experience and understanding of self and world."[35] Rather than expressing a prior experience, religions are thus seen to (ideally) shape the perception and experiences of believers. And rather than in terms of their correspondence to an objective state of affairs, the truth of religious teachings is determined intrasystemically, or in terms of their place and coherence within the larger religious grammar and in the lives of believers.[36]

Insofar as the questions of truth and understanding are shaped by the internal framework and logic of a religious tradition, the epistemological status of other religions remains, in an important sense, undecided. From the perspective of one's own religious tradition, the competing claims of other religions can of course not be considered true or valid. But this judgment is based on the a priori truth claims of a tradition or on a faith perspective that does not necessarily assume the status of propositional truth. It is understood that each religion (or nonreligious ideology) claims ultimate and unsurpassable truth. However, "there are no universal or foundational structures and standards of judgment by which one can decide between different religious and nonreligious options."[37] Lindbeck here uses the term incommensurability to refer to the fact that the competing claims to unsurpassability "cannot be judged either better or worse, inferior or superior, because they lack any common measure acceptable to both by which they can be compared."[38] It is thus "impossible" for religions to have a "productive dialogue about either their truth or falsity."[39] Lindbeck does suggest that the reasonableness or truth of a religion may be judged on the basis of its assimilative power.[40] But he admits in the end that different religions may argue for the superiority of their own tradition even in this regard.

The epistemological gap between religions is also expressed in terms of the difficulty, if not the impossibility, of fully understanding the religious other within his or her own frame of reference. Insofar as the meaning of particular teachings and practices is derived from a whole lifestyle and way of being, it can never or rarely be fully grasped from the outside. This does not mean that all interreligious understanding is rendered mute or impossible, but rather that it is always colored by one's own religious framework.

The implications of this particularist and postliberal approach to religious truth for comparative theology have been variously assessed. Some have argued that the postliberal approach represents a serious impediment to all constructive engagement between religions. Jeannine Hill Fletcher, for example, interprets Lindbeck's notion of incommensurability in terms of the impossibility of "bridging the distance between persons of different religions." "What is missing from his theology", she states, "is a way for people of differing faith perspectives to converse with and learn from one another."[41] She thus judges the cultural-linguistic approach to be ineffective in addressing questions of religious plurality and interreligious engagement. Marianne Moyaert also views postliberalism as "a quite thoroughgoing hermeneutical and theological deconstruction of the whole project of interreligious dialogue."[42] In emphasizing the radical difference between religions as various language-games, "not only does the cultural-linguistic model undermine the hermeneutical possibility of interreligious dialogue; the theological importance of such dialogue is also minimalized" and other religions are rendered "theologically meaningless."[43] If all meaning and truth is derived from the internal structure and grammar of a religion, it would be difficult to imagine how religious teachings or practices might grow or change, and how other religions might become an occasion for such change. Moyaert believes that the main concern of postliberalism is "to protect the identity of a religious tradition against possible erosion and relativization from outside."[44]

Some theologians have indeed used particularist notions to reject the very possibility of constructive engagement between religions. In his article with the telling title "The End of Dialogue," John Milbank, for example, emphasizes the fact that religions represent mutually exclusive answers or solutions to some of the same existential questions, and that "the incommensurability of these solutions helps to reconfirm the futility of 'dialogue.'"[45] Rather than seeking mutual understanding and learning, he suggests that relationship between religions ought to take the form of "mutual suspicion." This would involve not only challenging other religions to live up to their own highest goals, but also "subverting other discourses at the very point of their denial of otherness."[46] The extreme interpretation of particularism in terms of an unbridgeable epistemological gap between religions indeed leaves little room for constructive comparative theology.

However, the postliberal and particularist approach does not preclude constructive engagement with other religions. Lindbeck himself in fact developed his intrasystemic approach to doctrine precisely to "oppose the boasting and sense of superiority that destroys the possibility of open and mutually enriching dialogue."[47] Though the truth of religious doctrines is determined intrasystemically, and though religious teachings shape religious perception rather than the other way round, he also fully recognized the possibility of the development of doctrine, "not as proceeding from new experiences, but as resulting from the interactions of a cultural-linguistic system with new situations."[48] Lindbeck also admits to a certain dialectical or reciprocal relation between language and experiences. He refers in particular to the ways in which cultural patterns of experience have shaped religious identities in different parts of the world.[49] This thus leaves some room for the possibility of religious innovation and change. For Lindbeck, belief in the ultimate truth and unsurpassability of one's own religion does not preclude a recognition of elements of truth in other religions:

> To hold that a particular language is the only one that has the words and con-
> cepts that can authentically speak of the ground of being, the goal of history,
> and true humanity … is not at all the same as denying that other religions have
> resources for speaking truths and referring to realities, even highly important
> truths and realities, of which Christianity as yet knows nothing and by which it
> could be greatly enriched.[50]

Elsewhere, he also states that "partly false religions may contain truths of an important though subordinate nature that are not initially present in the highest religion and can therefore enrich it."[51] He thus views religions as complementary, in the sense that "they provide guidance to different but not incompatible dimensions of existence." By way of example, he suggests that "perhaps … Buddhists know more about contemplation and Christians about social action, and perhaps they can learn from each other in these domains while retaining their categorically different notions of the maxi-mally important."[52] It is thus clear that a postliberal and particularist approach to religious truth allows for the possibility of constructive engagement with other religions.

Characteristic of a particularist comparative theology is its emphasis on the epistemological primacy of one's own tradition. This means not only that the truth of other religions will be judged in terms of its continuity and compati-bility with one's own tradition, but also that its teachings will be interpreted from within one's own hermeneutical framework. The postliberal approach to comparative theology emphasizes the particularity of all understanding and appropriation of the teachings or practices of the other religion. This does not imply a denial of the alterity of the other religion. Rather it reflects an epistemological realism (and humility) in acknowledging the impossibility of escaping one's own historical and religious context in the process of constructively engaging the other.

For comparative theology, this also means that theologians can only focus on advancing the truth of their own tradition. On the rare occasion Lindbeck speaks of missionary engagement with other religions, he states that "one of the ways in which Christians can serve their neighbors may be through helping adherents of other religions to purify and enrich their heritages, to make them better speakers of the languages they have."[53] This would mean encouraging "Marxists to become better Marxists, Jews and Muslims to become better Jews and Muslims, and Buddhists to become better Buddhists."[54] He immediately qualifies this last statement by admitting that "their notion of what a 'better Marxist', etc., is will be influenced by Christian norms." However, Lindbeck does not go beyond this by suggesting what others might actually learn from Christianity.

An example of particularist or postliberal comparative theology may be found in the work of Mark Heim. In his work *Salvations*, Heim establishes the particularity and distinctiveness of the various religious ends, and the validity of the various religious paths and practices as leading to their respective ends.[55] In *The Depth of the Riches*, he first argues for the superiority of the Christian conception of salvation in terms of participation in the life of the triune God. Heim sees this as the most encompassing understanding of the ultimate end.[56] However, he then explores ways in which the Christian understanding of the Trinity may be deepened and expanded through engagement with the conceptions of ultimate reality in other religious traditions. He focuses in particular on the conceptions of ultimate reality in the Hindu tradition of Advaita Vedānta and in Islam. While the former focuses on the non-personal and immanent nature of ultimate reality, the latter emphasizes the personal transcendent and relational dimension of the divine. Since each of those religions have developed in greater detail dimensions that are present in the Christian Trinitarian understanding of ultimate reality, he states that "Christians need humble apprenticeship to other religions in regard to dimensions of the triune life that those faiths grasp with profound depth."[57] While, from a Christian perspective, the ultimate ends of other religions can only be regarded as "penultimate," their full body of religious teachings and attendant practices may still make a significant contribution to Christian theological self-understanding.

The particularist approach to the truth of other religions may thus leave ample room for constructive engagement with other religions. It is based on a modest epistemology that recognizes the alterity of the religious other without precluding the possibility of learning. It is faithful to the self-understanding of religious traditions as claiming ultimate truth and ideally shaping the believer's perception and experience of the world. And it acknowledges the plurality of claims to ultimacy and unsurpassability and the possibility of engaging in comparative theology from multiple religious perspectives.[58] The particularist perspective thus draws attention to the perspectival nature of all comparative theology.

2.3   Closed Inclusivism and Comparative Theology

The inclusivist approach to the question of religious truth recognizes the possible presence of truth in other religions insofar as it may be reconciled with the truth of one's own religion. The teachings and practices of one's own tradition here thus constitute the ultimate norm or criterion for discerning truth in other religious traditions. Only those teachings that are continuous with, or that do not contradict, one's own tradition may be potentially considered true. This is a fairly common and coherent religious position. It avoids the contradiction of an exclusivist rejection of teachings in other religions that are occasionally the same as one's own. And it does not threaten epistemic confidence or conviction of the ultimate truth of one's own tradition. It differs from particularism in that it assigns a greater cognitive or propositional value to one's own truth claims, and also to those of other religions.

The term closed inclusivism is used for inclusivist approaches that emphasize the fullness of truth of one's own tradition and that recognize truth in other religions only insofar as it corresponds to the truth of one's own tradition. Here, the teachings and practices of one's own tradition function as a maximal norm or, to use the terminology of Roger Haight, as "positive norm," that "positively rules out what does not agree with it."[59] Only those teachings or practices in other traditions that are the same or essentially similar to one's own may thus be considered to be true. It thus severely limits the possibility of discovering anything new in other religions that might be theologically relevant or enriching. Insofar as religious teachings and practices are always embedded in different contexts, they are of course rarely identical across religious traditions. Though elements of truth may be found in other religions, for inclusivists they are generally seen to find their fulfillment within one's own religious tradition.

The Christian theologian most often associated with this type of inclusivism is Karl Rahner (1904–84). His views of other religions led to major changes in the Church's attitude to other religions, providing the theological basis for the Vatican II document *Nostra aetate*. Though the Church had long recognized the possibility of salvation of non-Christian individuals, Rahner was one of the first Catholic theologians to also recognize the positive role of the religions themselves in the process of salvation. He refers to other religions as "lawful," insofar as they represent "a positive means of gaining a right relationship to God."[60]

> Until the moment when the gospel really enters into the historical situation of an individual, a non-Christian religion (even outside the Mosaic religion) does not merely contain elements of a natural knowledge of God, elements, moreover,

mixed up with human depravity which is the result of original sin and later aberrations. It contains also supernatural elements arising out of the grace which is given to men as a gratuitous gift on account of Christ. For this reason, a non-Christian religion can be recognized as a *lawful* religion (although only in different degrees) without thereby denying the error and depravity contained in it.[61]

Rahner's qualified recognition of the presence of truth in other religions was based on his emphasis on the historical and communal dimensions of human nature. Thus, if individuals could be saved, this could not but be at least in part through (and not in spite of) their religious traditions. However, these elements are only valid until Christianity "enters with existential power and demanding force into the realm of another religion and – judging it by itself – puts it in question."[62] The Church remains for Rahner the model and the arbiter of truth, or "the historically tangible vanguard and the historically and socially constituted explicit expression of what the Christian hopes is present as a hidden reality even outside the visible Church."[63] The teachings and practices of other religions may thus be recognized as true only insofar as they correspond to Church teachings. Hans Küng also states that from a Christian perspective, "a religion is true and good if and insofar as it allows us to perceive the spirit of Jesus Christ in its theory and practice."[64] Even though the notion of "the spirit of Jesus Christ" may be open to interpretation, it is clear that the teachings of other religions will be mainly assessed on the basis of their similarities with Christian teachings.

Comparative theology from the perspective of closed inclusivism will thus mainly focus on similarities or analogies between one's own religion and other religions. This requires no less of a serious scholarly engagement with the other tradition. Surface similarities often conceal profound differences, while apparent differences may reveal important similarities. The goal of this type of comparative theology may be to confirm the presence of truth in the other religion and/or to affirm the superior truth of one's own tradition. In contrast with Barth, the similarities between the Christian and the Pure Land Buddhist emphases on love and grace are seen by theologians such as Choan-Seng Song as a sign of God's saving presence and truth in the Buddhist tradition.[65] And Peggy Starkey sets out more broadly to demonstrate that the Christian ideal of *agape* is manifest in many other religious traditions, thus providing evidence of the working of the spirit of Christ beyond the Christian tradition.[66]

The attempt to establish the superiority of Christianity over other traditions is in evidence in much of the work of late nineteenth- and early twentieth-century theologians who attempted to engage other religions with a more open mind without compromising Christian claims to ultimacy. While engaging in an in-depth study of Pure Land Buddhism, and evoking the beauty and power of the figure of Amida in poetic terms, Henri de Lubac still asserts that "the beauty itself of the worship of Amida, and the depth derived from the Buddhist faith to which it remained faithful, only serve to put this teaching [of the universal transformation through the Incarnation of Jesus Christ] in a more shining light."[67] And in one of the earliest systematic attempts at Hindu-Christian comparative theology, the Jesuit Pierre Johanns engages in a thorough study of the various philosophical traditions of Vedānta. While finding elements of truth or partial truth in each of the philosophical schools, he argues that the fullness of truth is only to be found in the Christian system of Thomism:

> We have said that in the Catholic philosophy of Saint Thomas, we find all the important doctrines met with in the Vedānta. But in the Thomistic system we have an organic whole. It is one harmony in which the different Vedāntic systems find their proper setting. Their discordance disappears. The loose members combine into one organism, one harmonious body of truth.[68]

He refers to the different philosophical systems as "stragglers on the road, not yet in the possession of Truth, which all admit to be one."[69]

Since the teachings of other religions are here generally seen as a pale reflection of one's own, there is little chance for constructive engagement with the other religion. The discovery of truth only in teachings or practices that are similar will not lead to new theological insights or to theological development. However, one may still speak of comparative theology in so far as the engagement with the other does prompt a new attention to traditional teachings and a new consideration of traditional claims to superiority. In comparing Meister Eckhart to the Hindu Shankara, Rudolf Otto, for example, attempts to rehabilitate the former as a legitimate example of Christian mysticism by establishing both similarities and differences between their concepts of God and their implications for moral life.[70] Viewing Eckhart through the lens of Shankara moreover draws attention to particular elements otherwise unnoticed, and introduces new possibilities for understanding and interpretation. Thus, comparative theology rooted in closed inclusivism may still lead to subtle changes.

The primary focus on recognizing truth in similarities moreover does not preclude some attention to differences or variations that might also inform or enrich one's own tradition. Gavin D'Costa refers to the discovery of truth in other religions in terms of the "non-identical repetition of the revelation which is given."[71] Though rejecting the possibility of discovering new truths or new revelations in other religions, he recognizes that engagement with other religions may lead to "a deepening appreciation, and therefore possibly different practices and articulations of the faith."[72] This may emerge from practices of inculturation, where the engagement with the language and symbols of local cultures implicitly involves engagement with the religions that originally shaped those cultures. But it may also evolve from the reality that any similarity between religions always remains couched in a broader context of difference, and that these variations may also deepen or enhance the faith. D'Costa speaks here of "mutual fulfillment," in the sense that "it is not only the other religions that are fulfilled in (and in one sense, radically transformed) their *preparatio* being completed through Christianity, but also Christianity itself that is fulfilled in receiving the gift of God that the Other might bear."[73] This thus moves closer to the attitude of open inclusivism.

When done within the framework of closed inclusivism, comparative theology will focus mainly on the similarities between one's own and the other religion. It may at times shed new light on established teachings or practices, focus attention on particular neglected dimensions, and lead to subtle shifts in self-understanding. But it will rarely lead to significant theological development or change. Some may question whether one should speak here of comparative theology at all. Insofar as it views the other religion entirely through the lens and in function of its own established conceptions of truth, it does not answer to a commonly cited characteristic of comparative theology, that it should reflect the self-understanding of the religious other.[74] Arguably, it thus represents the "old" rather than the "new" comparative theology.[75]

2.4   Open Inclusivism and Comparative Theology

Like closed inclusivism, open inclusivism engages other religious traditions on the basis of the normative teachings and practices of one's own tradition. Here, however, one's central teachings function as a minimal norm, or what Roger Haight calls a "negative norm" ruling out "only those alternatives which contradict it."[76] This allows for the possible recognition of truth in any teachings or practices that are not in contradiction with one's own tradition and for the discovery of new forms and expressions of truth. It thus also opens greater possibility for theological development and growth.

Recognition of truth in difference represents a challenge for most religious traditions. It seems to imply a limitation or incompleteness of one's own understanding of the truth which runs against the grain of religious self-understanding. It thus presupposes some theological or religious creativity in retrieving religious resources that generate doctrinal or epistemological humility and recognize other religions as possible sources of distinctive truth.

In the Christian tradition, theologians have generally focused on the notion of the "Logos," the word or will of God that was active in the world prior to the incarnation, and/or on the continued activity of God in the world in the Holy Spirit. Pneumatology or Spirit-Christology have thus been major resources for an open inclusivist approach to other religions.[77] Jacques Dupuis, for example, advances a "Trinitarian Christology"[78] which would "be able to account for God's self-manifestation and self-gift in human cultures and religious traditions outside the orbit of influence of the Christian message, without, for that matter, construing Christology and pneumatology into two distinct economies of divine-human relationships for Christian and for the members of other religions, respectively."[79] He rejects all "talk about 'absoluteness' … with regard both to Jesus Christ and, a fortiori, to Christianity" since it represents "an attribute of the Ultimate Reality of Infinite Being which must not be predicated of any finite reality, even the human experience of the Son-of-God-made-man."[80] In addition to this, Dupuis focuses on the eschatological understanding of the Kingdom of God as the basis for recognizing both the incompleteness of the Christian understanding and realization of truth, and the possibility and importance of engaging other religions in the pursuit of such truth. He states that

> There is, perhaps, nothing which provides interreligious dialogue with such a deep theological basis and such true motivation, as the conviction that in spite of the differences by which they are distinguished, the members of different religious traditions, co-members of the Reign of God in history, are traveling together toward the fullness of the Reign, toward the new humanity willed by God for the end of time, of which they are called to be co-creators with God.[81]

However, Dupuis also insists that "a keen discernment needs to be observed to sift divine truth from untruth" and that in the process, Christ remains the "norma normans":[82] "For the Christian the normative criterion for such a discernment is unmistakably the mystery of the person and event of Jesus Christ, who is the Truth (Jn. 14:6). Whatever is in contradiction with him who is '*the* Word' cannot come from God who sent him."[83] Each tradition engaging religious others from an open inclusivist perspective will of course discern elements of truth in other religions on the basis of its own set of norms, or in terms of their continuity and compatibility with its own established teachings and practices. Theologians who recognize the presence of distinctive truth in other religions often speak of a complementarity between religions. Since open inclusivism is based on the epistemological privilege and priority of one's own religion, Dupuis here speaks of an "asymmetrical" complementarity.[84]

Though the notion of the complementarity of religions was explicitly rejected by the magisterium of the Catholic Church,[85] the Vatican II document *Nostra aetate* may be read as recognizing the possibility of distinctive truth in other religions when it states that "The Catholic Church rejects nothing that is true and holy in these religions. She regards with sincere reverence those ways of conduct and of life, those precepts and teachings which, *though differing in many aspects from the ones she holds and sets forth*, nonetheless often reflect a ray of that Truth which enlightens all men."[86]

Later Vatican documents such as *Dialogue and Proclamation* (1991) also open the way for constructive engagement with other religions. This document states that "Christians must be prepared to learn and to receive from and through others the positive values of their traditions."[87] One may thus argue with Paul Griffiths that open inclusivism represents the implicit position of the Catholic Church:

> Since the Church already acknowledges that she needs to learn some of what she must teach from those outside her boundaries, and that alien religions teach truths, there would need to be pressing reasons to deny that some of what the Church needs to learn is already to be found among the teachings of alien religions – which is precisely open inclusivism.[88]

Open inclusivism represents the theological basis for most of the work of confessional comparative theologians. It allows the comparative theologian to remain faithful to the self-understanding of a particular tradition while being open to constructive engagement with other religious traditions. Recognition of distinctive truth in other religions raises not only the possibility, but the necessity, of engaging that truth in a constructive way. Thus, having realized the validity and truth of the Hindu spiritual experience of Advaita Vedānta, Henri Le Saux, the early pioneer of Christian comparative theology, argues that "if Christianity should prove to be incapable of assimilating Hindu spiritual experience from within, Christians would thereby at once lose the right to claim that it is the universal way of salvation"[89] and that "the pleroma of Christ will never be the fullness that it is intended to be, either in the individual believer or in the church at large, so long as that experience has not been integrated by Christianity."[90] Le Saux experimented throughout his years in India with various strategies for reconciling the Christian understanding of the Trinity with the teachings of Advaita Vedānta.[91] In the series Christian Commentaries on Non-Christian Sacred Texts, described in Chapter 1, Christian theologians mine the foundational texts of other religions in search of new insight and inspiration for advancing Christian theological reflection.[92] The authors thus approach the sacred text of the other religion as a possible repository of authentic and distinctive religious truth, while also recognizing that they always assess this truth from a Christian normative position.

The distinctive truth of other religions may take various forms, from particular ritual expressions or meditative practices that have not been developed in one's own tradition to entire philosophical systems that might lead to a reinterpretation of one's basic religious beliefs, and from compatible ethical teachings to more fully developed accounts of aspects of one's own tradition. Christian comparative theologians such as William Johnston, Aloysius Pieris or Bede Griffiths have long found in Buddhist and Hindu forms of spiritual practice a source of enrichment for Christian practice, and John Keenan[93] and Joseph O'Leary[94] have found in the Mādhyamika Buddhist philosophy a resource for coming to terms with some of the challenges of traditional Christian metaphysics, and with the very reality of religious plurality. Klaus von Stosch studies the work of some Muslim thinkers to examine the ways in which it might stretch and challenge Christian thought on certain common theological questions.[95] His project "Jesus in the Qur'an" involves a new approach to the traditional contentious discussion around the representation of Jesus in the sacred text of Islam.[96] Rather than dismissing the Qur'anic verses on Jesus as erroneous or misguided, he attempts to delve deeper into the historical and exegetical context of these verses as an occasion for constructive dialogue with Muslim scholars. Without compromising their basic faith convictions, Christians might then also possibly learn from the Muslim understanding of Jesus.

This draws attention to the fact that, though confessional comparative theology engages other religions on the basis of the normativity of one's own tradition, the meaning or understanding of one's own norms may also shift and become themselves enriched as a result of the dialogue. While Jesus Christ remains the ultimate criterion of truth for Christians, theologians engaged in dialogue with other religions have at times come to develop new conceptions of the meaning of Christ. Dupuis also refers to the normativity of the word of God in Christianity as a "dynamic reality, calling for interpretation in the specific context of interfaith encounter."[97] In his comparative theological engagement with Mahāyāna Buddhism, John Keenan thus interprets the person and message of Jesus through the Mādhyamika Buddhist categories of emptiness and dependent origination.[98] And engagement with the Hindu tradition has led several Christian theologians to interpret Jesus' expression of oneness with the Father through the Advaita Vedānta category of nonduality.[99] These reinterpretations of the Christian norm may in turn affect the way in which it is used in further comparative theological engagement.

If other religions are recognized as a potential source of significant religious truth, then comparative theologians play a vital role within their respective religious traditions. They help to expand the epistemological horizons of a tradition and allow a tradition to grow. To be sure, the discernment of distinctive truth in other religions is never a simple or straightforward matter. It requires the collaboration of theologians and scholars, and ultimately a broader reception of certain teachings and practices by the religious tradition at large. But comparative theology is here central to the theological enterprise of a tradition.

2.5   Pluralism and Comparative Theology

The pluralist approach to questions of religious epistemology is based on the premise of the equivalence of all religions in matters of truth. This does not mean that all religions are equally true with regard to all religious questions. But the truth of one or the other tradition on a particular topic is to be determined a posteriori, as a result of serious study, dialogue, and debate, and on the basis of neutral or common criteria, rather than the a priori norms of a particular tradition.

This attitude may arise as a reaction against traditional forms of exclusivism that have led to violence and exploitation and to the demonization of the religious other. Christian pluralist theologians such as John Hick, for example, point to the destructive effects of the Christian claims to superiority in particular in the relationships between European and North American Christians and peoples in other continents, and between Christians and Jews.[100] It is viewed as the source of antisemitism, colonialism, racism, and Western imperialism. Awareness of these dynamics may thus lead to reticence about imposing one's own judgment on the teachings of other religions. Pluralism here thus represents an attempt to compensate for the distortions in understanding and judgment that have colored the history of interreligious engagement.

The attitude of religious pluralism has evolved largely as a result of developments in religious studies and in the understanding of other religions. The study of the texts, teachings, and history of other religions leads to an awareness of the immense diversity, richness, and depth of these traditions. Pluralism states plainly that no religious tradition has a monopoly on sainthood,[101] and that different religious traditions represent a mixture of truth and error. It would be impossible, on purely scientific grounds, to establish the superiority of one tradition over the others or of one savior over others. Furthermore, since different religious teachings often address different questions, it would also be inappropriate to judge one religion according to the criteria of another. Insofar as theologians engaged with questions of religious plurality are often also historians of religions, it is not surprising that the attitude of methodological agnosticism that has dominated the historical study of religions also comes to be applied consciously or unconsciously to theological questions.

Pluralism is also often regarded as the only basis for a real dialogue between religions in that it establishes a level playing field. Langdon Gilkey, for example, calls for a "rough parity" between religions, without which "a serious discussion of diversity and its theological meaning would not be undertaken, nor would serious and authentic dialogue between religions be possible."[102] Paul Knitter also believes that attachment to the superiority of one's own tradition or focus on one's own criteria cannot but stifle the dialogue.[103] Any criteria or norms used in the engagement between religions will be "multiple, correctable, expandable – and always established within the dialogue."[104] Rather than judging one tradition on the basis of criteria of another, pluralism thus seeks to establish neutral or common criteria, or else move between the criteria of different religions in various areas of theological judgment.

Pluralism may require some reinterpretation of the self-understanding of religious traditions. It is based on a radically transcendent or ineffable understanding of ultimate truth, and a rejection of all religious claims to exclusive or superior understanding and expression of that truth. Within the Christian tradition, this requires rethinking the traditional understanding of the uniqueness of Jesus Christ. Theologians such as John Hick and Paul Knitter have tended to sidestep or overlook the traditional Christian understanding of the redemptive suffering of Jesus Christ and have furthermore made a focused effort to question or relativize the early Christian interpretations of the divinity of Jesus Christ. John Hick, for example, argues that the early metaphorical use of the title son of God in the course of time and under influence of Greek thought "hardened into prose and escalated from a metaphorical son of God to a metaphysical God the Son, of the same substance as the Father, within the triune Godhead."[105] Though this language was adequate for its time and place, Hick suggests a new Christological model that would preserve the divinity of Jesus Christ without excluding the possibility of divine saviors and salvific truth in other religions:

> We want to say of Jesus that he was *totus Deus*, "wholly God," in the sense that his *agape* was genuinely the *agape* of God at work on earth, but not that he was *totum Dei*, "the whole of God," in the sense that the divine *agape* was expressed without remainder in each or even in some of his actions.[106]

Knitter also embraces this distinction between *totus Deus* and *totum Dei*, and he discusses replacing the traditional understanding of the meaning of

Jesus as "full, definitive and unsurpassable" with the more open categories of "universal, decisive and indispensable," leaving room for recognizing equivalent truth in other religions.[107] Though he recognizes that, for Christians, the person of Jesus Christ will necessarily remain the decisive norm, he argues that "a decisive norm … may rule out *some* other norms, but it need not exclude *all* other norms."[108] Knitter also agrees with Roger Haight who proposes the notion of "mutual normativity":

> If one maintains that Jesus is normative for one's own salvation as a human being, one must, by the principle of noncontradiction, assert that Jesus is universally relevant and normative for all human beings. But … the explanation of the status of Jesus must be such that it not be exclusive. It must also allow for the possibility of other figures of equal status and who may also reveal something about God that is normative.[109]

Knitter thus suggests a "multinormed"[110] approach to questions of religious truth or validity. In calling upon Christianity (and presumably other religions as well) to "move emphatically from the confessional to the truth-seeking stance in dialogue"[111] John Hick turns to what he believes to be a common or generic criterion of religious truth and validity in the capacity to bring about a "transformation of human experience from self-centeredness to Reality-centeredness."[112]

This pluralist view of religious diversity forms the basis for the meta-confessional approach to comparative theology. Here, comparative theologians pursue what they perceive to be valid and important religious insights from whatever religious tradition they may derive, and regardless of whether they are consistent with the overall claims of any one single tradition. Comparative theology is here conceived not so much as serving or advancing the self-understanding of one particular tradition, but as contributing to a more universal understanding of truth. Perry Schmidt-Leukel thus envisions the development of "an 'inter-faith theology' or 'world theology,' 'global theology,' 'universal theology'"[113] in which "theological questions are raised and discussed not only on the basis of the Christian tradition, but in consideration of other religious traditions" and in which each tradition considers "its possible contribution to a global, interreligious colloquium."[114]

Pluralist approaches to comparative theology have resulted in highly creative personal syntheses of insights gained from different religious traditions. Since they are not grounded in or addressed to a specific religious tradition, their appeal rests largely in the personal power of persuasion of the theologian, or in the ability of the theologian to give voice to more broadly held views of the relative validity and truth of different religions.

Pluralist theologians tend to themselves identify with more than one religion, and they may speak to other individuals who claim a similar multiple religious belonging. As such, the work of Raimon Panikkar or Paul Knitter resonates with individuals who feel allegiances with both Christianity and the nondualist traditions of Hinduism and Buddhism.

In the actual practice of comparative theology, theologians here at times draw from common criteria, from external social or scientific criteria, or alternately from the criteria from one and the other tradition. And they may focus on similarities and/or on differences in judging their respective truth. Comparative theologians might focus on a particular worldview or philosophical system that they believe to be more coherent than others, and then draw from different religious traditions to support that system. This is the case, for example, in the development of Perennial Philosophy, which may be regarded as an early form of pluralist comparative theology. Here, philosophers from different traditions (Aldous Huxley, Ananda Coomaraswamy, Frithjof Schuon, etc.) attempted to develop universal philosophical and theological systems based on the teachings of nondualism in different religious traditions. Huxley describes the essential characteristics of their approach, which also became the basis for discerning truth in other texts and traditions:

> The metaphysic that recognizes a divine Reality substantial to the world of things and lives and minds; the psychology that finds in the soul something similar to, even identical with, divine Reality; the ethic that places man's final end in the knowledge of the immanent and transcendent Ground of all being – the thing is immemorial and universal.[115]

This nondualist philosophy continues to inspire the work of more contemporary comparative theologians such as Panikkar, Knitter, and O'Leary.

The criteria for judgment in pluralist comparative theology may also focus on common and/or external beliefs and concerns such as ecological issues, gender, economic development, and the like, drawing from different religious traditions and assessing each according to the degree to which they are judged to either serve or impede progress in these areas. Wesley Wildman, for his part, argues that science might become the starting point for a transreligious theology, testing religious hypotheses and claims and providing the basis to adjudicate the greater validity or plausibility of the teachings of one religion over the other.[116] This approach to normativity in comparative theology resonates with cognitive approaches to the study of religion. Wildman believes that in fact transreligious theology "best comprehends" the results of the cognitive theories of religion since "they address the entire human species" and that hence "the scientific study of religion is potentially the single most important aspect of multidisciplinary engagement for inspiring and supporting transreligious theology."[117] In his comparative theology, Joseph Bracken has also focused on science as the basis for linking theological concepts from different religions and for developing a unified notion of the divine reality.[118]

Finally, pluralist comparative theologians may go back and forth between the criteria of different religions. In his engagement in Buddhist-Christian comparative theology, Schmidt-Leukel argues that the different norms or criteria of truth of the different religions may themselves be complementary, rather than hierarchical or exclusive:

> The fact that the criteriological emphasis of Buddhism and Christianity in their assessment of other potential mediators of transcendence is different, does not necessarily entail a claim to superiority. For … the Buddhist emphasis on the fostering of non-attachment and the Christian emphasis on the fostering of love can be seen as complementary and mutually qualifying. Detachment without loving involvement would not be a sign of liberation but at best a form of indifferent complacency. And loving involvement without detachment seems but a barely concealed form of self-centeredness.[119]

Paul Knitter also recognizes the normativity of Christianity when it comes to questions of social justice, and Buddhism in the areas of philosophy and spirituality.[120] Knitter and Schmidt-Leukel focus on roughly the same areas in which Christianity and Buddhism might each become normative in the process of comparative theology, and other comparative theologians, both Buddhist and Christian, have focused on the same relative areas of strength and normativity.[121] This may thus lead to new forms of comparative theological agreement within and across religious traditions. In order to prevent a purely subjective or relativist approach to religious truth, J. R. Hustwit proposes relying on "the relative consensus of a community of experts" to adjudicate the truth of different religions.[122] He does not specify, however, how such community would be constituted.

2.6   Postcolonialism and Comparative Theology

While the epistemological models discussed presume a classical understanding of religions as more or less self-contained and bounded realities that may reflect on the status of other religions, postcolonialism tends to question the very notion of religious boundaries and the existence of distinct religious identities. This of course has important implications for comparative theology. Postcolonialism views the category of religion and the concept of "world religions" as a Western and colonial construct that does not reflect the reality of religious life and history. It is indebted to Edward Said's critical study in his influential *Orientalism*, which exposed the way in which power and knowledge have conspired throughout history to create and proliferate particular images of the other.[123] In *The Invention of World Religions*, Tomoko Masuzawa applies this critique to the way the category of "world religions" came into use, and to the way in which the various religions were judged and classified in relation to Christianity.[124] A number of scholars (Vasudha Dalmia, Robert Fryckenberg, John Hawley, Brian Smith, Heinrich von Stietencron, etc.) have argued that the term Hinduism is no more than a British colonial construction.[125] And Timothy Fitzgerald dubs the term religion itself part of "our cognitive imperialism" and the prominence of categories such as theology and soteriology as reflective of the "de facto institutional dominance of western theology through the auspices of phenomenology."[126] In his work on the early history of Christianity and its separation from Judaism, Daniel Boyarin points to the ways in which the very formation of religious identities often involve the creation of false dichotomies between self and other.[127]

These critiques have left a mark on the study of religion and theology alike. It has drawn attention to the intersections between religion, culture, gender, and race relationships and it has generated various types of critical reflection on traditional forms and sources of theology. In the area of theology of religions, postcolonial thinkers have criticized the fact that the traditional paradigms of exclusivism, inclusivism, and pluralism have largely been developed by white theologians in the Western academy, and do not reflect the lived religious experiences of individuals.[128] Ursula King, for example, argues that these categories are "too narrow, static, and insufficiently differentiated to capture the organic, fluid and dynamic reality of religion at a personal and social level."[129] In *Postcolonial Imagination and Feminist Theology*, Kwok Pui-lan develops some of the basic principles and the framework of a postcolonial theology of religious difference. This would begin with the question of how to "deal with the fact that Western Christian theological discourse about religious difference is constructed in such a way as to justify a hierarchical ordering of religious traditions, which always puts Christianity at the top?"[130] She argues that the traditional focus on questions of religious truth, and on the unity or diversity of religious experiences and goals, has in fact diverted attention from the ways in which religions construct difference. For her, "the question before us is not religious diversity, but religious difference as it is constituted and produced in concrete situations, often with significant power differentials."[131] Besides a critique of such power differentials, postcolonial theology of religious difference focuses on lived experiences and on the social and cultural dimensions of religion. Kwok Pui-lan suggests that such theology should "attend to the transformation of religious symbols and institutions in migration, exile, diaspora and transnationalism."[132] Rather than focusing on institutional questions of religious identity and belonging or doctrinal questions of truth, postcolonial theology thus takes seriously the reality of hybrid religious identities as resource for theological reflection.

Jeannine Hill Fletcher also takes issue with the isolation and the prioritization of religion in the formation of personal identities and with the very notion of uniform and stable religious identities. She emphasizes that "there is no 'Christian' identity, only Christian identities implicated by race, gender, class, ethnicity, profession, and so on."[133] Since every person represents a confluence of various biological, social, and cultural factors, "The hybrid identity of each member produces a religious community of infinite internal diversity."[134] This emphasis on the inner diversity within religions directs attention away from the larger doctrinal questions dividing religious traditions and toward those elements that may serve to create bridges and alliances across religions. Hill Fletcher focuses on concrete experiences of embodiment that may generate profound empathy and understanding between individuals from various traditions. She points, for example, to the experience of a young Muslim mother who, in sharing the very physical and stressful event of childbirth and breastfeeding with women of other faiths, found a connection which "transcended the boundaries of religion that had so long distanced her from her coworkers and neighbors in the conflict."[135] A postcolonial approach to the religious other thus attempts to destabilize the notion of otherness and to expose the power dynamics attendant on the creation of dichotomies between self and other. It thus circumvents the strictly theological questions of conflicting claims to truth in religious teachings and practices.

This approach to religious diversity leads to a questioning of the very pursuit of comparative theology as developed from within the previous paradigms and perceptions of the religious other. Any conception of religions as bounded realities engaging one another from within distinct and more or less stable frames of reference is regarded as hegemonic and apologetic. It is seen to be based on a conscious denial of, or an unconscious oblivion toward, the history of the formation of oppositional identities and the power relationships involved in this. Hugh Nicholson and Judith Gruber both take issue with the comparative theological approach of Francis Clooney, which they regard as enmeshed in hegemonic and apologetic identity politics. Though Nicholson recognizes Clooney's attempt to overcome the radical distinctions and claims of uniqueness between religions by focusing on similar texts and teachings, he is still judged to contribute to the classical Christian apologetic enterprise by ignoring the history and politics of Christian identity formation. "Clooney's choices of what to compare with what," he states, "are determined in part by Christianity's past attempt to distinguish itself from various rivals. In this respect, the contemporary practice of comparative theology remains inscribed in an apologetic tradition even when the comparative theologian assumes a critical stance vis-à-vis that tradition."[136]

Judith Gruber is more severe in her critique of Clooney's comparative theology. She accuses him of engaging in the "politics of essentialism" by calling for a crossing of religious boundaries and the cultivation of hybridity which, according to Gruber, "ultimately serve only to reestablish and reinforce the idea of undebatable religious identities and untransgressable borders between religions."[137] She also charges him with "silencing the diversity inherent in traditions,"[138] and concealing the fact that "his choices of representative texts are active moments in the formation of religious identity" and that "questions of representation are ultimately tied to questions of power."[139] From such a postcolonial perspective, any constructive theological engagement with another religious tradition is thus regarded as suspect, since it presupposes the existence of distinctive religious traditions, and since it does not deal with the genealogy of religious beliefs and with the infinite internal diversity of religious traditions.

Comparative theology may here take the form of "deconstructing dichotomous typifications"[140] between religious traditions. Nicholson develops what he calls a "dialectical model of comparative theology" which involves describing "how Christian identity is constructed 'politically' through apologetic contrast with rival religious communities" and de-essentializing or deconstructing "the oppositional contrasts constructed in the first, political moment of identity formation."[141] He thus views comparative theology as a way to depoliticize and denaturalize religious identities and to demythologize apologetics:

> Thoughtful comparison exposes this basic need to establish religious identity by invalidating many of the representations through which this need has been at once expressed and concealed. We might say that comparative theology represents the demythologization of apologetics, where demythologization is understood in Rudolph Bultmann's sense as the recognition of an expressive function underneath an appearance of objective description.[142]

Nicholson focuses on instances where theologians have attempted to enforce or create particular markers of their own identity by juxtaposing or opposing them to those of other traditions, such as Albert Schweitzer's binary opposition between the life-affirming traditions of the West and the world-denying religions of India, or Rudolf Otto's attempt to rehabilitate Meister Eckhart by magnifying the contrast between his theism and Shankara's pantheism. Nicholson counters this by delving deep into the writings and historical context of Shankara in order to "highlight the theist and realist aspects of the former that have been suppressed by the orientalist character-ization of his teaching as illusionistic pantheism."[143] Comparative theology is here thus conceived as "a critical, anti-essentializing discourse"[144] which seeks to enhance "our awareness of the contingency, and therefore the changeability of religious beliefs, practices, and institutions."[145]

Gruber also believes that the main goal of comparative theology should be "an exposure of its constitutive ambivalence and internal diversity." Then, she states, "comparative theology can fully unfold its dangerously unsettling potential: it can show that traditions have always already been forged out of hybridity through powerful negotiations of in- and exclusion."[146]

Some comparative theologians sensitive to a postcolonial critique of reli-gion and theology, while recognizing the constructed nature of religious dif-ferences and the similarities across religious traditions, continue to engage in constructive theology. This sort of constructive theological enterprise is dis-tinguished by its attention to subaltern theological methods and traditions and to marginalized or minority groups within a religious tradition and their ways of experiencing and expressing their relationship to the divine. For example, in "Liberative Service: A Comparative Theological Reflection on Dalit Theology's Service and Swami Vivekananda's Seva," Christopher Conway focuses on Indian liberation theology and ways in which it might be enriched through engagement with contemporary Hindu thought.[147] Since Dalit Theology has traditionally been strongly antagonistic toward Hindu and in particular Brahmanical forms of thinking, this type of comparative theology also represents a way of overcoming religious dichotomies, or of bridging the divide between religious traditions. However, it still recognizes and respects the boundaries drawn by religious individuals and groups, such as the Dalit Christians themselves. Other examples of postcolonial compara-tive theology may be found in third world feminist theologies that often draw from local concepts, symbols, and practices to develop a more holistic approach to theology.[148] Rather than focusing on questions of doctrinal orthodoxy, Hill Fletcher proposes measuring the "truth" of Catholic compar-ative theology in terms of whether it has exhibited "features of the sacramental embrace of the messiness of concrete reality as a vehicle for the divine, and if it participates in the prophetic care for the least."[149] It is also reflected more generally in the new attention to indigenous religions as resources for theological reflection and in the move away from texts and teachings as the only focus for comparative theology.[150]

2.7   Dialogue between Perceptions of the Religious Other

Though there is a clear correlation between different theological conceptions of the epistemological status of other religions and the practice of comparative theology, its procedure and goals, these are not necessarily monolithic and fixed. It is true that some view of the truth of other religions is always operative, implicitly or explicitly, in the engagement with another religion. But these views may vary, depending on the religion involved. In addition, one's perception of the truth of the other religion may also shift and change in the process of engaging a particular religion. This is why Francis Clooney states that "Only when an interreligious theological conversation is actually taking place can there be progress in drawing conclusions from it and about it, either to reaffirm or revise established theological positions."[151] The relationship between theology of religions and comparative theology is thus a circular one in which each continuously informs the other. After studying another religion and recognizing elements of truth that are not easily subsumed under existing religious truths, a closed inclusivist might veer toward a more open inclusivist view. And the particular epistemological stance one adopts may differ depending on the tradition engaged. Thus, pluralist theologians might end up adopting an exclusivist epistemological stance toward certain religions, or certain aspects of a religion.

Some comparative theologians may be hesitant about or resistant to declaring their epistemological and theological presuppositions about the other. This may have to do with an aversion for a priori and sweeping statements about other religions, with a fear of distorting one's understanding of the other, or of resisting change.[152] The reticence about embracing one or the other form of theology of religions may also be regarded as a form of prudence, adopted in light of the variable and unstable epistemological reality of other religions. On the other hand, Kristin Beise Kiblinger calls for comparative theologians "to be self-conscious and forthcoming about the effects of their theology of religions on their comparative theology," in particular for the purpose of "easing the hegemony concern by framing work in terms of more politically sensitive theology of religions."[153] This presumes a more or less fixed and static understanding of the truth of other religions in general, and the possibility of doing comparative theology only from within certain theological and epistemological paradigms (in particular "new forms of inclusivism and pluralism.")[154]

I have tried to demonstrate that one may engage in comparative theology from within any of the conceptions of the truth of other religions, although each will determine its nature and form, and surface particular aspects of comparative theology. Exclusivism will emphasize apologetics, particularism the situated nature of all comparative theological work, closed inclusivism the natural focus on finding truth in similarities, open inclusivism the possibility of discovering truth in difference while remaining committed to the normative truth of one's own tradition, and pluralism the ineffability of ultimate truth and the need for religions to participate in a public discourse on questions of truth. The postcolonial approach to comparative theology also plays an important critical function in warning against the essentializing of religions and pointing to the flexibility and permeability of religious borders.

Since each of these epistemological positions and approaches to comparative theology may exist within any particular tradition, dialogue and engagement between these different approaches is all the more important. It is important for the discipline of comparative theology that theologians with different presuppositions and different approaches share and discuss their findings with one another so that they may challenge and correct one another, and it is also important that the epistemological presuppositions be challenged by insights or findings that might arise from different presuppositions. As such, the dialogue between different perceptions of the status of other religions and different approaches to comparative theology is necessary for theological development and growth and for the advancement of the field of comparative theology itself.

Notes

1. Catherine Cornille, *The Im-Possibility of Interreligious Dialogue* (New York: Crossroad, 2008), 9–58.
2. For a critique of the term religion, see Timothy Fitzgerald, "A Critique of Religion as a Cross-Cultural Category," *Method and Theory in the Study of Religion 9*, no. 2 (1997): 91–110. Comparative theology generally adopts a critical realist understanding of religion that acknowledges its Western roots but recognizes sufficient structural similarities to warrant its use across cultures.
3. The notion of truth is here to be understood to refer not only to the origins and contents of certain teachings but also to the efficacy of certain practices, or the evocative power of certain symbols or forms.
4. While the terminology and the general paradigms of this area of theological specialization have been developed mainly in the context of Christian theology, they have also come to be adopted as a terminology in other religious traditions, such that one may speak of a Jewish theology of religions, a Buddhist theology of religions, etc.
5. James Fredericks, *Faith among Faiths: Christian Theology and Non-Christian Religions* (New York: Paulist Press, 1999), 166; James Fredericks, *Buddhist and Christians: Through Comparative Theology to Solidarity* (Maryknoll: Orbis Books,

2004), 99; James Fredericks, "Introduction," in *The New Comparative Theology: Interreligious Insights from the Next Generation*, ed. F. Clooney (London: T&T Clark, 2010), xiv. Fredericks also cites Francis Clooney, Klaus von Stosch, and Norbert Hintersteiner as supporting his position. However, Clooney states that "theology of religions can usefully make explicit the grounds for comparative theology, uncovering and clarifying the framework within which comparative theology takes place." Francis Clooney, *Comparative Theology: Deep Learning across Religious Borders* (Oxford: Wiley-Blackwell, 2010), 14.

6. This is my summary of his arguments in Fredericks, "Introduction," xiv and xv.

7. John Berthrong and Francis Clooney, "Editors' Introduction to *European Perspectives on the New Comparative Theology*," *Religions 3* (2012): 1195.

8. See Catherine Cornille, "Soteriological Agnosticism and the Future of Catholic Theology of Interreligious Dialogue," in *The Past, Present, and Future of Theologies of Interreligious Dialogue*, ed. T. Merrigan and J. Friday (Oxford: Oxford University Press, 2017), 201–15; Catherine Cornille, "Soteriological Agnosticism and Interreligious Dialogue," in *From Vatican II to Pope Francis: Charting a Catholic Future*, ed. P. Crowley (Maryknoll: Orbis Books, 2014).

9. Paul Knitter, *Introducing Theologies of Religions* (Maryknoll: Orbis Books, 2002), 202–14.

10. Kristin Beise Kiblinger, "Relating Theology of Religions and Comparative Theology," in *The New Comparative Theology*, ed. F. Clooney (London: T&T Clark, 2010), 42.

11. Gabriel Almond, R. Scott Appleby, and Emmanuel Sivan, *Strong Religion: The Rise of Fundamentalisms around the World* (Chicago: University of Chicago Press, 2003), 102.

12. Paul Griffiths, *Problems of Religious Diversity* (Oxford: Blackwell, 2001), 54.

13. Trent Pomplun, *Jesuit on the Roof of the World: Ippolito Desideri's Mission to Eighteenth-Century Tibet* (New York: Oxford University Press, 2010), *82*, 95.

14. Hendrik Kraemer, *The Christian Message in a Non-Christian World* (London: Edinburgh House Press, 1938), 135.

15. Karl Barth, *Church Dogmatics, vol. 1: The Doctrine of the Word of God, part 2* (London: T&T Clark, 1961), 350.

16. Barth, *Church Dogmatics, vol. 1, part 2*, 326–27.

17. Barth, *Church Dogmatics, vol. 1, part 2*, 339.

18. He is aware of the distinction between the Pure Land ("Yodo-Shu") and the True Pure Land ("Yodo-Shin-Shu") schools of Buddhism and the difference between the cat school and the monkey schools of the Hindu Bhakti tradition. Barth, *Church Dogmatics, vol. 1, part 2*, 340–44.

19. Barth, *Church Dogmatics, vol. 1, part 2*, 342.

20. Barth, *Church Dogmatics, vol. 1, part 2*, 343.

21. Sven Ensminger, *Karl Barth's Theology as a Resource for a Christian Theology of Religions* (London: Bloomsbury, 2014), 221.

22. Ensminger, *Karl Barth's Theology*, 237.

23. Ensminger, *Karl Barth's Theology*, 237.

24. Ensminger, *Karl Barth's Theology*, 221.

25. See Hugh Nicholson, *Comparative Theology and the Problem of Religious Rivalry* (Oxford: Oxford University Press, 2010), 70–105.

26. Paul Griffiths, *An Apology for Apologetics: A Study in the Logic of Interreligious Dialogue* (Maryknoll: Orbis Books, 1991), 3.

27. Griffiths, *An Apology for Apologetics*, 14.

28. Griffiths, *An Apology for Apologetics*, 83–108.

29. See Paul Williams, *The Unexpected Way: On Converting from Buddhism to Catholicism* (London: T&T Clark, 2002) and the ensuing debate in John D'Arcy May, ed., *Converging Ways?* (Sankt Ottilien: EOS, 2007), 67–154.

30. Francis Clooney, *Hindu God, Christian God* (Oxford: Oxford University Press, 2001), 161.

31. Clooney, *Hindu God, Christian God*, 158.

32. Clooney, *Hindu God, Christian God*, 146.

33. Clooney, *Hindu God, Christian God*, 158.

34. Clooney, *Hindu God, Christian God*, 160.

35. George Lindbeck, *The Nature of Doctrine* (Louisville: Westminster John Knox Press, 2009), 18, originally published 1984.

36. Lindbeck, *The Nature of Doctrine*, 87.

37. Lindbeck, *The Nature of Doctrine*, 116.

38. Lindbeck, *The Nature of Doctrine*, 132.

39. Lindbeck, *The Nature of Doctrine*, 133.

40. Lindbeck, *The Nature of Doctrine*, 117.

41. Jeannine Hill Fletcher, *Monopoly on Salvation? A Feminist Approach to Religious Pluralism.* (New York: Continuum, 2005), 76, 75.

42. Marianne Moyaert, "Absorption or Hospitality," in *Interreligious Hermeneutics*, ed. C. Cornille and C. Conway (Eugene: Wipf & Stock, 2010), 68.

43. Moyaert, "Absorption or Hospitality," 70.

44. Marianne Moyaert, *In Response to the Religious Other* (Lanham: Lexington Books, 2014), 133.

45. John Milbank, "The End of Dialogue," in *Christian Uniqueness Reconsidered*, ed. G. D'Costa (Maryknoll: Orbis Books, 1990), 185.

46. Milbank, "The End of Dialogue," 190.

47. Lindbeck, *The Nature of Doctrine*, 59.

48. Lindbeck, *The Nature of Doctrine*, 25.

49. "The warrior passions of barbarian Teutons and Japanese occasioned great changes in originally pacifistic Christianity and Buddhism." Lindbeck, *The Nature of Doctrine*, 19.

50. Lindbeck, *The Nature of Doctrine*, 47.

51. Lindbeck, *The Nature of Doctrine*, 35.

52. Lindbeck, *The Nature of Doctrine*, 39.

53. Lindbeck, *The Nature of Doctrine*, 47–48.

54. Lindbeck, *The Nature of Doctrine*, 40.
55. Mark Heim, *Salvations: Truth and Difference in Religion* (Maryknoll: Orbis Books, 1995).
56. Though he could have simply recognized the particularity of his own faith perspective, he argues for the superiority of the Christian understanding of the ultimate end on the basis of Jerome Gellman's thesis that "The attempt at harmonization should be guided by the desire to accommodate as much of the appearances as is possible as indicative of reality. Any adjudication which in this regard saves more phenomenal content than another is to be preferred, everything else being equal." Jerome Gellman, *Experience of God and the Rationality of Theistic Belief* (Ithaca: Cornell University Press, 1997), 112, quoted in Mark Heim, *The Depth of the Riches: A Trinitarian Theology of Religious Ends* (Grand Rapids: Eerdmans, 2001), 38.
57. Heim, *The Depth of the Riches*, 213.
58. Lindbeck circumvents possible accusations of relativism by still allowing for the possibility of correspondence between religious truth claims and objective reality.
59. This is the terminology used by Roger Haight in *Jesus, Symbol of God* (Maryknoll: Orbis Books, 2000), 409.
60. Karl Rahner, "Christianity and the Non-Christian Religions," in *Theological Investigations*, vol. 5 (London: Darton, Longman & Todd, 1966), 125.
61. Rahner, "Christianity and the Non-Christian Religions," 121.
62. Rahner, "Christianity and the Non-Christian Religions," 118. Rahner realized that the mere knowledge of Christianity was not sufficient to recognize its superiority and thus disqualify one's old religion. It is only when "an existentially real demand is made by the absolute religion in its historically tangible form" that a certain obligation exists to embrace it (119).
63. Rahner, "Christianity and the Non-Christian Religions," 133.
64. Hans Küng, *Theology for the New Millennium* (New York: Doubleday, 1988), 248.
65. Choan-Seng Song, *Third-Eye Theology: Theology in Formation in Asian Settings* (Maryknoll: Orbis Books, 1991), 90.
66. Peggy Starkey, "Agape: A Christian Criterion for Truth in the Other World Religions," *International Review of Mission 74* (1985): 425–63.
67. Henri de Lubac, *Amida* (Paris: Seuil, 1955), 10.
68. Pierre Johanns, *To Christ through Vedānta* (Bangalore: United Theological College, 1996), 5–6, originally published 1929.
69. Johanns, *To Christ through Vedānta*, 6.
70. Rudolf Otto, *Mysticism East and West* (New York: Collier Books, 1962). The comparison sheds particular light on Eckhart's apophaticism, even if Otto ultimately emphasizes its grounding in a clear theistic tradition.
71. Gavin D'Costa, *The Meeting of Religions and the Trinity* (Maryknoll: Orbis Books, 2000), 122.
72. D'Costa, *The Meeting of Religions and the Trinity*, 122.
73. D'Costa, *The Meeting of Religions and the Trinity*, 114.

74. Hugh Nicholson, "The New Comparative Theology and Theological Hegemony," in *The New Comparative Theology*, ed. F. Clooney (London: T&T Clark, 2010), 58–59; Klaus von Stosch, "Comparative Theology and Comparative Religion," in *Interreligious Comparisons in Religious Studies and Theology*, ed. P. Schmidt-Leukel and A. Lehring (London: Bloomsbury, 2016), 165.

75. As we will see in the discussion of comparative theological hermeneutics, the difference between the two types of comparative theology is often a matter of degree, rather than a radical distinction.

76. Haight, *Jesus, Symbol of God*, 409.

77. Christian theologians who have developed a Trinitarian and pneumatological approach to theology of religions are Amos Young in his books *Hospitality and the Other* (Maryknoll: Orbis Books, 2008) and *Beyond the Impasse: Toward a Pneumatological Theology of Religions* (Eugene: Wipf & Stock, 2014); as well as Dermot Lane, *Stepping Stones to Other Religions: A Christian Theology of Inter-Religious Dialogue* (Maryknoll: Orbis Books, 2011).

78. Jacques Dupuis, *Toward a Christian Theology of Religious Pluralism* (Maryknoll: Orbis Books, 1997), 205ff.

79. Dupuis, *Toward a Christian Theology*, 207.

80. Dupuis, *Toward a Christian Theology*, 282.

81. Dupuis, *Toward a Christian Theology*, 346.

82. Dupuis, *Toward a Christian Theology*, 249.

83. Dupuis, *Toward a Christian Theology*, 252.

84. Jacques Dupuis, "Complementarity and Convergence," in *Many Mansions? Multiple Religious Belonging and Christian Identity*, ed. C. Cornille (Eugene: Wipf & Stock, 2010), 61–75.

85. Congregation for the Doctrine of the Faith, "Notification on the Book *Toward a Christian Theology of Religious Pluralism* by Jacques Dupuis, S.J.," January 24, 2001, article 6.

86. *Nostra aetate* (1965), para. 2, in *Vatican Council II*, ed. A. Flannery (New York: Costello, 1975), 739, emphasis added.

87. Pontifical Council for Inter-Religious Dialogue, *Dialogue and Proclamation* (1991), article 49, http://www.vatican.va/roman_curia/pontifical_councils/interelg/documents/rc_pc_interelg_doc_19051991_dialogue-and-proclamatio_en.html.

88. Paul Griffiths, *Problems of Religious Diversity* (Oxford: Blackwell, 2001), 63. Though Paul Griffiths believes that the Church has no explicit position on either closed or open inclusivism, he argues that the burden of the proof lies on those who would defend closed inclusivism. Griffiths thus suggests that the Church "ought to adopt a properly modalized open inclusivism, of the following form: It is possible that alien religions teach truths of religious significance to the Church, and that some of these are not yet explicitly taught or understood by the Church."

89. Abhishiktānanda, *Saccidānanda* (London: ISPCK, 1974), 49.

90. Abhishiktānanda, *Saccidānanda*, 70.

91. The challenges of achieving this reconciliation are evident not only in books such as *Saccidānanda*, but also and more poignantly in his journal, Abhishiktānanda, *La montée au fond du coeur. Le journal intime du moine chrétien-sannyasi hindou, 1948–1973* (Paris: OEIL, 1986).

92. All volumes are published by Peeters in Leuven.

93. John Keenan, *The Meaning of Christ: A Mahāyāna Theology* (Maryknoll: Orbis Books, 1989); John Keenan, *The Gospel of Mark: A Mahāyāna Reading* (Maryknoll: Orbis Books, 1995); John Keenan, *The Emptied Christ of Philippians: Mahāyāna Meditations* (Eugene: Wipf & Stock, 2015); John Keenan and Linda Keenan, *I Am / No Self: A Christian Commentary on the Heart Sutra* (Leuven: Peeters, 2011)

94. Joseph O'Leary, *Religious Pluralism and Christian Truth* (Edinburgh: Edinburgh University Press, 1996); Joseph O'Leary, *Conventional and Ultimate Truth: A Key for Fundamental Theology* (South Bend: Notre Dame University Press, 2015); Joseph O'Leary, *Buddhist Nonduality, Paschal Paradox: A Christian Commentary on The Teaching of Vimalakīrti* (Leuven: Peeters, 2017), 273.

95. Klaus von Stosch, *Herausforderung Islam: Christliche Annäherungen* (Paderborn: Ferdinand Schöningh, 2017), 153–79; Klaus von Stosch, *Komparative Theologie als Wegweiser in der Welt der Religionen* (Paderborn: Ferdinand Schöningh, 2017); Klaus von Stosch, "Developing Christian Theodicy in Conversation with Navid Kermani," in *Comparing Faithfully*, ed. M. Voss Roberts (New York: Fordham University Press, 2016), 89–106.

96. "Qur'anic Approaches to Jesus Christ in the Perspective of Comparative Theology," see https://pluriel.fuce.eu/thematique/approches-du-coran-a-jesus-christ-dans-la-perspective-de-theologie-comparee/?lang=en.

97. Dupuis, *Toward a Christian Theology of Religious Pluralism*, 294.

98. Keenan, *The Meaning of Christ*.

99. For just two examples of this: Abhishiktānanda, *Saccidānanda*; Dupuis, *Toward a Christian Theology of Religious Pluralism*, 268–75.

100. John Hick, "The Non-Absoluteness of Christianity," in *The Myth of Christian Uniqueness*, ed. J. Hick and P. Knitter (Maryknoll: Orbis Books, 1987), 18.

101. Hick, "The Non-Absoluteness of Christianity," 23–35.

102. Langdon Gilkey, "Plurality and Its Theological Implications," in *The Myth of Christian Uniqueness*, ed. J. Hick and P. Knitter (Maryknoll: Orbis Books, 1987), 37.

103. Leonard Swidler, John Cobb, Paul Knitter, and Monika Hellwig, *Death or Dialogue? From the Age of Monologue to the Age of Dialogue* (London: SCM Press, 1990), 32.

104. Paul Knitter, *Jesus and the Other Names* (Maryknoll: Orbis Books, 1996), 19.

105. John Hick, "Jesus and the World Religions," in *The Myth of God Incarnate*, ed. J. Hick (London: SCM Press, 1977), 176.

106. John Hick, *God and the Universe of Faiths* (New York: St. Martin's Press, 1973), 159.

107. Knitter, *Jesus and the Other Names*, 72–80.

108. Knitter, *Jesus and the Other Names*, 77.

109. Roger Haight, "The Case for Spirit Christology," *Theological Studies 53* (1992): 280–81. This idea is further developed in Haight's *Jesus, Symbol of God*, 395ff.

110. Knitter, *Jesus and the Other Names*, 18.

111. John Hick, *God Has Many Names* (London: Macmillan, 1980), 126.

112. John Hick, "On Grading Religions," *Religious Studies 17* (1981): 463.

113. Perry Schmidt-Leukel, *Transformation by Integration* (London: SCM Press, 2009), 5.

114. Reinhold Bernhardt and Perry Schmidt-Leukel, eds., *Interreligiöse Theologie: Chancen und Probleme* (Zurich: Theologischer Verlag Zurich, 2014), 12–13.

115. Aldous Huxley, *The Perennial Philosophy* (New York: Harper & Brothers, 1945), vii.

116. At the American Academy of Religion meeting in 2016, Wildman developed the example of the human person who is conceived in science as a bacterial organism. This, he argued, pushes one into the no-self doctrine.

117. Wesley Wildman, "Theology without Walls: The Future of Transreligious Theology," *Open Theology 2* (2016): 244–45.

118. See, for example, Joseph Bracken, *The Divine Matrix: Creativity as Link between East and West* (Eugene: Wipf & Stock, 2006); Joseph Bracken, *The World in the Trinity: Open-Ended Systems in Science and Religion* (Minneapolis: Fortress Press, 2014).

119. Schmidt-Leukel, Transformation by Integration, 145.

120. Paul Knitter, "Comparative Theology Is Not 'Business-as-Usual Theology,'" *Buddhist-Christian Studies 35* (2015): 185–91.

121. For just one example from the Buddhist side, see John Makransky, "Thoughts on Why, How, and What Buddhists Can Learn from Christian Theologians," *Journal of Buddhist-Christian Studies 31* (2011): 119–33, and John Makransky, "A Buddhist Critique of, and Learning from Christian Liberation Theology," *Theological Studies* (2014): 635–57.

122. J. R. Hustwit, *Interreligious Hermeneutics and the Pursuit of Truth* (Lanham: Lexington Books, 2014), 115.

123. Edward Said, *Orientalism* (New York: Vintage Books, 1979).

124. Tomoko Masuzawa, *The Invention of World Religions: Or, How European Universalism Was Preserved in the Language of Pluralism* (Chicago: University of Chicago Press, 2005).

125. For a thorough debate over this, see J. E. Llewellyn, ed., *Defining Hinduism: A Reader* (New York: Routledge, 2005).

126. Timothy Fitzgerald, "A Critique of 'Religion' as a Cross-Cultural Category," Method and Theory in the Study of Religion 9, no. 2 (1997): 99.

127. Daniel Boyarin, Border Lines: The Partition of Judeo-Christianity (Philadelphia: University of Pennsylvania Press, 2004).

128. This critique has been voiced by feminist thinkers such as Ursula King, Maura O'Neill, Jeannine Hill Fletcher, and Kwok Pui-lan.

129. Ursula King, "Feminism: The Missing Dimension in the Dialogue of Religions," in Pluralism and the Religions: The Theological and Political Dimensions, ed. J. D'Arcy May (London: Cassell, 1998), 40.

130. Kwok Pui-lan, *Postcolonial Imagination and Feminist Theology* (Louisville: Westminster John Knox Press, 2005), 205.

131. Kwok, *Postcolonial Imagination*, 205.

132. Kwok, *Postcolonial Imagination*, 206.

133. Hill Fletcher, *Monopoly on Salvation?* 88.

134. Hill Fletcher, *Monopoly on Salvation?* 89.

135. Jeannine Hill Fletcher, *Motherhood as Metaphor* (New York: Fordham University Press, 2013), 71.

136. Nicholson, *Comparative Theology and the Problem of Religious Rivalry*, 104.

137. Judith Gruber, "(Un)Silencing Hybridity: A Postcolonial Critique of Comparative Theology," in *Comparative Theology in the Millennial Classroom*, ed. M. Brecht and R. Locklin (New York: Routledge, 2016), 28. Gruber also believes that this affirming of essential religious identities and a relegating of comparative theology to the margins of the Christian tradition is a way for Clooney "to claim a place for comparative theology within his home tradition" (29).

138. Gruber, "(Un)Silencing Hybridity," 29. It is somewhat ironical that Gruber accuses Clooney of this, since he is highly conscientious about acknowledging the particularity of his choices of texts within the whole of the traditions, and since he always includes a variety of interpretations of the same text.

139. Gruber, "(Un)Silencing Hybridity," 30.

140. Nicholson, *Comparative Theology and the Problem of Religious Rivalry*, 94.

141. Nicholson, *Comparative Theology and the Problem of Religious Rivalry*, 84.

142. Nicholson, *Comparative Theology and the Problem of Religious Rivalry*, 210.

143. Nicholson, *Comparative Theology and the Problem of Religious Rivalry*, 198.

144. Nicholson, *Comparative Theology and the Problem of Religious Rivalry*, 95.

145. Nicholson, *Comparative Theology and the Problem of Religious Rivalry*, 102.

146. Gruber, "(Un)Silencing Hybridity," 31.

147. Christopher Conway, "Liberative Service: A Comparative Theological Reflection on Dalit Theology's Service and Swami Vivekananda's Seva," Dissertation, Boston College, 2014.

148. See some of the articles in Kwok Pui-lan, ed., *Hope Abundant: Third World and Indigenous Women's Theology* (Maryknoll: Orbis Books, 2010).

149. Jeannine Hill Fletcher, "What Counts as 'Catholic'? What Constitutes 'Comparative'? Embodied Practice as a Site for Comparative Catholic Theology," *Studies in Interreligious Dialogue 24*, no. 1 (2014): 79.

150. See Marianne Moyaert and Joris Geldhof, eds., *Ritual Participation and Interreligious Dialogue* (London: Bloomsbury, 2015).

151. Clooney, *Hindu God, Christian God*, 28.

152. These are the arguments advanced by James Fredericks in his "Introduction" to *The New Comparative Theology*, xiv–xv.

153. Kiblinger, "Relating Theology," 42.

154. Kiblinger, "Relating Theology," 42.

3

Comparative Theological Hermeneutics

A combination of various fields or types of inquiry, the discipline of comparative theology is built on various epistemological foundations and hermeneutical approaches. It contains both explicitly normative and more descriptive or historical elements, and it involves a continuous negotiation of various perspectives: one's own, that of the other tradition, and that of one's home tradition. It also presupposes a broad theory of understanding which engages not only texts but also ritual practices, oral traditions, and material culture. As such, comparative theology is based on types of understanding that set it apart from both classical theology and religious studies.

The different approaches to comparative theology have largely reflected the background from which they arose. Whereas nineteenth-century comparative theology grew out of religious apologetics and continued to exhibit a strongly normative bent, the new comparative theology has been more indebted to the disciplines of religious studies and area studies, and has been less inclined to assess the value of the teachings and practices of other religions. It has been strongly concerned with historical accuracy and with faithfulness to the self-understanding of the other tradition. Two characteristics that are often said to typify the new comparative theology are the desire to understand other religions "on their own terms" while on the other hand acknowledging "its own normative commitments and interests." This encapsulates the tensions within comparative theological hermeneutics.

Comparative theologians have generally turned to the tradition of philosophical hermeneutics in order to establish a foundation for comparative theological hermeneutics. Paul Hedges, for example, draws from Hans-Georg Gadamer in order to "help us understand in philosophical terms the process by which the mutual interpretations of religions may take place."[1] David Tracy also believes that Gadamerian hermeneutics still "represents the

Meaning and Method in Comparative Theology, First Edition. Catherine Cornille.
© 2020 John Wiley & Sons Ltd. Published 2020 by John Wiley & Sons Ltd.

most persuasive model for interpretation-hermeneutics" although in need of "qualifications, expansions and even radical corrections or interruptions, especially for interreligious dialogue."[2] He turns in particular to Paul Ricoeur's hermeneutical model of "understanding-explanation-understanding" in order to expand Gadamer's hermeneutical approach. Marianne Moyaert and J. R. Hustwit also believe that Paul Ricoeur's textual hermeneutics "may lend a necessary hermeneutical credibility to comparative theology."[3]

We will here approach comparative theological hermeneutics as a complex interplay between seeing the other through oneself and seeing oneself through the other, dissecting the various elements that go into each. Interreligious understanding is shaped by preconceptions or prejudices that determine the choice of a particular tradition, text, or practice, as well as its interpretation. Though hermeneutical privilege is granted to the self-understanding of the other, comparative theology is based on the basic hermeneutical principle of the indeterminacy of texts, teachings, and practices, and their openness to ever new interpretation. Even when the understanding of the comparative theologian remains colored by certain religious and other prejudices, it may still generate creative insight that may inspire and enrich not only the comparative theologian, but at times also the other.

A central purpose of comparative theology is to expand one's self-understanding by also seeing oneself and one's own tradition through the eyes of the other. This requires transposing oneself into the religious worldview and experience of the other, and attempting to understand oneself and one's own tradition from that perspective. I will here focus on sympathy and the imagination as the two conditions and capabilities that allow individuals to rise above given, familiar categories to grasp, intuit or experience something different or new. This allows both a defamiliarization and a reconceptualization of one's own tradition. Participation in the ritual life and daily practice of the other religion can also play an important role in the process of identifying with and understanding the other. Not only does this serve to stimulate and ground the imagination, but rituals, artistic expressions, and other aspects of material religious culture may become the direct object of comparative theological reflection.

Hermeneutical questions in comparative theology involve not only the processes of understanding, but also the processes of borrowing across religious traditions. In learning from another religion, comparative theologians may appropriate or adopt certain symbols, categories, teachings or practices in order to enrich their own religious understanding. Since no two religions fit seamlessly into one another, this transposition of elements from one religious context into another inevitably involves semantic shifts which must be taken into consideration in comparative theological hermeneutics.

All this may raise critical questions regarding the deontology or propriety of comparative theology. It may lead to charges of syncretism as elements from seemingly incompatible traditions are being combined. And it may cause suspicion and critique of religious hegemony, imperialism or domestication, as teachings and practices of the other are considered for the theological edification and growth of another religion, rather than in their own right. These are legitimate concerns that must be addressed by comparative theological hermeneutics.

3.1 Understanding the Other through the Self

It has come to be broadly recognized in comparative theology as well as in religious study in general that there is no neutral vantage point from which to study religions, and that one's understanding of the other is shaped by personal, religious, cultural, linguistic, and other factors.[4] While this is still treated as something of a liability in the secular study of religion, it is fully embraced in comparative theology as part of the hermeneutical process. The comparative theologian approaches other religions from a clear religious location, and/or with particular religious questions, bringing his or her arsenal of religious insights and experiences to the understanding of the other. Pre-understanding or prejudice thus plays an important role in comparative theological hermeneutics, as in all hermeneutics. While the notion of prejudice acquired negative connotations in light of the Enlightenment ideal of objectivity, Gadamer argued that "all understanding inevitably involves some prejudices."[5] This is particularly the case in the human sciences, where experience and understanding are based in language and history and where one thus always brings foreknowledge and fore-meanings to the understanding of the other. In the case of understanding a text, Gadamer states that: "A person who is trying to understand a text is always projecting. He projects a meaning for the text as a whole as soon as some initial meaning emerges in the text. Again, the initial meaning emerges only because he is reading the text with particular expectations in regard to a certain meaning."[6]

Prejudices thus play a constitutive and productive role in the process of understanding. This is all the more the case with religious texts and practices, where certain categories and references can only be grasped or approximated through some prior religious knowledge and experience, or as answering to particular religious questions. In comparative theology, religious prejudice or pre-understanding plays a role in the choice of traditions, texts or objects for comparative theological engagement, as well as in their interpretation.

The world of religious plurality offers an endless diversity of traditions, texts, and practices for potential engagement. As has been pointed out before, the choice of tradition and the object of theological comparison involves some arbitrariness.[7] Educational context and access to particular traditions undoubtedly play a role. But the choice of particular texts, teachings, and practices will be determined in light of their relevance for one's own tradition. This relevance may derive both from their similarity with or difference from one's own teachings and practices. Francis Clooney states that the work of comparative theology "ordinarily starts with the intuition of an intriguing resemblance that prompts us to place two realities – texts, images, practices, doctrines, persons – near one another so that they may be seen over and again, side by side."[8] Though differences are not ignored, it is the similarities that here direct theological reflection. Comparative theologians may, however, also be moved and inspired by the differences between their own religion and the other. These differences may still be measured in terms of certain basic or minimal similarities. But the comparative theological exercise is here based on some meaningful contrast or sense of complementarity between one's own tradition and the other. Certain texts or practices may be meaningful because they add theological leverage or weight to one's own, or because they address religious questions or areas of experience either lacking or underdeveloped in one's own tradition or past experience. As such, the choice is partially determined by the relevance of the elements from the other religion for one's own. Traditions, teachings, and practices that are not perceived to have any bearing on one's own will be left outside of the purview of comparative theology. Christian comparative theologians have thus engaged other religions on such topics as divine embodiment, theodicy, divine providence, loving surrender, the experience of divine presence and absence, the feminine divine, the origin of evil, the human predicament, pilgrimage, the tripartite structure of reality, etc., all topics relevant to the Christian tradition.

Secondly, prejudices play a role in constructing the comparison and interpreting the other religion. Each religious text, teaching, and practice contains multiple layers of meaning depending in part on the way it is read or understood in relation to other elements of the tradition. Comparative theology tends to lift particular elements outside of their original context and relate them to one's own particular tradition. This thus sheds sharp light on certain meanings while ignoring others. Hugh Nicholson understands comparison as "a way of construing or redescribing one thing in terms of another in order to highlight aspects of the former that are of particular interest to the scholar." The goal of redescription "may be either to overcome the incomprehensibility of an unfamiliar phenomenon, or, alternatively, it may be to unsettle a sense of familiarity that has dulled one's perception of a phenomenon."[9] He refers to the element to be redescribed as the variable, and the term forming the redescription as the constant.[10] In comparative theology, the constant generally represents a familiar religious teaching. The redescription of the other involves a matter of emphasis or focus, rather than a complete reinterpretation. But religious prejudice certainly plays a role in this selective focus.

More broadly, the other religion will be interpreted in comparative theology on the basis of one's own set of religious categories and experiences. In the process of understanding and comparing, comparative theologians start from familiar categories and experiences relevant to themselves and to their respective traditions. These are emptied of their particularity in order to serve as a more neutral comparative category, able to identify similar or analogous phenomena in the other religion. However, some of the familiar connotations and associations of the categories will inevitably linger and color the understanding and interpretation of the other religion. To be sure, comparative theologians may also focus on religious differences, but these will again be defined and understood by way of contrast with one's own, rather than on their own terms.

All this raises the question of the role of religious traditions and religious identity in comparative theological hermeneutics. One's religious identity may be seen to represent only one among different components of one's set of prejudices or pre-understandings shaping the understanding of the other. There are any number of personal, social, and cultural factors that may play a role. Religious identity is itself a matter of hermeneutical engagement with the sources of one's particular tradition. This means that the comparative theologian always engages in several layers of interpretation: first of his or her own tradition, and secondly of the tradition of the other.

In his narrative approach to the person, Ricoeur also considers religious traditions as only one element constituting the more stable part (*idem*) of personal identity. However, individual identity is also dynamic (*ipse*) and constantly formed in relationship with others and with one's environment, and "implies no assertion concerning some unchanging core of the personality."[11] It is this notion of hermeneutical agency which renders Ricoeur's philosophy appealing to comparative theologians such as Moyaert and J. R. Hustwit.[12] "Underlying Ricoeur's approach to the question of personal identity," Moyaert states, "is an anthropology that understands the human being as a creative hermeneutical being who is always in search of meaning. It is not the conformity to tradition that has been passed on but the creativity of the believers that is striking here. Identity is continually being formed."[13] Different comparative theologians with the same religious background may then understand and interpret elements from the other tradition in different ways, depending on an inscrutable combination of intellectual, social, and emotional factors.

Though it is undoubtedly true that the understanding and interpretation of another religion is not shaped solely by one's religious identity, what is distinctive about confessional comparative theology is its deliberate assumption of a particular normative perspective as the lens through which the meaning and importance of the other tradition are filtered and interpreted so as to render elements from the other tradition intelligible and relevant, not only for oneself but for one's own religious tradition more broadly.

Most religious traditions, at least as an ideal, seek to shape the entire worldview and experience of believers in accord with their own teachings and values. This is where Lindbeck's postliberal theology may shed light on the possibilities and limits of comparative theological hermeneutics. In his understanding of religion, religious traditions (ideally) provide the language for interpreting believers' experience of the world and by extension of other religions. This does not mean that other religions are utterly unintelligible or that interreligious dialogue would be "theologically meaningless," as has been argued.[15] Lindbeck recognizes that "religions may be complementary in the sense that they provide guidance to different but not incompatible dimensions of existence."[16] He also states explicitly that "other religions have the resources for speaking truths and referring to realities, even highly important truths and realities, of which Christianity as yet knows nothing and by which it could be greatly enriched."[17] Lindbeck merely emphasizes the fact that all religious truth and meaning is derived from within the grammatical structure of a particular tradition, and that since the ultimate claims of different religions are incommensurable (in the sense that they cannot be true at the same time), one religion will always interpret and evaluate the other from within its own hermeneutical framework.[18] This cultural-linguistic approach thus points to the contours, to the possibilities and limits of comparative theological hermeneutics when done from within the parameters of particular confessional traditions.

While seeing the other through oneself thus plays a constitutive role in comparative theology, prejudices may also distort the other in problematic and unproductive ways and must thus be checked against the self-understanding of the other. Negative prejudices in particular tend to various types of misunderstanding: essentialization, generalization, exaggeration, and projection.[19] Each of these may be used for different reasons and to varying effect, but they often focus primarily on elements that put their own beliefs and practices in a better light. Essentialization usually aims at contrasting elements of one's own religion with that of others, generalization ignores the internal diversity of the other, exaggeration tends to overblow particular events or elements that are despised, and projection involves the superimposition of categories and interpretations of one's own tradition onto the other. Samples of each of these types of misrepresentation are in evidence in Said's *Orientalism*.[20] To be sure, not all negative or critical assessment of the other is based on misunderstanding, and negative prejudice does not always lead to misunderstanding. One may have a fairly accurate understanding of another religion and yet be critical of it, and in spite of their generally negative prejudice toward other religions, some Christian missionaries left behind invaluable information about other religions.[21] Though misunderstanding of the religious other generally arises from negative prejudice, positive prejudice or idealization of the other may at times also lead to distortion. It may exaggerate certain traits that are particularly laudable from one's perspective, and ignore or downplay traits that may be generally viewed as more problematic.[22] While less pernicious, idealization also ultimately involves a limited or faulty understanding of the other religions.

Comparative theological hermeneutics thus involves a balance between fully mobilizing one's pre-understanding and keeping it in check by means of the self-understanding of the other, and between acknowledging and engaging one's own religious presuppositions and engaging and studying the other tradition on its own terms. Clooney also points to this tension when he states that "If we do our work well, grounding scholarly commitments in faith, we will always be on the edge of failing in scholarship or failing in faith. Then we will be properly conflicted theologians, comparative theologians."[23]

In comparative theology, as in the study of religion in general, prejudices need to be checked against the self-understanding of the other. Comparative theologians, as all hermeneutical thinkers, are attentive to "the all-important fact that the focus of hermeneutical philosophy must be on the other as an alterity, not as a projected other of the self."[24] Gadamer already draws attention to the difference between legitimate and illegitimate prejudices, and the need for prejudices and projections to be revised in confrontation with the other:

> A person trying to understand something will not resign himself from the start to relying on his own accidental fore-meanings, ignoring as consistently and stubbornly as possible the actual meaning of the text until the latter becomes so persistently audible that it breaks through what the interpreter imagines it to be. Rather, a person trying to understand a text is prepared for it to tell him something. That is why a hermeneutically trained consciousness must be, from the start, sensitive to the text's alterity. But this kind of sensitivity involves neither "neutrality" with respect to content nor the extinction of one's self, but the foregrounding and appropriation of one's own fore-meanings and prejudices.[25]

This is where David Tracy believes that Ricoeur's approach to hermeneutics "expands and partly corrects Gadamer's hermeneutics" by acknowledging the "interruptions" and distortions in the process of understanding and by offering "a hermeneutical way to render more coherent the meaning of a text."[26] Ricoeur's hermeneutical arc of understanding-explanation-understanding introduces a critical and self-critical moment in the hermeneutical process. It allows for all of the tools of historical and critical study to be brought to bear on the understanding of a phenomenon.

J. R. Hustwit also argues that Ricoeur's approach to hermeneutics emphasizes the alterity of sacred texts and the need to grapple with genuine difference:

> Because the guess must answer to the independent structure of language, an interpreter cannot simply assimilate a text into her own horizon but must confront and grapple with something potentially unfamiliar and heretofore unencountered. The structural determinacy of texts resists the simple projection of preconception and not only challenges but draws the interpreter outside of her own horizon if her naïve guess is found to be wanting. The challenge of explanatory validation is the impetus for critical distance, horizon transcendence and novelty in interpretation.[27]

In addition to errors that may be readily corrected through historical study, Tracy points to the ways in which our perception of the other may be distorted through "*ressentiment* from unadmitted or even noticed racism, sexism, classism, colonialism, imperialism, or Eurocentrism."[28] In addition to the tools of critical theory, Tracy points out that religions themselves contain resources that may "serve as hermeneutics of suspicion on our self-delusions and intractable egotism, including our communal egotisms."[29] He refers in particular to the Christian notion of sin and the Buddhist notion of *avidya* (ignorance) as internal religious cautions against faulty projections and distortions of the other. But religions may also offer constructive resources for recognizing and welcoming the other through categories of "justice, compassion, love" and through affirming the other as "the friend, the family, the neighbor, the stranger, the forgotten and oppressed; even, at the limit, the enemy."[30] Comparative theology may thus also draw from its own religious sources to recognize the alterity of the other and remain vigilant of one's own conscious and unconscious distortions.

One way in which comparative theologians attempt to minimize distorting projection and generalization is through its focus on particular texts or teachings that are carefully circumscribed and studied within their own religious context.[31] They accord a certain hermeneutical priority to the self-understanding of the other, and attempt to avoid simply superimposing its own interpretation onto a text or teaching by engaging indigenous interpretations and submitting itself to correction and redress by religious insiders. In the end, however, the comparative theologian remains an outsider and his or her understanding and interpretation will be colored by particular questions and presuppositions.

Though the goal of comparative theology is to approach the self-understanding of the other, the perspective of the outsider may also yield theological fruit, even for the insider. There are numerous examples in the history of religions of what might be called "creative misunderstanding," from Plotinus's and the neo-Platonic understanding of Plato, to Aquinas's understanding of Aristotle, and from classical Hindu interpretations of the meaning and role of the Buddha, to more modern interpretations of the meaning and role of the person of Jesus Christ. While these interpretations and uses may be regarded as misunderstanding from the perspective of the original tradition, they also represent moments of philosophical and theological creativity that may occasionally also come to inform and inspire the tradition of origin. In his dialogical approach to hermeneutics, Mikhail Bakhtin emphasizes the importance of the outsider perspective (*exotopy*) when he states that:

> There is an enduring image that is partial, and therefore false, according to which to better understand a foreign culture one should live in it and, forgetting one's own, look at the world through the eyes of its culture. As I have said, such an image is partial. To be sure, to enter in some measure into an alien culture and look at the world through its eyes is a necessary moment in the process of understanding; but if understanding were exhausted in this moment, it would have been no more than a simple duplication and would have brought nothing new or enriching. Creative understanding does not renounce its self, its place in time, its culture; it does not forget anything. The chief matter of understanding is the exotopy of the one who does the understanding – in time, space, and culture – in relation to what he wants to understand creatively … In the realm of culture, exotopy is the most powerful lever of understanding. It is only to the eyes of an *other* culture that the alien culture reveals itself more completely and more deeply (but never exhaustively, because there will come other cultures, that will see and understand even more).[32]

While no outsider perspective is normative or conclusive, each may contribute to deepening the self-understanding of the insider. This may occur by shedding light on the particularity of certain beliefs and practices, by drawing attention to underdeveloped or unnoticed dimensions or aspects of one's own tradition, or by offering new frameworks for interpretation. Interreligious hermeneutics may thus represent what Bakhtin calls a "surplus of seeing."[33]

Bakhtin in fact assigns a certain privilege to the position of the outsider. "Creative understanding," he states, "does not renounce itself, its own place, time, its own culture, and it forgets nothing. In order to understand it is immensely important for the person who understands to be located outside the object of his or her creative understanding – in time, in space, in culture."[34]

One of the basic principles of comparative theological hermeneutics, as of all hermeneutics, is the idea of the semantic indeterminacy of religious texts, teachings, and practices. Ricoeur speaks in this regard of the fourfold distanciation of a text from the act of speaking, from the intention of the author, from its original historical and cultural context, and from its originally intended audience.[35] Applying these principles to comparative theology, Marianne Moyaert states that this "challenges the idea that insiders are the only true possessors of their tradition and hence the only ones authorized to read and interpret their religious texts. Because of the four-fold process of distanciation, a strange religious text can disclose its meaning to attentive readers, even if they do not belong to the community for which the text was originally meant."[36] Just as sacred texts and teachings are continuously reinterpreted within any particular religion, and just as these interpretations may differ significantly across time and traditions, comparative theologians may also offer their own distinctive perspective and interpretation of sacred texts and teachings, even if they do not adhere to the tradition in which they play a normative role. Paul Hedges also argues that the hermeneutical notion of the indeterminacy of texts justifies the practice of comparative theology:

> The act of interreligious interpretation or translation as practiced within Comparative Theology is therefore free to extend and develop the text and its meaning. We can see new things the author or original audience did not. That is to say, the Comparative Theologian may, as she employs a text or concept in her own tradition, come to new insights that extend it beyond the original meaning.[37]

This may represent a sensitive point since sacred texts, unlike literature, are often treated with extreme reverence and rules about who is entitled to access, let alone interpret a particular text. Their handling and reading by individuals who do not belong to the tradition may thus be regarded as sacrilege. Every religious tradition also tends toward a sense of ownership toward its own religious contents, and its interpretation by individuals who lack the faith necessary for proper understanding may thus be experienced as a threat. We will deal with the question of religious hegemony and ownership at the end of this chapter.

3.2   Understanding the Self through the Other

Comparative theology is premised on the possibility and promise of learning something new from another religion. This presupposes the ability to shift one's hermeneutical perspective, enter into the worldview of the other and understand oneself from that perspective. The texts, teachings, and practices of the other religion then become the catalyst for seeing oneself anew. One of the four characteristics of all hermeneutics, according to Tracy, is that "the hermeneutical self experiences an excess to its ordinary self-understanding that it cannot control through conscious intentionality or through desire for the same."[38] It is the element of surprise, and the discovery of a certain alternative, or a surplus of insight and experience in the other religion that also opens up new possibilities for one's own tradition. James Fredericks also insists that comparative theologians are to "go beyond their own religious tradition and expose themselves to teachings that may be strange, unsettling, or even disturbing."[39] The question, however, is whether and how this is possible. As pointed out, one's understanding of the other is always already colored by religious and other presuppositions. However, this does not preclude the discovery of religious ideas and expressions that are genuinely different or new.

The question of the possibility and limits of understanding other religions is not fundamentally different from that informing religious studies and the comparative study of religions in general. It first of all requires in-depth study of that religion, its history, languages, texts, teachings, and practices. The field of religious studies has moved through various stages, from naive optimism in the unlimited possibility of religious understanding, based on common human nature or universal mental structures (phenomenology of religion), through an emphasis on the epistemic particularity and incommensurability of religions (postmodern and postcolonial theory), to a new recognition of the need to find a middle way between "problematic universalism" and "problematic relativism."[40] Some scholars, such as William Paden, have come to rediscover the existence of religious patterns, not as "timeless archetypes carrying ahistorical values or meanings which are simply replicated in histor-ical material," but rather as "explanatory and refineable" categories which surface both similarities and differences between religions.[41] Others, such as Fabian Volker, even return to the idea of "universal reason" and "invariant structures of knowing" in order to argue for the possibility of understanding across religious differences.[42] In his "fractal theory of religious diversity," Perry Schmidt-Leukel argues that "the differences that can be observed at the inter-religious level are, to some extent, reflected at an intrareligious level in the internal differences discerned within the major religious traditions, and that they can be broken down at the intrasubjective level into different religious patterns and structures of the individual mind."[43] In order to understand the other religions, "one will be able to resort to some common ground found within the larger reservoir of one's own tradition" and this otherness "will thus be grasped in terms of a different emphasis and elaboration of features that are less developed or differently developed in one's own tradition."[44] Without presuming universal or uncritical intelligibility, the comparative study of religions is thus moving to a greater optimism about understanding religious others, not only in their similarity but also in their difference or particularity.

The two faculties that play a central role in understanding the other religion in its alterity are sympathy and the imagination. As Ricoeur states, "it is always through some transfer from self to other, in empathy and imagination, that the Other that is foreign to me is brought closer."[45] Sympathy here involves a positive disposition toward the coherence and meaningfulness of the teachings and practices of the other. This requires a general theology of religions that affirms in principle the possible validity and truth of other religions. But beyond this, comparative theologians tend to engage traditions they are particularly drawn to. Raimon Panikkar argues that real understanding of a particular religion requires a certain "convincement,"[46] or identification with the truth and validity of its teachings and practices. It is probably true that it is only if one has come to experience for oneself the power and impact of certain beliefs and practices that one can really claim to understand them. It is the fascination with particular teachings and practices that generates a desire to immerse oneself more deeply into the broader religious context and engage in a thorough study of the other religion. This sympathy may at times also lead to a personal identification with the other and to a sense of multiple religious identification. One may then move back and forth between different religious and hermeneutical perspectives, seeing one through the lens of the other. Sympathy may simply entail recognition of the plausibility of the teachings or practices of the other religion and of their possibility, not only for the other but also for oneself. David Tracy suggests that "to attend to the other as other, the different as different, is also to understand the different *as* possible … In such moments of recognition, what is both disclosed and concealed as other and different becomes appropriated as possibility."[47] This hypothetical possibility lends credibility to the other and both reflects and generates a deep level of understanding. It is of course possible that proper understanding of a particular teaching or practice leads to antipathy or rejection, and that certain negative prejudices may still yield fairly accurate understanding of the other. However, negative prejudices tend to generate the types of misunderstanding mentioned before, and would not likely lead to a constructive desire to see oneself through the other.

Sympathy for the religious other does not guarantee understanding. It also requires imagination, or the ability to rise beyond one's own given set of beliefs and experiences and conceive of significantly different possibilities. Though the imagination plays an important role in all of Ricoeur's thought, he defines it only in passing as "the faculty of moving easily from one experience to another if their difference is slight and gradual, and thus of transforming diversity into identity."[48] And in his treatment of metaphors, he emphasizes the role of the imagination as the "*ability* to produce new kinds of assimilation and to produce them not *above* the differences, as in the concept, but in spite of and through the differences."[49] The imagination thus serves to bridge the difference between actual and potential experiences and forms of being and thinking. Ricoeur also speaks of the "subversive force of the imaginary,"[50] pointing to its potential to break through the status quo and open up the realm of possibilities.

Imagination plays a central role in religious life in general. It is through the imagination that believers are lifted beyond their mundane existence into the realms of religious possibilities and ideals. Sacred texts and religious rituals allow believers to identify imaginatively with particular religious ideals which shape their overall religious life and behavior. The very concreteness and particularity of one's own religious views may also at times point the imagination to alternate possibilities. Certain religious beliefs or practices imaginatively contain their opposite within themselves, monotheism evoking the specter of polytheism, or dualism the possibility of nondual conceptions of the relationship between the human and the divine. As such, one's own concrete beliefs and practices may become the basis for entering imaginatively into the realm of the religious other.

Though imagination represents primarily a mental faculty, embodiment and bodily metaphors may provide a conduit for the imagination. Ricoeur speaks of the prereflexive nature of the pairing of one's own body with that of the other, prior to any linguistic expression.[51] Richard Kearney also speaks of "a special grammar of carnal hermeneutics across distance, gaps and difference."[52] This "proto-hermeneutics of the flesh," while representing only one element in the process of interreligious hermeneutics, may still contribute to the logic of understanding across religious traditions. Prior to cultural and religious differences, we are embodied beings with particular needs and desires and with physical capabilities that both open up and delimit the range of possibility for religious expression and communication. In perceiving the forms and movements of the other, one may thus gain a certain preliminary access to their possible impact on the life and experience of the other. Following George Lakoff and Mark Johnson's conceptual metaphor theory, Michelle Voss Roberts argues that primary metaphors which derive from human embodiment may serve in particular as a vehicle for understanding across cultures and religions: "Theological metaphors ensure intelligibility by drawing upon (near) universal bodily experiences to express abstract concepts and values. Thus they offer a basis for interreligious (and intergeneric) comparison."[53] Though themselves the fruit of the imagination, metaphors may indeed serve to guide the imagination into the realm of the other. Voss Roberts focuses on the metaphors of fluidity and fluids designating the relationship between the human and the divine and allowing for a reconceptualization of this relationship in the work of both Hindu and Christian female mystics.[54]

While the imagination plays a central role in entering into a new religious universe, it may also at times falter, due to personal limitations or to the radical alterity of the other. It may also run wild and lose any grounding in the self-understanding of the other. Participation in the religious life of the other therefore plays an important role in both stimulating and grounding the imagination. One's own imaginative understanding may also be checked and verified against the self-understanding of the other. In the attempt to understand oneself through the eyes of the other, comparative theologians may of course simply ask members of the other tradition how they perceive or interpret one's own religious teachings and practices. But it is only by understanding and experiencing for oneself the meaning and power of particular teachings and practices that they may become the occasion for reenvisioning one's own tradition or for developing new religious syntheses.

The attempt to stretch the imagination and see oneself through the eyes of the other tradition may sharpen, deepen, and enhance theological understanding in a variety of ways. First of all, it brings about a process of defamiliarization. Religious and theological reflection typically operates on the basis of a set number of texts and within an established set of categories that are handed down from one generation to the next. This creates a firm sense of theological identity and security. But it also limits theological creativity and the possibilities of innovation and growth. It may also lead to a distorted sense of the universal relevance and meaning of one's own hermeneutical framework. Seeing oneself through the eyes of another thus sheds new and sometimes sharper light on teachings and practices otherwise drowned in familiarity. It may raise new religious questions and problems that may not appear within the self-contained system of a particular religion. It also puts into sharp relief the particularity (and at times also the peculiarity) of one's own familiar beliefs. Awareness of the particularity of one's own beliefs and practices may at times generate a sense of theological humility. But it may also produce a renewed appreciation of the importance, beauty, and meaning of particular teachings and practices, and stimulate a new attempt to render them meaningful, credible or plausible not only for one's own tradition but also for other traditions.

Seeing oneself through the eyes of the other may also lead to religious reimagination or reconceptualization. Different religious traditions are based not only on differing and at times competing religious beliefs and practices, but also on different foundational events and questions, and on different hermeneutical frameworks. Some religions may have a more developed understanding of and approach to certain areas of religious life than others. And different hermeneutical frameworks and categories are not necessarily incompatible. Comparative theological hermeneutics may thus open up and enlarge the hermeneutical horizon of the comparative theologian and broaden the possibilities for understanding and interpretation. It may also shed light on areas of religious thought and practice that are underdeveloped and that may profit from the expertise and the experience of the other religion. In Chapter 4, I will focus in greater detail on the different types of learning that may take place by understanding one's own religious tradition through the eyes of the other.

Jon Paul Sydnor states that "much of the power of comparative theology is derived from its capacity to generate tension, stimulate the imagination, stir the subconscious, doubt the obvious, and interrogate the familiar."[55] In his own comparative theological understanding of Schleiermacher through the Hindu philosopher Rāmānuja, he comes to new insight into the particularity of Schleiermacher's phenomenology when seen in light of Rāmānuja's ontology. Similarly, Klaus von Stosch's study of Jesus in the Qur'an confronts traditional Christology with new questions and insights and allows Christians to "discover themselves anew through the other and generate deeper self-understanding."[56] The very attempt to see oneself through the eyes of the other may thus open up new hermeneutical horizons, and generate new theological insight.

3.3 Participation and Understanding

Comparative theological hermeneutics, like hermeneutics in general, has focused primarily on the understanding of texts. This is not surprising since sacred texts play a central role in the so-called "world religions."[57] Though there is something arbitrary about this designation, it does tend to refer to the numerically larger religious traditions, and sacred texts play a role in this. They facilitate the dissemination and translation of the teachings of a religion, and they form a relatively stable point of reference. Though the interpretation of texts may vary among different schools within a tradition, and change in the course of history, the text itself preserves its normative or authoritative status. There is also an intimate and complex connection between sacred texts and religious practices, with texts reflecting and/or prescribing ritual and ethical behavior, and providing the historical and philosophical ground for religious action. Comparative theological engagement with certain texts may thus also involve engagement with practices. And finally, sacred texts are more readily accessible to the comparative theologian, and more open to interpretation. They may be translated and privately consulted without breaking any rules of propriety or etiquette and without having to travel to foreign locations. Sacred texts also have great hermeneutical flexibility. Just as they have been subject to continuous interpretation and hermeneutical variation within their respective traditions, they may be interpreted anew across religious traditions. As such, there are good reasons, beyond mere convenience, for focusing mainly on texts in comparative theology.

However, this does not mean that comparative theologians should only focus on texts, or that oral traditions should not be engaged in comparative theological efforts. First, the understanding of sacred texts often requires participation in and resonance with their expression in the ritual life and lived experience of a tradition. It is in their use in ritual contexts and in daily practice that the meaning of certain texts becomes fully manifested. Whereas solitary reading of texts may lead to projection of one's own religious imagination and interpretation onto the other, participation and actual exchange with representatives of a particular tradition tames the imagination and keeps it focused on the self-understanding of the other. At the same time, it may also broaden the imagination and draw attention to realities and details that might otherwise have been missed. Some religious practices have no textual variant. This applies in the first place to traditions whose teachings and practices have been handed down orally for centuries. But it also applies to scriptural traditions of which certain aspects or dimensions cannot be rendered in words. Just as religious learning and pedagogy in one's own tradition requires tutoring and physical proximity, learning from another religion also presupposes apprenticeship and immersion in the broader sensory context of a tradition. Hearing the recitation of a text not only gestures to its use in a particular tradition, but may also open up new layers of meaning that are not evident in historical and exegetical study.

In addition to supporting, correcting or strengthening the understanding of sacred texts, participation in the religious life of the other may thus generate a level and type of understanding that simply cannot emerge from the reading of texts. In his critique of the almost exclusive focus on texts in philosophical and interreligious hermeneutics, John Maraldo draws attention to the nonlinguistic dimensions of religions. He points out that some practices are "done for their own sake or for the sake of a goal inseparable from their very performance," and that some are not merely the expression of conceptual thought, but geared toward overcoming all discursive thinking.[58] Understanding these types of religious practices is thus only possible through participation and direct personal experience. Maraldo argues that engaging in practices may "not only increase the amount of content understood; it can change the very way one understands."[59] Since religion is about more than conceptual knowledge or rational understanding, participation may generate nonverbal and experiential forms of understanding that may themselves also inform comparative theological reflection.

The dominant focus on sacred texts has also been a point of critique within comparative theology itself. Marianne Moyaert, for example, takes issue with the fact that comparative theologians have paid almost no attention to the ritual practices of other religious traditions, or engaged them in a constructive way.[60] She argues that the preference for texts in comparative theology is not innocent but is "rooted in a long and complex history in which mind (reason, reading, texts) was privileged over body (senses, performance, symbolic practices)."[61] She points to the intimate interconnection between texts and rituals, and to the important role of rituals in not only reflecting, but shaping, religious beliefs and attitudes and suggests that "by paying attention to the material and ritual practices of traditions, we will start asking different questions and maybe even develop new theological concepts."[62] For Paul Hedges, "there is certainly a need therefore to move comparative theology away from textual analysis, or even the supposition that this represents the best way to undertake the discipline."[63] Laurel Schneider points to alternative types of engagement taking place with Native American traditions in, "When the Book Is a Coyote."[64] Some comparative theologians have in fact focused on ritual practices. Albertus Bagus Laksana, for example, has engaged in an in-depth study of some of the shared pilgrimage sites and practices of Muslims and Christians.[65] And both John Thatamanil and Mark Heim have reflected theologically on the adoption of and participation in Hindu and Buddhist meditative practices by Christians.[66] Here, the work of comparative theology represents a second-order reflection on spontaneous forms of interreligious ritual participation and ritual borrowing.

Another nontextual or nonlinguistic way of engaging in comparative theology is through artistic expression. Here, artists may use symbolic elements and images of different religious traditions in order to enlarge and enrich the religious imagination and the visual religious experience of any one tradition. The Indian Christian artist Jyoti Sahi, for example, has throughout his career engaged in the broadening of the Christian esthetic experience through the integration of elements from Hinduism, and more recently also from Buddhism, Islam, and Indian tribal religions. These artistic expressions are at times a reflection of theological developments taking place,[67] but at times also create new and creative visual expressions that may in turn engender new forms of comparative theological reflection.[68]

Though comparative theology may focus on ritual practices and artistic expressions, and though the understanding of the other may be enriched, nuanced, and even shaped by ritual participation, it remains itself, like all theology, a linguistic exercise. It involves a systematic commentary on existing forms of learning from other religions, or else a proposal for ways in which elements from other religions might be integrated in thought, practice or in the material religious culture more broadly. As such, comparative theology is itself limited to what can be expressed in words. There are other reasons why ritual and practice may be less engaged in comparative theology. If comparative theology is approached as a constructive exercise, or as a process of religious development and change through learning from other religions, rituals, symbols and material culture are generally more religion-specific, or particular, and more difficult to transpose from one religious context into another. Rituals are also slower or more resistant to change, and comparative theology will mainly constitute a theological reflection on spontaneous forms of borrowing. While comparative theologians may themselves experiment with possibilities for learning from the practices of other religious traditions, such experimentation only bears fruit when it comes to affect or change the ritual life within a particular religion.

Though ritual participation plays an important role in understanding the other and in shaping comparative theological reflection, there are also limits to the possibility of such participation. Not only are certain rituals exclusively reserved for initiated members of a particular religion, but any participation in the ritual life of another religion also raises questions regarding the propriety of joining in the physical expression of the faith of the other.[69] It may be regarded as a betrayal of one's own faith and religious tradition, and an expression of inauthenticity with regard to the other. The challenges of inter-riting may differ, depending on the form and content of the ritual itself.[70] The more aniconic, apophatic or nonlinguistic, the easier it is to participate. The more rituals are a reflection of a different set of beliefs, the more their participation requires some degree of theological justification, both on the part of one's own tradition and on the part of the other. These restrictions point to the limits not only of comparative theological engagement with ritual, but of interreligious understanding in general.

3.4 Dynamics of Interreligious Borrowing

In the process of engaging another religious tradition, comparative theologians may come to adopt or borrow elements from the other religion in order to expand and enrich their own religious understanding and experience. This generally involves a semantic shift in which the meaning of certain teachings or practices changes to fit the new religious context. Insofar as religious symbols, teachings, and practices derive their meaning from their place within the broader religious context, their transposition into a different religious context cannot happen without a certain loss of original meaning. Its reinterpretation within a new religious context may also be regarded as a source of semantic enrichment, at least by and for the borrowing tradition.

Religious borrowing has been taking place throughout history, as religions tend to take in thoughts and practices from prior and surrounding religions in forming their own distinct identity. Scholars such as Daniel Boyarin have pointed out how Christian identity came to be formed by borrowing from, building upon, and (artificially) distinguishing itself from the rabbinic tradition.[71] Islam borrowed from Judaism and Christianity, adapting biblical creation stories, and adopting both canonical and apocryphal narratives to fit its own central message. While distinguishing itself from the Vedic tradition, Buddhism retained much of its basic worldview, and Hinduism in time appropriated religious and philosophical ideas that had been developed in a Buddhist context. Religions have incorporated saints and copied ascetical practices from other religious traditions.[72] In the process of enculturation, inculturation, or adaptation to new cultural contexts, religions have readily adopted categories, symbols, and ritual elements from the religions that shaped that particular culture. The process of interreligious borrowing has only intensified as religions have come to interact with one another more directly and learned from ways in which other religions have adapted to social and cultural changes.[73]

What is distinctive about the process of borrowing in the context of comparative theology is its deliberate, systematic, and self-conscious nature. Whereas religious borrowing in the course of history often happened unconsciously and/or without acknowledging its source, comparative theology openly recognizes and credits the tradition from which it borrows. While historically borrowing may have often reflected an attitude of superiority or supersessionism, regarding the other tradition as obsolete, comparative theology affirms the continued relevance of the other tradition, and the distinct meaning of a borrowed idea or practice within its own religious context. Comparative theology also seeks to preserve as much as possible of the original meaning of a particular teaching or practice so as to allow it to inform and enrich one's own tradition. Thus, when Joseph O'Leary introduces the Buddhist term *upāya* to interpret the status of Christian doctrine as skillful means, he does not merely reinterpret the term to fit a traditional Christian understanding of doctrine, but he rather uses it to challenge the traditional propositional understanding of doctrine and to propose an alternative approach.[74] Conversely, when Masao Abe uses the Christian notion of *kenosis* in a Buddhist context, it comes to acquire certain Buddhist connotations without entirely losing its Christian meaning.[75]

When elements originating in one religious context are transplanted into another, this inevitably leads to certain semantic shifts, since the religious frameworks in which they are embedded and from which they derive their meaning are never perfectly compatible. This is what Lindbeck had in mind when he emphasized the incommensurability of religions and impossibility of transposing elements from one religion into another unscathed. Though not without some exaggeration, he states that "when affirmations or ideas from categorically different religions or philosophical frameworks are introduced into a given religious outlook, these are either simply babbling or else, like mathematical formulas employed in a poetic text, they have vastly different functions and meanings than they had in their original settings."[76] In his critique of inclusivism, Gavin D'Costa also argues that

> what is thus included from a religion being engaged with, is not really that religion *per se*, but a reinterpretation of that tradition in so much as that which is included is now included within a different paradigm, such that its meanings and utilization within that new paradigm can only perhaps bear some analogical resemblance to its meaning and utilization within its original paradigm.[77]

The challenges involved in interreligious borrowing are an extension of the more basic challenge of translation between religions and between languages in general. As Panikkar puts it, "we cannot properly translate words" since "words reflect a total human experience and cannot be severed from it." Speaking of transplanting religious categories, he states that "We can only transplant them along with a certain surrounding context that gives them meaning and offers the horizon over against which they can be understood, that is, assimilated within another horizon. Even then the transplanted word, if it survives, will soon extend its roots in the soil and acquire new aspects, connotations, and so forth."[78] The process of borrowing from another religion inevitably involves a process of semantic loss and gain. Symbols, teachings, and practices lose some of their original meaning and connotation, while accruing new meanings and references in becoming part of a new hermeneutical context. There is thus no semantic gain without a certain loss.

Turning to Ricoeur's theory of the untranslatability of languages, Moyaert also points out that "There is no such thing as a perfect translation, understood as a simple doubling of the original. Shifts in meaning, even a loss of meaning, cannot be avoided, precisely because there is no reservoir of meaning that can be lifted undamaged out of its original context and transferred to a new context."[79] This happens in the juxtaposition of texts, or the reading of one text in light of another. For Moyaert, Ricoeur's theory of metaphor and the process of metaphorization may here provide the basis for semantic innovation in comparative theological hermeneutics. Just as a metaphor represents an "odd predication that transgresses the semantic and cultural codes of a speaking community"[80] and that resolves the tension between things that do not fit, in the same way, intertextuality involves "the work of meaning through which one text in referring to another both displaces this other text and receives from it an extension of meaning."[81]

Comparative theology may involve the borrowing of practices, categories or entire hermeneutical frameworks. In this process of borrowing, meanings move in all directions; not only is the borrowed element reinterpreted to fit the new religious context, but this context is also itself changed by integrating new categories and experiences. The desire to learn from the other religion is based on the recognition of a surplus value or meaning in a particular category, teaching or practice, and the goal of comparative theology is to stretch one's hermeneutical horizon and open the religion to new possibilities for religious thought and expression. This is why comparative theologians seek to preserve as much as possible of their original meaning and connotation. Thus, when Abhishiktānanda uses Hindu categories such as *saccidanada* (being-consciousness-bliss) or *guru* to understand the meaning of the Trinity or the role of Jesus as teacher, he explores the possibility for reinterpreting Christianity in those terms as much as the other way around. With regard to understanding Jesus as guru, for example, he states:

> Why feel so uneasy in addressing myself to Christ as to my guru, the one who brings about the passage, the passer of the soul, the taraka? He lived in reality, he passed to the center. And in attaining the center, he made it accessible to all. And men have called him God precisely because he attained pure being.[82]

He also comes to interpret the Christian belief in the uniqueness of Jesus Christ increasingly in Hindu terms. Similarly, when John Keenan, Joseph O'Leary or Raimon Panikkar interpret Christianity through Mādhyamika, Yogacara or Advaita philosophical categories, these tend to bring about a significant change in traditional Christian self-understanding, or a creative tension between the traditional self-understanding and the new possibilities opened up by these types of borrowing.[83]

Elements borrowed from another religion may at times simply fill a gap or tend to underdeveloped areas in one's own tradition. In *Tastes of the Divine*, Michelle Voss Roberts introduces the Hindu *rasa* theory, or theory of religious emotions, to develop a more holistic Christian theology of emotions. She explores the nine principal rasas (the erotic, the comic, the pathetic, the furious, the heroic, the terrible, the odious, the marvelous, and peace) in the Hindu approaches to the emotion so as to "critically evaluate their religious usefulness, and to pursue them as potential tastes of the divine."[84] Though Voss Roberts recognizes that certain emotions are more resonant with Christian devotion, and that "some of the feelings emblematic of Christian experience, such as contrition or gratitude, have been set aside," she seeks to "attend to sentiments often treated as peripheral and to reframe those seen as central."[85] Here, borrowed categories may thus come to enlarge the Christian pallet of religious emotions. In borrowing categories from other religious traditions, comparative theologians may thus tap into new dimensions of their traditions.

As believers are increasingly exposed to the teachings and practices of other religious traditions, the process of interreligious borrowing often occurs spontaneously or from the ground up, leaving comparative theologians with the task of reflecting critically and constructively on such borrowing. This may involve a gradual process in which new ideas and practices germinate and are considered from the perspective of their theological coherence and fit.

Though the subtle or significant semantic shifts that occur in the process of borrowing may be regarded as nothing but a gain for the borrowing individual or tradition, it must be acknowledged that it is generally regarded as a loss or devaluation by the tradition of origin. The Christian use of Hindu or Buddhist forms of prayer, for example, may be regarded by Christians as a new and enriching way to draw attention to the role of the body and the relationship between mind and body in prayer, and to raise new theological and anthropological questions. However, insofar as they come to be interpreted as auxiliary practices, or a means to an end, rather than an end in themselves, they may be simply seen as misused or even abused from the perspective of the tradition of origin. On the other hand, elements of interest to one religion may not be at the heart of another. As Jacques Scheuer points out, "to the 'borrower,' a religious item (text, teaching, ritual, symbol) may appear significant and worthy of interest in spite of the fact that the lending tradition considers it less important, marginal, or even unorthodox or unacceptable."[86] The lending tradition may then be less affected by the semantic shifts that occur.

While meanings may shift in different directions, in the process of borrowing, one religious tradition remains dominant, setting the parameters for what and how elements from other religious traditions come to be integrated.

Some religious teachings and practices are incompatible and no amount of reinterpretation would relieve those tensions. Hence, only those elements that are ultimately compatible with the broader religious framework or with the teachings and practices of that particular tradition will be targeted. This use or instrumentalization of other religions for the purpose of one's own religious development and growth may be regarded as a form of religious hegemony or colonization. We will address this critique at the end of the chapter. But first we will address the risk of syncretism, as elements from different religious traditions are brought together.

3.5 The Problem of Syncretism

One of the possible concerns with regard to the process of borrowing in comparative theological hermeneutics is that of religious syncretism. The term syncretism has been used in the history of religions as "the coexistence of elements foreign to each other within a specific religion, whether or not these elements originate in other religions or in social structures"[87] or as "the temporary ambiguous coexistence of elements from diverse religious and other contexts within a coherent religious pattern."[88] It may refer to a state or to a process, as when it is defined as "the variation of the significance of any phenomenon, occurring in the dynamic of religions, while its form remains quite unaltered."[89] Here, syncretism is understood as an integral part of the history of religions. As religions develop and grow, they often absorb elements from other religious traditions that at first sight or for some time may seem incompatible. The semantic tensions which exist in the original combining of elements of different religions tend to get resolved in the course of time, as meanings shift and become part of a new integrated whole.

In theology, the term syncretism is generally used with negative connotations as the illegitimate mixing of incompatible ideas or practices. This critique of syncretism arises from a focus on the stability and incompatibility of religious traditions. If the meaning of religious symbols, teachings, and practices is believed to be fixed and inexorably linked to their original religious context, their use in other religious traditions cannot but be regarded as problematic. And if religions are approached as radically distinct and unchanging systems of belief and practice, any introduction of new elements will be regarded as intrusive and unacceptable. New religions tend to be accused of syncretism by older religions, and various forms of cultural adaptation will be regarded as syncretism by religious conservatives. The popular tendency to adopt practices of different religions without concern for their conceptual, philosophical or theological consistency or coherence has been called syncretism.

And the term syncretism has also come to be used for the type of religiosity that in the late twentieth century was designated as "new age," and that in the twenty-first century has come to be referred to as "spiritual but not religious," as "religious hybridity," or as "spiritual fluidity." Here, elements from different religious traditions are being selected and combined, based on personal taste and judgment.

It is unsurprising that the comparative theological engagement with texts, teachings, and practices of different religions would be regarded as a form of syncretism. From a purely descriptive point of view, it does indeed involve the combination of elements that are in one way or another incompatible. Even when the form of particular teachings or practices seems analogous or compatible, their respective point of reference is not. And insofar as religious elements ultimately derive their meaning from their place in a larger whole, their juxtaposition with elements from other religious traditions cannot but cause some form of hermeneutical friction. The charge of syncretism may arise from different religious traditions involved in comparative theology, as one may be worried about the introduction of foreign or alien elements that might disturb the status quo, and the other may be concerned with the misuse or misinterpretation of its own cherished beliefs and practices within a different religious context.

However, comparative theology may be seen to resist or overcome syncretism in several ways. First, some comparative theologians engage the other tradition mainly as a catalyst to discover new dimensions of their own tradition, either by way of similarity or difference. Daniel Sheridan, for example, engages the Hindu *Nārada Sūtras* of loving devotion to God as a catalyst to rediscover Christian texts and traditions of loving devotion.[90] And in understanding the Christian belief in the virginity of Mary in light of the Muslim belief in the illiteracy of Mohammed, Daniel Madigan comes to a new and sharp realization that "The doctrine of the virginity (at least *ante partum*) is a statement about divine origin and divine intervention, rather than a statement about marriage, sexuality and the body."[91] Here, the fundamental differences and incompatibilities between Christianity and the other religions are recognized and remain untouched, while still generating new insight and understanding. Comparative theology involves different types of learning (which will be discussed in Chapter 4), some of which do not involve explicit borrowing or the introduction of new or foreign elements within existing religious systems.

Second, if syncretism involves the mixing of incompatible elements, comparative theologians tend to focus on elements in other traditions that are compatible, either in terms of their similarity or in terms of their complementarity. Confessional comparative theologians will focus on elements that are not in contradiction with their normative traditions, whereas meta-confessional comparative theologians will focus on teachings and practices that fit within their own larger synthesis.

Third, as pointed out, comparative theology involves a dynamic hermeneutical process in which elements from one tradition eventually come to be reinterpreted in terms of another and adapted to a new hermeneutical context. Since the purpose is to learn from the other tradition, rather than simply reduce the other tradition in one's own familiar terms, comparative theologians may live for some time with the tensions and the frictions between the different hermeneutical frameworks. But in the end, meanings will shift and become adapted to a new hermeneutical context, either that of an established tradition, or that of a new synthetic whole.

While acknowledging the original meaning of teachings and practices, comparative theology is based on a dynamic understanding of religious traditions and on the hermeneutical flexibility of religious teachings and practices. The work of comparative theology involves an attempt to overcome semantic tensions and religious incompatibilities by demonstrating the relevance of a particular teaching or practice, and by adjusting religious beliefs and practices until some form of integration or theological coherence is attained. This may involve a process of experimentation. For example, a good number of Christian comparative theologians have attempted to integrate the Hindu and Buddhist notions of nonduality and emptiness in Christian theological reflection. At first sight, this philosophy may appear to be radically opposed to the traditional Christian dualism that emphasizes the discontinuities between human and divine realities. However, these theologians seek to demonstrate that Christianity may be interpreted through that new hermeneutical lens without losing its essential message. Whether such efforts will bear fruit, or rather be regarded as an unacceptable form of syncretism, will depend on their reception within the larger tradition.

Comparative theology does not presume the endless malleability and adaptability of religious ideas and practices. Certain religious ideas and practices may be genuinely incompatible and/or belong to the heart of another tradition such that they may never be able to shed their original meaning when interpreted in a new religious context. This is why comparative theologians focus mainly on beliefs and practices that are already in some continuity with their own basic religious beliefs.

Charges of syncretism are generally in the eye of the beholder. The use of one's own cherished symbols, ideas and practices within a different religious context tends to generally be regarded as illegitimate or sensed as a loss. And changes occurring in one's own tradition are often regarded as a threat. In 1989, the magisterium of the Catholic Church stated in a letter to the bishops: "With the present diffusion of eastern methods of meditation in the Christian world and in ecclesial communities, we find ourselves faced with a pointed renewal of an attempt, which is not free from dangers and errors, *to fuse Christian meditation with that which is non-Christian.*"[92] The letter goes on to discuss various ways in which theologians and practitioners attempt to integrate and justify such practices and states that "these and similar proposals to harmonize Christian meditation with eastern techniques need to have their contents and methods ever subjected to a thorough-going examination so as to avoid the danger of falling into syncretism." Traditional theologians may thus be weary of the way comparative theology may lead to syncretism. However, comparative theology may also shed new light on syncretism as an integral part of theological development and growth.

3.6   The Problem of Hegemony

A second critical concern with comparative theology involves the propriety of using the contents of one religious tradition for the theological edification of another. This may be regarded as a form of instrumentalization or domestication of the other religion for one's own religious purposes. Considering the power relationships that have informed, and often continue to inform, the relationship between religious traditions, comparative theology inevitably opens itself to charges of religious hegemony. Hugh Nicholson, for example, argues that even though comparative theology advertises itself "as a non-hegemonic form of interreligious theological discourse," it still perpetuates forms of religious hegemony.[93] Gavin Flood recognizes that "to perform a Christian theological reading of a non-Christian sacred text is fraught with difficulty, especially given the history of Christian readings of non-Christian traditions so often implicitly linked to imperial power."[94] And David Tracy also warns that "every intercultural and interreligious dialogue may need the Western participant to hesitate before entering to analyze whether some unconscious Western colonialist, imperialist attitude to the other is present despite goodwill."[95]

Hugh Nicholson argues that the very attempt of at least some comparative theologians to separate themselves from theology of religions already reflects a form of hegemony, which is only enhanced by the fact that they continue to inscribe themselves in particular apologetic traditions.[96] The fact that comparative theology remains up to the present a predominantly Christian theological exercise does not help matters.

Religious hegemony refers to an uneven power dynamic in which certain religious traditions consciously or unconsciously dominate, determine the public discourse, and subsume other religious traditions or positions into itself. The comparative theological attempt to learn from other religions and to enrich one's own tradition by integrating what is considered to be the best of other religions may indeed appear hegemonic. Since the new comparative theology has been developed mostly in Christian theological circles, and since Christianity remains one of the largest and most influential traditions in the world, the perception or threat of hegemony is unavoidable. Other religious traditions with less social and political influence may feel like they are being subsumed within a larger tradition, their own teachings and practices stolen and reinterpreted to fit the dominant religious framework. Insofar as comparative theology has focused mainly on texts, it has been accused of contributing "to the continued valorisation and prioritisation of the elite textual traditions at the expense of the religion of subalterns."[97] Comparative theology must be constantly attentive to these charges.

However, there are various characteristics of comparative theology that militate against the problem of hegemony. First, comparative theologians approach other religions with an attitude of epistemological and theological humility.[98] One engages the religious other not "as someone with something to add to them," but "as someone with something yet to discover."[99] In learning from other religious traditions, the comparative theologian recognizes the partiality or the perfectibility of his or her own religious understanding. Though the other tradition may be "used" to advance one's own self-understanding, the focus is not on changing the other religion, but rather one's own. Gavin Flood thus argues that the reading of the Christian tradition through the lens of another text "is not a metaphorical colonialism for it uses the other tradition to illuminate Christianity, to help clarify difference and to bring into focus dimensions of the Christian tradition that would otherwise remain hidden."[100] The comparative theologian also at times puts his or her tradition at risk in engaging the religious other. In learning from the other religion, comparative theology may challenge one's own traditional self-understanding and lead to critical debate within one's own tradition. The comparative theologian thus approaches the other religion not from a position of power, but from a position of vulnerability, and with an openness to recognizing the superiority of the other religion in certain areas of religious thought or practice.

This humility also applies to one's understanding of the other. Comparative theology involves what I have called "humility of place," a recognition that one approaches the religious other from the outside and with questions, insights, and interpretations that are not necessarily those of the insider.[101] J. R. Hustwit speaks in this regard of a "fallibilist hermeneutics" in which once "the individual becomes aware of her own finitude and situatedness, the perspective of the interpreter does not result in the oppressive clash of conflicting dogmas, but in the transformative phenomenon of genuine conversation."[102] In recognizing one's positionality or place as a guest in relation to the other religion, the comparative theologian thus assumes an attitude of grateful appreciation, rather than domination. This is a far cry from the notion of imposing on or abusing the other religion for one's own purposes. It is of course true that comparative theology involves using and reinterpreting elements from another religious tradition. But this may happen in every direction as sacred texts, teachings, and practices have become part of the public domain, and every religious tradition may borrow from the other. Just as nineteenth-century Hindu reformers borrowed from biblical themes and found inspiration in the person of Jesus Christ, Christians have come to use Hindu categories and practices in order to enrich their own tradition, without seeking to diminish Hinduism.

This respect for the integrity and the irreducibility of the other tradition is an integral characteristic of comparative theology. Whereas hegemonic approaches would impose a particular interpretation on the religious other, comparative theology acknowledges the alterity and the autonomy of the other religion. Comparative theology does not claim to improve on, supplant or abrogate its original meaning, but rather recognizes its enduring validity and truth within its own religious context. In focusing on particular texts and teachings, it also resists the temptation to generalize, which, as Nicholson recognizes, mitigates against both internal religious hegemonies and against interreligious hegemonies.[103] It prevents particular dominant texts or teachings from being regarded as representative for the tradition as a whole, which in turn becomes "an effective means of deconstructing dichotomous typifications"[104] of religions: "The comparative juxtaposition of cultural-religious formations sets up resonances between the two whereby prominent features of the one bring to light parallel features of the other that may have been suppressed by various hegemonic discourses, whether those of indigenous orthodoxies or those of Western scholarship."[105] Comparative theology thus respects the internal diversity of the other religion and the particularity of religious ideas and practices within their broader religious context.

In the process of learning from the other, comparative theology also grants a certain priority or hermeneutical privilege to the self-understanding of the other.[106] It seeks to preserve as much as possible of the original meanings attached to symbols, teachings, and practices. Rather than uncritically imposing its own hermeneutical framework on the other or reducing the other to the same – as would be the case with domestication – it seeks to save or preserve as much as possible the self-understanding of the other in the process of interreligious hermeneutics. Comparative theology is informed, as

Moyaert puts it, by a "fear of inflicting violence on the other"[107] or by a sense of "responsibility to understand the other, as much as possible, as the other understands himself, and to both attribute to and receive from the text (tradition, symbol, rite) the most charitable reading possible."[108] In her engagement with the Hindu theory of emotions, Michelle Voss Roberts seeks to combat hegemony by granting epistemological priority or privilege to Hindu categories and meanings: "In a deviation from Western epistemological hegemony, the Christian theology of the emotions developed here *begins* with categories that originate in Indian aesthetic theory. This borrowing does not replicate the original theory but considers its relevance in other contexts."[109] Clooney similarly states that he opposes "a consumerist mining of texts in service of a preconceived agenda neglectful of the text's own purposes"[110] and he advocates a dual accountability, toward the other as well as toward one's own tradition.[111] Comparative theologians thus practice what Bruce Marshall calls "generous hermeneutics," "affirming as much truth as possible about the other from within one's own hermeneutical horizon."[112]

The critique of comparative theology as hegemonic is based on the notion of ownership of religious texts, ideas, and practices. It presumes that certain texts or teachings are the property of certain religions, and that their interpretation or appropriation in different religious contexts represents a form of illegitimate encroachment by one tradition upon another. Though it is true that certain symbols, texts, and practices are strongly identified with particular religions, some are also themselves the fruit of a complex history of religious interaction and borrowing. As such, it is not always clear who the original owner or creator might have been of particular ideas or practices. While religions may at times be protective of their teachings and practices, and averse to their reinterpretation in different religious contexts, they may also be gratified by the appeal of their tradition and of its importance and usefulness in the theological development of another religion. This is expressed in Paul Knitter's critical consideration of his use of Buddhist texts and teachings:

> Might it be another, more subtle, example of Western Christians falling into their colonial propensities to take advantage of other cultures and religions for their own benefit? No doubt, that's a proven propensity and a real danger. But exploitation happens when one side of a transaction is left impoverished or harmed. What I'm "taking" from Buddhism isn't in any way diminishing Buddhism; in fact, the Buddhist teachers I've known have been happy to give it away.[113]

It is true that the discipline of comparative theology has developed mainly within Christian theological circles. This may be partly an attempt to reverse (and repent for) older colonialist and imperialist attitudes toward other religions and cultures. But it is also due to the place of theology and religious studies in the Western academy, and to the opportunities to study other religions in a systematic way while reflecting critically and constructively on one's own theological presuppositions. Though there are different ways of approaching comparative theology (as pointed out in Chapter 2), it is generally based in theological presuppositions that preclude the hegemonic appropriation of the other.

As increasing numbers of comparative theologians from other religious traditions or with no single religious background become part of the academy and engage other religions from within their own normative frameworks, they also may come to profit from the insights and practices of other religious traditions. It is indeed through mutual borrowing and lending, and through reciprocal hospitality, that each religion may develop and grow. Reinhold Bernhardt speaks in this regard of "mutual hermeneutical inclusivism" which is an expression of epistemological realism, rather than theological superiority.[114] Even though the use of one's own cherished texts, teachings, and practices by another religious tradition may be regarded as unsettling, it may also be seen as an honor to have served as inspiration for another religious tradition.

If all forms of understanding or interpretation of another from within one's own normative perspective are deemed hegemonic, then comparative theology is certainly guilty as charged. But this view would stifle all possibility for an open and mutually constructive engagement between religions and ignore the ways in which religions have absorbed and continue to consciously and unconsciously absorb elements from one another for their mutual edification. As religious texts, teachings, and practices have become part of the heritage of humanity, it would seem futile to prohibit the circulation and mutual fecundation of religious ideas out of an exaggerated sense of protectiveness, however noble its intentions. Rather than diminishing or domesticating the other religion, comparative theology may in fact contribute to the affirmation and valuation of the other tradition.

Notes

1. Paul Hedges, "Comparative Theology and Hermeneutics: A Gadamerian Approach to Interreligious Interpretation," *Religions 7*, no. 7 (2016): 13.
2. David Tracy, "Western Hermeneutics and Interreligious Dialogue," in *Interreligious Hermeneutics*, ed. C. Cornille and C. Conway (Eugene: Wipf & Stock, 2010), 2.

3. Marianne Moyaert, *In Response to the Religious Other* (London: Lexington Books, 2014), 160; J. R. Hustwit, *Interreligious Hermeneutics and the Pursuit of Truth* (Lanham: Lexington Books, 2014).

4. Hugh Nicholson in fact argues that there is little difference between comparative religion and comparative theology, in "The Reunification of Theology and Comparison in the New Comparative Theology," *Journal of the American Academy of Religion 7*, no. 3 (2009): 609–46.

5. Hans-Georg Gadamer, *Truth and Method*, transl. revised by J. Weinsheimer and D. Marshall (New York: Continuum, 1995), 270.

6. Gadamer, *Truth and Method*, 267.

7. Francis Clooney, *Comparative Theology: Deep Learning across Religious Borders* (Oxford: Wiley-Blackwell, 2010), 11.

8. Clooney, *Comparative Theology*, 1.

9. Hugh Nicholson, *Comparative Theology and the Problem of Religious Rivalry* (Oxford: Oxford University Press, 2011), 130.

10. Clooney, *Comparative Theology*, 13.

11. Paul Ricoeur, *Oneself and Another* (Chicago: University of Chicago Press, 1992), 3.

12. Hustwit, *Interreligious Hermeneutics and the Pursuit of Truth*, 43.

13. Marianne Moyaert, "Absorption or Hospitality: Two Approaches to the Tension between Identity and Alterity," in *Interreligious Hermeneutics*, ed. C. Cornille and C. Conway (Eugene: Wipf & Stock, 2010), 82.

14. George Lindbeck, *The Nature of Doctrine* (Louisville: Westminster John Knox Press, 2009), 18.

15. Moyaert, "Absorption or Hospitality," 69–70.

16. Lindbeck, *The Nature of Doctrine*, 39.

17. Lindbeck, *The Nature of Doctrine*, 47.

18. Lindbeck, *The Nature of Doctrine*, 87.

19. Catherine Cornille, "Types of Misunderstanding in Interreligious Hermeneutics," in *Antisemitism, Islamophobia and Interreligious Hermeneutics: Ways of Seeing the Other*, ed. E. O'Donnell (Leiden: Brill, 2018).

20. Edward Said, *Orientalism* (New York: Vintage Books, 1979).

21. See, for example, Abbe J. A. Dubois, *Hindu Manners, Customs and Ceremonies* (Oxford: Clarendon Press, 1906).

22. See, for example, Huston Smith, *The World's Religions* (San Francisco: Harper, 1958). It attempts to put every religion in its best light and to facilitate empathy, mainly for a Western and modern reader.

23. Clooney, *Comparative Theology*, 30.

24. Tracy, "Western Hermeneutics," 3.

25. Hans-Georg Gadamer, *Truth and Method*, 269.

26. Tracy, "Western Hermeneutics," 12.

27. Hustwit, *Interreligious Hermeneutics and the Pursuit of Truth*, 47.

28. Tracy, "Western Hermeneutics," 14.

29. Tracy, "Western Hermeneutics," 17.

30. Tracy, "Western Hermeneutics," 16.

31. Hugh Nicholson, "The New Comparative Theology and the Problem of Theological Hegemonism," in *The New Comparative Theology*, ed. F. Clooney (New York: T&T Clark, 2010), 58.

32. Tzvetan Todorov, *Mikhail Bakhtin: The Dialogical Principle* (Minneapolis: University of Minnesota Press, 1984), 109, emphasis in the original.

33. Michael Holquist, *Dialogism: Bakhtin and His World* (London: Routledge, 1990), 36.

34. Mikhail Bakhtin, *Speech Genres and Other Late Essays*, ed. C. Emerson and M. Holquist, trans. V. McGee (Austin: University of Texas, 1986), 7. Caryl Emerson points out that, far from overcoming differences, Bakhtin is "wholeheartedly positive about boundaries, thresholds, delineations, delimitations, drawing them wherever possible and as often as possible, between life and art, between one consciousness and another, between one person's language and another. He advises us to draw a line, cross it, then consider what we can offer the far side from our perspective." In Caryl Emerson, *The First Hundred Years of Mikhail Bakhtin* (Princeton: Princeton University Press, 1997), 238.

35. Paul Ricoeur, *Hermeneutics and the Human Sciences* (Cambridge: Cambridge University Press, 1981), 91–94.

36. Moyaert, *In Response to the Religious Other*, 175.

37. Hedges, "Comparative Theology and Hermeneutics," 12.

38. Tracy, "Western Hermeneutics," 3.

39. James Fredericks, *Faith among Faiths* (New York: Paulist Press, 1999), 169.

40. See the articles in Perry Schmidt-Leukel and Andreas Nehring, *Interreligious Comparisons in Religious Studies and Theology* (London: Bloomsbury, 2016); the notion of "a problematic universalism and a problematic relativism" is used in the article by Gavin Flood, "Religious Practice and the Nature of the Human," 138.

41. William Paden, "Elements of a New Comparativism," in *A Magic Still Dwells*, ed. K. Patton and B. Ray (Berkeley: University of California Press, 2000), 186.

42. Fabian Volker, "On All-Embracing Mental Structures," in *Interreligious Comparisons in Religious Studies and Theology*, ed. P. Schmidt-Leukel and A. Nehring (London: Bloomsbury, 2016), 153.

43. Perry Schmidt-Leukel, *Religious Pluralism and Interreligious Theology* (Maryknoll: Orbis Books, 2017), 233.

44. Schmidt-Leukel, *Religious Pluralism and Interreligious Theology*, 235. Schmidt-Leukel thus believes that "it is not unlikely that comparative theology may continue where comparative religion stopped, that is, with the discernment of fractal patterns in religious diversity" (232).

45. Paul Ricoeur, *Time and Narrative*, vol. 3, trans. K. Blamey and D. Pellauer (Chicago: University of Chicago Press, 1988), 184.

46. Raimon Panikkar, *The Intra-Religious Dialogue* (Mahwah: Paulist Press, 1999), 34.

47. David Tracy, *Plurality and Ambiguity* (San Francisco: Harper & Row, 1987), 20, 93.

48. Ricoeur, *Oneself as Another*, 127. He does reiterate the role of the imagination in various ways and in various texts: "It is always through some transfer from Self to Other, in empathy and imagination, that the Other that is foreign to me is brought closer." Ricoeur, *Time and Narrative*, 184.

49. Paul Ricoeur, "The Metaphorical Process as Cognition, Imagination, and Feeling," in *On Metaphor*, ed. S. Sacks (Chicago: University of Chicago Press, 1979), 146.

50. Paul Ricoeur, *Hermeneutics and the Human Sciences: Essays on Language, Action and Interpretation*, trans. J. Thompson (Cambridge: Cambridge University Press, 1981), 93.

51. Ricoeur, *Oneself as Another*, 334–35.

52. Richard Kearney, "The Wager of Carnal Hermeneutics," in *Carnal Hermeneutics*, ed. R. Kearney and B. Trainor (New York: Fordham University Press, 2015), 54.

53. Michelle Voss Roberts, *Dualities: A Theology of Difference* (Louisville: Westminster John Knox Press, 2010), 14–15.

54. She focuses in particular on Mechthild of Magdeburg and Lalleśwarī of Kashmir.

55. Jon Paul Sydnor, *Rāmānuja and Schleiermacher: Toward a Constructive Comparative Theology* (Eugene: Wipf & Stock, 2011), 215.

56. See in this regard Klaus von Stosch's dialogue project on Jesus in the Qur'an, which attempts to go beyond apologetics and denunciation of the position of the other religion to genuine learning from one another. The project itself is still ongoing, but a reflection of this work may already be found in Klaus von Stosch, *Herausforderung Islam: Christliche Annäherungen* (Paderborn: Ferdinand Schöningh, 2016), 153–78.

57. For a discussion of the randomness of this concept, see Tomoko Masuzawa, *The Invention of World Religions* (Chicago: University of Chicago Press, 2005).

58. John Maraldo, "A Call for an Alternative Form of Understanding," in *Interreligious Hermeneutics*, ed. C. Cornille and C. Conway (Eugene: Wipf & Stock, 2010), 113.

59. Maraldo, "A Call for an Alternative Form of Understanding," 114.

60. Marianne Moyaert, "Towards a Ritual Turn in Comparative Theology: Opportunities, Challenges, and Problems," *Harvard Theological Review 111*, no. 1 (2018).

61. Moyaert, "Towards a Ritual Turn," 2.

62. Moyaert, "Towards a Ritual Turn," 11.

63. Paul Hedges, *Comparative Theology: A Critical and Methodological Perspective* (Leiden: Brill, 2017), 39.

64. Laurel Schneider, "When the Book Is a Coyote: Some Challenges and Possibilities for Comparative Theology from the Study of Native American Traditions," Lecture at the Center for the Study of World Religions, Harvard Divinity School, April 7, 2015.

65. Albertus Bagus Laksana, *Muslim and Catholic Pilgrimage Practice: Explorations through Java* (Farnham: Ashgate, 2014).

66.   John Thatamanil, "Eucharist Upstairs, Yoga Downstairs: On Multiple Religious Participation," in *Many Yet One?* ed. P. Jesudason, R. Rajkumar, and J. Prabhakar Dayam (Geneva: World Council of Churches, 2016), 5–22; Mark Heim, "On Doing as Others Do: Theological Perspectives on Multiple Religious Practice," in *Many Yet One?* ed. P. Jesudason, R. Rajkumar, and J. Prabhakar Dayam (Geneva: World Council of Churches, 2016), 27–44.

67.   Sahi was strongly influenced in his early career by the theological insights of Bede Griffiths, Henri Le Saux, and Raimon Panikkar, who attempted to integrate Hindu spiritual ideas in their Christian theological reflection.

68.   Sahi is also a theologian in his own right who has written eloquently on his own work. See, for example, his "Yoga and the Wounded Heart," in *Traversing the Heart: Journeys in the Interreligious Imagination*, ed. R. Kearney and E. Rizo-Patron (Leiden: Brill, 2010), 43–80.

69.   Catherine Cornille, "Interreligious Hospitality and Its Limits," in *Hosting the Stranger between Religions*, ed. R. Kearney and J. Taylor (New York: Continuum, 2011), 35–45.

70.   See Marianne Moyaert and Joris Geldhof, *Ritual Participation and Interreligious Dialogue: Boundaries, Transgressions and Innovations* (London: Bloomsbury, 2015).

71.   Daniel Boyarin, *Border Lines: The Partition of Judeo-Christianity* (Philadelphia: University of Pennsylvania Press, 2004).

72.   See the oft retold story of Barlaam and Josaphat, Christian saints who were widely revered during the Middle Ages and whose legend refers back to the story of the Buddha. See Wilfred Cantwell Smith (1981), *Toward a World Theology*, (Maryknoll: Orbis Books), 3–20.

73.   For examples of this, see Catherine Cornille and Stephanie Corigliano, eds., *Interreligious Dialogue and Cultural Change* (Eugene: Wipf & Stock, 2012).

74.   Joseph O'Leary, "Skillful Means as a Hermeneutic Concept," in *Interreligious Hermeneutics*, ed. C. Cornille and C. Conway (Eugene: Wipf & Stock, 2010), 163–83.

75.   Masao Abe, "Kenotic God and Dynamic Śūnyatā," in *The Emptying God: A Buddhist-Jewish-Christian Conversation*, ed. J. Cobb and C. Ives (Maryknoll: Orbis Books, 1990), 3–68.

76.   Lindbeck, *The Nature of Doctrine*, 35.

77.   Gavin D' Costa, *The Meeting of Religions and the Trinity* (Maryknoll: Orbis Books, 2000), 22–23. He raises this critique with regard to the paradigm of inclusivism in theology of religions. Though I do not believe it disqualifies inclusivism as D'Costa argues (since inclusivists do not claim to be able to fully recognize the other religion in its self-understanding), it does raise important questions for comparative theology.

78.   Panikkar, *The Intra-Religious Dialogue*, 20.

79.   Moyaert, "Absorption or Hospitality," 86.

80.   Paul Ricoeur, *Figuring the Sacred* (Minneapolis: Fortress Press, 1995), 160–61.

81.   Ricoeur, *Figuring the Sacred*, 53.

82. Abhishiktānanda, *La montée au fond du coeur. Le journal intime du moine chrétien-sannyasi hindou, 1948–1973* (Paris: OEIL, 1986), 163.

83. John Keenan, *The Meaning of Christ: A Mahāyāna Christology* (Maryknoll: Orbis Books, 1989), and all of his other works up until his latest, *The Emptied Christ of Philippians: Mahāyāna Meditations* (Eugene: Wipf & Stock, 2015). Joseph O'Leary's latest works include *Conventional and Ultimate: A Key for Fundamental Theology* (South Bend: University of Notre Dame Press, 2015) and *Buddhist Nonduality, Paschal Paradox: A Christian Commentary on The Teaching of Vimalakīrti* (Leuven: Peeters, 2018). Raimon Panikkar, *The Rhythm of Being* (Maryknoll: Orbis Books, 2010).

84. Michelle Voss Roberts, *Tastes of the Divine: Hindu and Christian Theologies of Emotion* (New York: Fordham University Press, 2014), 161.

85. Voss Roberts, *Tastes of the Divine*, 179.

86. Jacques Scheuer, "Comparative Theology and Religious Studies in a Non-religious Environment," *Religions 3* (2012): 979.

87. Jacques Kamstra, *Synkretisme: Op de Grens tussen Theologie en Godsdienstfenomenologie* (Leiden: Brill, 1970), 9–10.

88. Michael Pye, "Syncretism and Ambiguity," *Numen 18* (1971): 93.

89. Gerardus Van der Leeuw, *Religion in Essence and Manifestation*, trans. J. E. Turner (New York: Harper & Row, 1963), 610–11.

90. Daniel Sheridan, *Loving God: Kṛṣṇa and Christ: A Christian Commentary on the Nārada Sūtras* (Leuven: Peeters, 2007).

91. Daniel Madigan, "God's Word to the World: Jesus and the Qur'an, Incarnation and Recitation," in *"Godhead Here in Hiding": Incarnation and the History of Human Suffering*, ed. T. Merrigan and F. Glorieux (Leuven: Peeters, 2012), 167.

92. Congregation for the Doctrine of the Faith, "Letter to the Bishops of the Catholic Church on Some Aspects of Christian Meditation," October 15, 1989, article 12 (emphasis in the original), http://www.vatican.va/roman_curia/congregations/cfaith/documents/rc_con_cfaith_doc_19891015_meditazione-cristiana_en.html.

93. Nicholson, *Comparative Theology and the Problem of Religious Rivalry*, 29–105.

94. Gavin Flood, "Reading Christian Detachment through the Bhagavad Gītā," in *Song Divine: Christian Commentaries on the Bhagavad Gītā*, ed. C. Cornille (Leuven: Peeters, 2007), 10.

95. Tracy, "Western Hermeneutics," 14.

96. See Nicholson, "The New Comparative Theology," 43–62.

97. Hedges, *Comparative Theology*, 45.

98. Catherine Cornille, *The Im-Possibility of Interreligious Dialogue* (New York: Crossroad, 2008), 9–59.

99. Reid Locklin and Hugh Nicholson, "The Return of Comparative Theology," *Journal of the American Academy of Religion 78*, no. 2 (2010): 499.

100. Flood, "Reading Christian Detachment," 11.

101. Catherine Cornille, "Interreligiöse Theologie und die Bescheidenheit des Ortes: Überlegungen zu den 'Christian Commentaries on Non-Christian

Sacred Texts," in *Interreligiöse Theologie: Chancen und Probleme*, ed. R. Bernhardt and P. Schmidt-Leukel (Zurich: Theologischer Verlag Zurich, 2013), 161–80.

102. Hustwit, *Interreligious Hermeneutics and the Pursuit of Truth*, 104.
103. Nicholson, "The New Comparative Theology," 58.
104. Nicholson, *Comparative Theology and the Problem of Religious Rivalry*, 96.
105. Nicholson, *Comparative Theology and the Problem of Religious Rivalry*, 95.
106. In the series Christian Commentaries on Non-Christian Sacred Texts, being published by Peeters in Leuven, theologians will thus first attempt to elucidate the meaning of the text and its own religious and historical context before turning to its meaning and relevance from within the Christian tradition.
107. Moyaert, *In Response to the Religious Other*, 168.
108. Moyaert, *In Response to the Religious Other*, 69.
109. Voss Roberts, *Tastes of the Divine*, xxi, emphasis in the original.
110. Francis Clooney, *The Truth, the Way, the Life: Christian Commentary on the Three Holy Mantras of the Śrīvaiṣṇava Hindus* (Leuven: Peeters, 2008), 8.
111. Clooney, *Comparative Theology*, 13.
112. Bruce Marshall, ed., *Theology and Dialogue: Essays in Conversation with George Lindbeck* (South Bend: University of Notre Dame Press, 1990), 75.
113. Paul Knitter, *Without Buddha I Could Not Be a Christian* (Oxford: Oneworld, 2009), 155.
114. Reinhold Bernhardt, "Comparative Theology: Between Theology and Religious Studies," *Religions 3* (2012): 971.

4

Types of Learning in Comparative Theology

The goal of comparative theology is the advancement of theological truth through a process of learning from and through other religious traditions. This is what distinguishes comparative theology from the comparative study of religions. While the latter focuses on understanding religion or religious phenomena through detailed and controlled comparisons, the former is oriented to gaining a deeper understanding of ultimate truth itself, as revealed either in or beyond any particular religion. The process of theological learning may occur through various means: through solitary reading of texts, study with a teacher, ritual participation, religious practice, or a combination of these. It may be the result of prolonged and systematic study or of sudden insight and intuition leading to further exploration.

Comparative theological learning may take various forms, depending on the subject matter, the level of truth attributed to the other religion, and the personal interest and disposition of the comparative theologian. Certain traditions and topics may lend themselves to particular types of learning. While Christian engagement with Judaism often involves a considerable amount of rectification, engagement with Hinduism and Buddhism have tended toward reinterpretation. The type and degree of learning also depends on the recognition of truth in the other religion, as discussed in Chapter 2. Whereas most types of learning require at least recognition of truth in teachings or practices similar to one's own, appropriation also requires some recognition of truth in difference. Some theologians may be drawn mainly to particular types of learning because of the traditions and topics they study, or else to particular topics because of the type of learning best suited to their theological and scholarly inclinations.

The types of learning delineated in this chapter apply mainly to confessional approaches to comparative theology. The learning taking place in

Meaning and Method in Comparative Theology, First Edition. Catherine Cornille.
© 2020 John Wiley & Sons Ltd. Published 2020 by John Wiley & Sons Ltd.

meta-confessional comparative theology does not allow for a single or stable reference point against which the degree and kind of learning may be measured. Within confessional comparative theology, on the other hand, the various types of learning are considered in relation to a particular religious tradition. We will here focus mainly on examples of learning within the Christian tradition. But the typology of comparative theological learning may be applicable to any other religious tradition.

The process of learning from other religious traditions is complex and multiform. It generally evolves from a deep personal resonance with a particular teaching or practice and from an experience of personal enrichment and transformation resulting from the encounter with the other. This may not necessarily lead to a desire to integrate a particular teaching or practice into one's own religious tradition. One may respect the differences between religious traditions and keep the experience to oneself, or else share one's experience of the other as other with members of one's own religion and beyond. Moreover, not all types of learning can be defined or grasped. There may be light or insight coming from another religion that cannot be categorized or integrated.[1] Comparative theology, however, is based on the belief that religions may grow in their understanding of truth, and that whatever truth is to be found in another religion may have validity and importance not only for the other, but also for one's own tradition. It is also based on a desire and a sense of responsibility on the part of the theologian to share the insights and experiences one has gained through engagement with the other with a broader theological and religious community. The types of learning delineated here represent an attempt to systematize the process of learning that occurs spontaneously or often unreflectively. Any particular topic may elicit different types of learning.[2] And comparative theologians may use different types of learning simultaneously in their work. This chapter's delineation of the various types of learning is meant to allow comparative theologians, regardless of their confessional background, to reflect on their own learning processes, and to situate them within the broader framework of potential avenues for interreligious learning and theological growth.

4.1   Intensification

One common approach to comparative theology involves the juxtaposition of similar texts or teachings of different religions, which may lead to reinforcement or intensification of their meaning and truth. The recognition of similarities between text and teachings of different religions does not in itself constitute an occasion for religious learning or growth. They may simply point to analogical patterns of religious thought and experience, and generate theories about the nature of religion or religious phenomena, as has been the case in the comparative study of religion. But when approached with a generous religious disposition, the recognition of similarities in other religious traditions and/or the intensity of expression and experience may lead to an amplification of the meaning and truth of one's own religious ideas and experiences.

This type of learning characterizes the work of Francis Clooney. From his early *Seeing through Texts* to *His Hiding Place Is Darkness*, he places selected texts from the Hindu and the Christian tradition side by side, reading one through the other. In reading the Three Holy Mantras of the Śrīvaiṣṇavas in relation to the Spiritual Exercises of Saint Ignatius, he argues that "Proximity enhances intensity, and with intensification, all their meanings become sharper and clearer, even as the possibilities of a single meaning and single conclusion seem all the more unlikely because now we see clearly what is involved."[3] Similarly, in focusing on the topic of loving surrender in St. Francis de Sales and Śrī Vedānta Deśika, he states that "although these two reading experiences do not require each other, once both are read in proximity this doubled intensity deeply affects the reader twice over, such that each text intensifies and magnifies the other rather than diluting its impact."[4] And in reading side by side the intense experiences of love in separation in the *Song of Songs* and in the medieval Hindu text *Tiruvyāmoli*, he again emphasizes that "This doubling of memories intensifies rather than relativizes the deep yet fragile commitments of our singular, first love."[5] Clooney thus believes that the reading of sacred texts with similar teachings amplifies or enhances the significance and meaning of each.

By strongly rejecting the relativizing or diluting effect of juxtaposing texts of different religions, Clooney at least implicitly admits to such possibility or risk. It may lead at least to a questioning of certain claims to uniqueness, and at times also to a strong identification with particular elements in the other tradition or to an unsettling of one's religious identity:

> The deeper learning sends an uncertain message, introducing doubt at the start of our own reflection, about what we have read and what we are supposed to do with it. The more we know, the less likely it is that we will be able to say with certainty if either story is our own, if this beloved, absent twice over, really belongs to us.[6]

For Clooney himself, the discovery of similarities does not constitute a threat since "noting even partial common ground can strengthen our confidence in the claims we make, clarify what is at stake and disabuse us of the notion that our theological insights are unparalleled."[7] This, however, presupposes a theology of religions that implicitly or explicitly recognizes the similarities in other religions as a confirmation of the presence of truth in those religions. The process of intensification occurs in both directions, the discovery of similarities confirming the truth of particular teachings in the other religion, and the recognition of such truth in turn reaffirming the truth of one's own. Clooney states that through comparing Christian and Hindu texts on divine longing a "Christian may intensify her desire for Jesus, a Jesus real enough to come near, to hide, and later become manifest again."[8] However, this does not diminish the validity or truth of a Hindu focusing such desire on Krishna, in fact it reinforces it. Beyond the particularities of each tradition, it also confirms the experience of divine longing, and the play of divine presence and absence as central to all devotional mystical life.

Learning through intensification often starts with the study of another religion and the discovery of teachings and practices reminiscent of one's own. For Clooney, comparative theology "ordinarily starts with the intuition of an intriguing resemblance that prompts us to place two realities – texts, images, practices, doctrines, persons – near one another, so that they may be seen over and over again, side by side."[9] This then leads to a more systematic juxtaposition of texts focused on a common theme such as loving surrender in *Beyond Compare* or love in separation in *His Hiding Place Is Darkness*, forms of theological reasoning in *Hindu God, Christian God* or adoration and worship of the feminine divine in *Divine Mother, Blessed Mother*. In the series Christian Commentaries on Non-Christian Sacred Texts, authors also tend to search for texts in the Christian tradition which evince significant resonance with the text of the other tradition. In his *Christian Commentary on Shankara's Upadeśasāhasrī*,[10] Reid Locklin juxtaposes the text mainly with excerpts of the Pauline letters. In this, he admits to a certain arbitrariness:

> my selection of scripts for dialogue in each of the following chapters will likely seem more than a little arbitrary and subjective, governed by my own personal interest in returning to Paul after a number of years working with the Upadeśasāhasrī in dialogue with other sources, by a modestly idiosyncratic commitment to chronological sequence in identifying those texts that extend Paul's insights into later Christian tradition from one chapter to the next, and by a generous dose of instinct.[11]

This is reminiscent of Jonathan Smith's critique of the ethnographic approach to the comparative study of religion as random and unsystematic, based solely on the "recollection of similarity":

> at some point along the way, as if unbidden, as a sort of déjà vu, the scholar remembers that he has seen "it" or "something like it" before; he experiences

what Coleridge described in an early essay in *The Friend* as the result of "the hooks-and-eyes of the memory." This experience, this unintended consequence of research, must then be accorded significance and provided with an explanation.[12]

Clooney also admits that his approach to comparative theology involves a "necessarily arbitrary and intuitive practice." He does not, however, take umbrage with this reality. Whatever the text or teaching selected, "we see ourselves differently, intuitively uncovering dimensions of ourselves that would not otherwise, by a non-comparative logic – come to the fore."[13] Any juxtaposition that intensifies one's own religious understanding and experience may thus represent a fruitful theological exercise. Every comparative theologian, however, also ultimately needs to justify the choice of texts in their own as well as in the other tradition in order to establish the broader pertinence or relevance of their comparative theological work.

While Clooney generally focuses on strong parallel texts and uses them to read each other, Locklin tends to piece together a variety of texts in order to address a particular question. He attempts to counter charges of idiosyncrasy by pointing out that Paul was after all the first and the greatest Christian theologian and that "if the goal of dialogue is creative transformation, then it does well to attend to this voice, which was so decisive in the creative transformation of the early Jesus movement into what we now recognize as Christianity."[14] Since no single Christian text presents a perfect analogue or parallel to the *Thousand Teachings* of Shankara, Locklin also invokes later Christian theologians such as Irenaeus, Augustine, Peter Lombard, Mary Ward, and J. B. Metz. In reading Peter Lombard's *Sentences* III.31.9, 2.2 in light of Shankara's doctrine of the reflection of the divine self in the infinite intellect (*ābhāsa*), for example, Locklin sheds new light on Lombard's understanding of perfect charity (*caritas*) as "ultimately non-different from the Holy Spirit and Spirit of Christ, God the divine self."[15] An interpretation of this teaching by means of the Hindu notion of *Ātman* may bring to the fore the idea that "insofar as we do love truly, we reveal the God who is that love, within and beyond its limited reflection in the embodied individual."[16] Rather than on the fundamental notion of nonduality or on the conception of ultimate reality and its relation to the world, which represent "one of the most difficult points of difference between Christianity and Advaita,"[17] Locklin focuses instead on certain practices as "therapies" or as "performative practice," studying them in juxtaposition with Christian texts and teachings. He purposefully follows Clooney's method, stating that "as texts and traditions are set side by side and read together, previously settled meanings become unsettled, reconfigured, and perhaps even reaffirmed in new ways, in and out of their mutual juxtaposition."[18] Here, however, it is not so much a particular theological theme as it is the overall purpose of the text that becomes the occasion for mutual intensification.

The process of intensification may also at times involve privileging one particular understanding or interpretation of a text over another within a particular tradition. This comes to the fore, for example, in Holly Hillgardner's juxtaposition of the Flemish mystic Hadewijch and the Hindu mystic Mirabai.[19] As opposed to Augustine's classical ideal of attaining ultimate peace or repose in God, she suggests that Mirabai sheds light on and reinforces Hadewijch's suggestion that longing itself may be seen to stand "at the heart of a radically relational anthropology" and may constitute the ultimate religious aim of "passionate non-attachment." "Longing, as it connects to theological anthropology, then, is an intense desire that can rupture the boundaries of the self to allow a recognition, if only a partial one, of how the 'I' does not exist without its entanglements with others."[20] Though "some paths within Hinduism and Christianity teach that desire should be solely satisfied in God, held lightly, or even completely eradicated," both Hadewijch and Mirabai point to "paths of attachment fueled by longing, yet sheltered from possession or consumption-based systems of desire by these very energies of longing."[21] The juxtaposition of texts for the purposes of intensification may thus include a certain political or normative stance or interpretation not always evident in any text read on its own terms. It may also reinforce certain critical views of one's own tradition, by noticing parallel attitudes or themes in other religions. As such, feminist critiques of one's religion may be reinforced by noticing analogous views and themes in other religious traditions.

Though the type of learning through intensification has been applied mainly to sacred texts, it also may be used to intensify the understanding and experience of particular ethical principles and religious rituals. Hans Küng's famous World Ethos project, for example, seeks to reinforce the importance of the fundamental ethical principles of the religions of the world by demonstrating their recurrence in different religious traditions. And the similarity between monastic disciplines or rules in various religious traditions reinforces the sense of their ascetical efficacy. In recognizing other religions as a source of truth, any type of similarity may thus lead to the reinforcement of the truth and efficacy of one's own religion.

In all forms of comparative theological learning through intensification, the meanings of the texts used for comparison are taken somewhat out of context and allowed to rub off on one another in order to fit particular needs. The comparative theologian nonetheless must strive to avoid distortion. It is only by remaining true to their original intention that different texts, teachings, and practices may effectively become the source of intensification. But it must be understood that the very selection of texts and teachings represents an outside set of interests and priorities that may not always correspond to their place and priority within their own tradition.

Intensification represents one of the more uncontroversial types of learning in comparative theology. It may apply to historical influences as well as to more serendipitous contemporary connections. David Burrell, for example, reinforces the meaning of concepts of human freedom, grace, providence, detachment, and eschatology by pointing to mutual influences of Jewish, Christian, and Muslim thinkers during the medieval period.[22] And though (or because) there may not have been any direct historical contingency, the recurrence of similar religious views and practices in different religions may be seen to confirm and amplify their meaning and truth. The very use of another tradition to reinforce the truth of one's own may be regarded as a betrayal, compromising the exclusive teachings and truth of one's own tradition. But constructive comparative theology requires recognition of at least some validity or truth in other religious traditions. And the recognition of truth in similarities forms the first step in opening traditions to the possibility of learning from the other.

4.2   Rectification

One of the types of learning that may be operative in comparative theology involves the restoration of proper understanding of the other, and thus a new understanding of one's own tradition in relation to the other. At first glance, this may not be regarded as a form of theological development and growth. However, insofar as one's self-understanding is often linked to one's understanding of the other in polarizing or oppositional terms, the rectification of traditional forms of misunderstanding of the other will often significantly change one's self-understanding. The encounter with different and competing religious systems often leads to a conscious or unconscious belittling and misrepresentation of the religious other in order to inflate the importance and truth of one's own tradition. Typical forms of misrepresentation involve exaggeration and generalization of traits considered unpopular, projection of one's own notions of heresy, and minimizing all similarities between one's own religion and the other. Some postcolonial theories argue that all religious identity is in fact forged in a "political act of exclusion," and of constructing artificial oppositional relations between one's own religious views and that of the other.[23] By studying the other religion in depth, comparative theology may point to its internal complexity and diversity and thus correct self-interested forms of essentialization or reification of the religious other. In restoring the other religion to its own self-understanding and in recognizing similarities and one's occasional indebtedness to the other, certain traditional claims to superiority and exclusivity may be disputed, and one's own religion reinstated in its proper relationship with the religious other. This type of comparative theology thus also involves significant theological learning affecting one's own tradition.

One of the recurring Christian depictions of Hindu and Buddhist forms of mysticism has been to typify them as passive or quietistic as opposed to the ethical and active forms of mysticism within Christianity. Rudolf Otto, for example, draws this dichotomy in his *Mysticism, East and West*,[24] and R. C. Zaehner also characterizes Shankara's mysticism as essentially passive.[25] In their *Mysticism, Buddhist and Christian*, Paul Mommaers and Jan Van Bragt explore in depth the question as to whether the traditional Christian critique of natural mysticism or mysticism of passivity could fairly be applied to Buddhist, and in particular Zen Buddhist forms of meditation.[26] In focusing on concrete details of the Christian critique (in particular that of Jan van Ruusbroec) and in specific Buddhist texts, they conclude that it is far too simplistic to identify natural contemplation with Buddhist teachings and practices, and that one finds in Buddhism no less than in Christianity a critique of the type of passivity or quietism that Ruusbroec raises. This type of comparative theology thus breaks through a particular sense of exceptionalism of Christian mysticism and restores it to its proper place among the different mystical traditions.

In his critical comparative theological work, Hugh Nicholson takes direct aim at Rudolf Otto's attempt to contrast Eckhart and Shankara in order to rehabilitate the former.[27] He revisits the works of both mystical thinkers in order to demonstrate the similarities rather than the differences between the two. Whereas Otto interprets Eckhart from the perspective of a certain reading of Shankara, Nicholson reads Shankara in terms of Eckhart, and states that: "By redescribing Sankara in terms of Eckhart, I have sought to highlight the theistic and realist aspects of the former that have been suppressed in the orientalist characterization of his teaching as illusionistic pantheism."[28] While Otto's intention was "to disambiguate Eckhart by making strategic use of the traditional essentializing dichotomy between East and West," his own purpose is "to 'ambiguate' Sankara with the aim of calling that dichotomy into question."[29]

Nicholson takes Otto particularly to task on the question of quietism. Otto uses Eckhart's notion of "living without a why" to call attention "to this one-sidedness of Sankara's mysticism."[30] Nicholson, on the other hand, demonstrates that there are in fact significant similarities between Shankara and Eckhart in terms of their conception of the relationship between ritual action and experience. Shankara's emphasis on renunciation was merely developed in opposition to certain prior teachings and practices (Vedic ritual and Pūrva Mīmāṃsa) that he viewed as exaggerating the relationship between action and knowledge. Nicholson thus exposes Otto's critique of Shankara as an expression of Christian apologetics and fulfillment theology: "Having taken on in this context a dimension of differential meaning, this teaching gives concise expression to Otto's Christian apologetic. Inasmuch as it encapsulates both moments of the Eckhartian dialectic, this formula implies a theology of Christian fulfillment whereby a philosophy of world and life denial finds its fulfillment in Christian mysticism."[31]

Though apologetics does not per se involve a misrepresentation of the other, polemics often does. It aims at attacking or denouncing the other and thus tends to exaggerate and distort certain traits of the other. The history of Christian polemics may thus provide ample material for comparative theological reflection and rectification. Reid Locklin also discusses ways in which Christians might misconstrue the teachings of Shankara through projecting other types of Christian heresies on them. He focuses in particular on Irenaeus of Lyons (second century) who, in his *Against Heresies* 5.19.2, mentions those who believe that "neither soul nor body can receive eternal life, but only the 'inner man,' which they identify with their mind, judging it to rise to perfection." Locklin may be seen to engage in a type of preemptive rectification by strongly arguing that Shankara's thought cannot simply be reduced to this form of heresy:

> Advaita Vedānta is not a Christian heresy, and it stands, at least in its self-understanding, opposed to any and all forms of dualism (*dvaita*); so perhaps it comes as no great surprise that Shankara's teachings do not quite match those which Irenaeus finds so offensive. Scandal it may well be, but the challenge Advaita offers is not so easily domesticated to familiar Christian categories. In fact, we might even ask whether the essential vision of this Hindu teacher may actually resonate more richly and more interestingly with Irenaeus' own notion of "recapitulation" than it does with the esoteric and cosmological theories of the Gnostics.[32]

In-depth study of another religion in comparative theology thus shatters simple denunciations of the religious other and forces the theologian to take honest stock not only of the other religion, but also of his or her own.

One area of comparative theology in which rectification plays a particularly important role is in Jewish-Christian comparative theology. Here, Christian comparative theologians have critically examined traditional Christian distortions of Judaism, and dismissals of Jewish self-understanding, seeking to reverse this long history of misrepresentation and neglect by engaging with Judaism in constructive ways. Marianne Moyaert, for example,

analyzes the way in which the identification of Christ with the suffering servant of Isaiah 53 has been appropriated by Christian theology to fit its own
Christological beliefs, ignoring and dismissing Jewish interpretations of the
text. She argues: "If it can be said that the suffering of Christ led to a problematic interpretation of God's covenant with Israel ... the suffering of Israel must
now lead to a revaluation of the role of Isaiah 53 in Christology."[33] The purpose
of this type of Jewish-Christian comparative theology "is not to Judaize
Christianity, but rather to formulate a Christology that ends a long tradition
of supersessionism."[34] In his *The More Torah, the More Life: A Christian
Commentary on Mishnah Avot*, Daniel Joslyn-Siemiatkoski also seeks to overcome supersessionism by engaging a rabbinic text as a vital source for
Christian theological reflection. Noting the many continuities between the
early rabbinic interpretation of the Torah and the teachings of Jesus and Paul,
he argues that "the wine of the Torah is still to be savored" by Christians and
that "knowing Torah and the moral life that has arisen out of it in Judaism can
deepen the theological, ethical and spiritual dimensions of contemporary
Christianity."[35] He is acutely aware that the recognition of "complementary
divine revelations in Torah and Christ" may challenge traditional Christian
conceptions of the uniqueness of Jesus. But since Jesus was himself a teacher
of Torah, serious engagement with the living tradition of Torah interpretation
may in fact be regarded as an expression of faithfulness to Jesus Christ. This
form of rectification or reversal of traditional Christian attitudes toward the
rabbinic tradition raises several theological questions and challenges that
Joslyn-Siemiatkoski mentions without fully developing them.[36] The responsibility for doing this lies indeed not only with comparative theologians but
with the broader theological community. Insofar as certain oppositional
views of the other belong to the core identity of a religious tradition, the
theological implications of the work of rectification may be profound and the
subject of prolonged theological reflection and discussion.

The purpose of this type of learning in comparative theology is not to
minimize or downplay the differences between religions. It is merely to
distinguish real from imagined or artificially imposed differences and oppo-
sitions that may become the basis for a more open and honest constructive
theological engagement with the religious other.

4.3   Recovery

Engagement with the teachings and practices of another religion often leads to
the recovery or rediscovery of figures, teachings or practices of one's own tradition that were neglected, forgotten, marginalized or even declared heretical.

Comparative theology in general tends to proceed by way of recognition or remembrance of similarities between the other tradition and one's own, which may then lead to the further exploration of possible differences. These similarities often involve familiar and well-established teachings and practices. But they may also at times point to aspects that had been submerged, sidelined, ignored or condemned within the history of a particular tradition. To be sure, some teachings and practices become ignored, condemned, and forgotten for good reasons, and their resemblance to elements from another religious tradition will not in itself constitute a source of learning or theological growth for one's own tradition. But the history of religion is rich with theological figures and ideas who were ignored for no discernable theological reason.[37] And the process of theological condemnation and exclusion is itself at times fraught and at times informed by less than purely theological motivations. In those cases, the recovery of forgotten or marginalized elements of one's own tradition may become a source of genuine theological learning and enrichment. Daniel Sheridan relates to the texts and teachings of other religions as "catalysts" which "can help to grasp afresh our own tradition and to make it our own in a way adequate to the demands and challenges of the modern culture that we live in."[38] This type of learning through comparative theology may thus be regarded, in Sheridan's words, as "part of a global religious *ressourcement* and re-foundation."[39]

In his *Loving God: Kṛṣṇa and Christ: A Christian Commentary on the Nārada Sūtras*, Sheridan focuses on the medieval Hindu sutras on loving God as a catalyst for recovering the rich Christian tradition of passionate loving surrender to God. Though the history of Christianity is replete with figures and texts expressing love of God, the notion that one may live a life entirely consumed by the love of God, or that being a disciple of Jesus means loving him with all one's heart and soul, has become somewhat alien, outmoded or even embarrassing for many Christians. While discussing various aspects of the love of God in an array of Christian theologians and spiritual teachers, Sheridan focuses in particular on Bernard of Clairvaux (1090–1153), "perhaps the greatest Catholic teacher on loving God."[40] Sheridan draws attention to dimensions of Christian faith and spirituality which, though not so much forgotten or obscured, may have been regarded as the particular prerogative of religious or monastics. Viewing them through the *Nārada Sūtras* reminds Christians that they belong to the very heart of Christian spirituality and thus ought to be the ultimate religious goal of all believers.

It is, as Nicholson points out, "something of a truism" in comparative theology that "a feature that is conspicuous in one tradition can be used as a heuristic template to focus attention on a parallel feature in another tradition that is either less pronounced or obscured because of the ideological blind spots of its tradition(s) of interpretation."[41] His own comparative theological study of Eckhart in light of Shankara serves to draw attention to "the polemical dimension of Eckhart's notion of 'living without a why,' a dimension which is otherwise difficult to discern because of its sublimated form."[42] Noting the parallel with Shankara's insistence on the sole importance of knowledge of Brahman as part of a polemical reaction against other authoritative Vedic voices and practices, he comes to identify Eckhart's notion of "living without a why" also as a reaction against both female religious movements claiming their own mystical authority, and against the institutional Church itself.[43] One tradition may thus surface certain hidden political motivations in another.

Bede Bidlack, for his part, believes that the birth narratives of the Daoist master Lord Lao "may serve as a possible model for resolving the tensions between low and high Christologies."[44] He thus also approaches the comparative theological method as a way for the theologian to "discover, or re-discover, insights from within his or her home tradition."[45]

Comparative theological engagement with the spiritual texts and teachings of Hinduism and Buddhism has led mainly to the recovery of mystical teachers and teachings in the Christian tradition. Henri de Lubac in fact regarded the new interest in Christian mysticism in the first half of the twentieth century as a direct response to the awareness of religious plurality. As mentioned earlier, Rudolf Otto sought to rehabilitate Meister Eckhart through his study of Shankara, much as R. C. Zaehner's study of Shankara led him to a new appreciation of Jan van Ruusbroec. While both of these authors continued to accentuate the differences between the Christian and Hindu spiritual teachings, other comparative theologians have focused more on resemblances to draw new attention to certain Christian mystical thinkers. Thus, noting certain structural similarities with the Buddhist experience of awakening, Paul Ingram focuses on one of the more controversial Beguines, Marguerite Porete (1250–1310), who became "his favorite mystical theologian."[46] In discussing her different stages of ascent to union with God in her work *The Mirror of Simple Souls*, Ingram draws attention to the similarities between her apophaticism, or emphasis on the need to go beyond doctrines and institutional strictures to attain the ultimate union with God, and the Buddhist conception of awakening. He exposes the social and political elements involved in her condemnation for heresy and her burning at the stake and revalidates her thought and experience as evidence of the idea that "Christians and Buddhists experienced a same reality named differently."[47] Comparative theology may thus at times challenge a tradition to reconsider its past theological judgments. Of course, this may not necessarily lead to a rehabilitation of movements and individuals condemned for heresy. But it does shed new light on the reasons for their condemnation and raise questions about their fit with orthodox Christian teachings.[48]

Besides shedding new light on old heresies, comparative theology may also bring certain figures or movements out of relative obscurity. In her book *Dualities*, for example, Michelle Voss Roberts focuses on two female theologians whose voices were "left out of the canon" of their respective traditions, and who may be regarded as "outsiders within" their religious traditions: Mechthild of Magdeburg and Lalleśvarī of Kashmir.[49] Her discussion of their particular use of theological imagery and metaphor is aimed not only at envisioning "duality without falling into world-denying dualisms"[50] but also at bringing new theological voices into normative theological debates, or changing "the degree of *difference* permitted under the umbrella of 'tradition.'"[51] Holly Hillgardner similarly draws attention to the particular conceptions of longing and detachment of two female mystics who, though less obscure, have not been part of mainstream theological reflection.[52] Through her comparative theological reading, she concludes that though detachment and desire are opposing forces in Hinduism and Christianity, "Hadewijch and Mirabai each illuminate, from their respective traditions, the integral, tensile relationship between desire and non-attachment."[53] Comparative theology may thus draw attention not only to forgotten figures but also to neglected strands of thought within particular religions.

Attending to a more traditional view of the relationship between detachment and desire, Gavin Flood's reading of the *Bhagavad Gītā* points him to the desert father Evagrius Ponticus (345–99), whose teachings were declared heretical by the fifth council of Constantinople.[54] Focusing on Ponticus's notion of *apatheia* through the lens of the *Gītā* allows him to "demarcate a sometimes underemphasized dimension" in Christian spirituality, in particular the relationship between detachment, cosmology, and the master. Thus, he states that "the Orthodox Christian reader might learn from the *Gītā* to revisit resources within Christianity which are neglected by modernity, namely a pattern of teaching about detachment which leads to love of the Lord and so freedom from bondage by the passions."[55] The comparative theological process of recovery may involve not only forgotten or marginalized figures and teachings, but also religious practices. Engagement with Hindu and Buddhist forms of meditation has led to a rediscovery of early Hesychast forms of Christian practice, which use repetition of a simple Christian mantra "Lord Jesus Christ, son of God, have mercy on me, a sinner" at the heart of their meditative practice.[56] While this use of the Jesus prayer has continued in some forms of Orthodox Christianity, it had not penetrated into most other denominations. It is engagement with Asian traditions which led to the use of this prayer in the World Community for Christian Meditation.

Founded in London by the Benedictine oblate John Main in 1975, it has spread throughout the world and teaches a Christian version of traditional Hindu and Buddhist forms of meditation, using the mantra "maranatha."[57] Inspired by the observances of Shabbat in Judaism and of fasting in Islam, some Christians also seek to return to stricter observances of Sunday rest and of Lent in Christianity. In some cases, it is not so much the mere existence of a particular idea or practice, but the intensity with which it is lived that forms the occasion for critical self-reflection and rediscovery.

Finally, in the sphere of ethics, or praxis and liberation, comparative theology may also lead to the recovery of liberative resources. Christopher Conway focuses on Christian Dalit theology and the ways in which engagement with Hinduism, in particular with the tradition of Vivekananda, may address some of the impasses currently experienced within that school of theology.[58] Contemporary Dalit theologians have expressed certain dissatisfaction with the exclusive focus on exemplary suffering of Dalits and seek alternative ways of maintaining Dalit theological identity while also offering a way out of and beyond suffering. Conway argues that Vivekananda's notion of "seva provides an alternative epistemological approach that is grounded in experience and revelation … but in which knowledge is arrived at by praxis."[59] Rather than fully appropriating Vivekananda's understanding of seva, Conway believes that "by understanding how seva functions theologically and practically in Vivekananda's thinking, we gain better insight into how service might function in Dalit theology."[60] "Seva," he states, "shapes liberative service by showing how identity and social vision can lead to realization or humanization."[61] It leads him to recover the Christian notion of *imago dei* which, in addition to affirming the dignity of all human beings, "establishes the connection between identity affirmation and liberative social vision."[62]

All this raises the question as to whether comparative theological learning as recovery involves a simple retrieval of what was known but neglected in a particular tradition, or rather a somewhat new understanding of traditional sources. Though the texts and teachings remain the same, the new lens through which they are recovered is likely to color their meaning. Reading Marguerite Porete by way of Buddhist notions of self-annihilation, Hadewijch in relation to Mirabai's dialectic of longing and detachment, or Christian meditation through Hindu or Buddhist practices adds a semantic layer to the process of recovery. Not only does it direct the focus to dimensions of ancient texts or practices which may not have been particularly central to traditional perceptions or interpretation, but it also broadens the semantic field with meanings and expressions derived from the tradition generating the recovery. Though building upon the ancient Hesychast tradition, contemporary Christian meditation often resembles its Hindu or Buddhist counterparts as much as it does its early Christian prototype. And the notion of fluidity that Michelle Voss Roberts recovers from Mechthild's works derives as much from her own theological imagination and synthesis of the writings of the two women as from Mechthild herself.[63] The process of recovery in comparative theology thus often involves some degree of innovative or creative theological reflection which, if acknowledged, in no way diminishes its value.

4.4 Reinterpretation

One of the more challenging types of learning pursued in comparative theology involves the reinterpretation of one tradition through the categories or philosophical framework of another. This may be seen to be part of the process of translation and inculturation where concepts derived from one religion are used to render another religion intelligible in a new cultural and religious context. However, while the categories of the other tradition have often been reinterpreted to fit one's own tradition, comparative theology seeks to learn from the other religion by preserving as much as possible the original meaning of symbols and categories and by reinterpreting one's own religion in terms of the other. This may take place in the use of discrete symbols and categories, as well as through a more wholesale reinterpretation of one's own tradition through the philosophical framework of another. The possibility and desirability of reinterpreting Christian categories and teachings through the framework of other religious traditions is based on a realization of the historical, cultural, and philosophical particularity of the Hellenistic worldview and categories through which Christianity has traditionally been interpreted. Hans Urs von Balthasar, for example, states that "there is therefore no cause for dismay in the idea that the truth of revelation, which was originally cast in Hellenistic concepts by the great Councils, could equally be recast in Indian or Chinese concepts."[64]

This type of learning through reinterpretation of one's own tradition in terms of the other may already be found in the work of figures such as Henri Le Saux/Abhishiktānanda (1910–74), who immersed himself deeply in the Hindu tradition of Advaita Vedānta, and attempted to interpret Christianity through its terms. For him, this process was not merely an adaptation to the Indian context, but an opportunity to establish the true universality of expression of Christianity, since:

> If Christianity should prove to be incapable of assimilating Hindu spiritual experience from within, Christians would thereby at once lose the right to claim that it is the universal way of salvation. Christianity could not be "another"

peak of spiritual experience alongside that of Vedānta, nor could its way of salvation be "another" parallel way. In their claim to be ultimate, Christianity and *advaita* are mutually exclusive. And yet, in its own sphere, the truth of *advaita* is unassailable. If Christianity is unable to integrate it in the light of a higher truth, the inference must follow that *advaita* includes and surpasses the truth of Christianity and that it operates on a higher level than that of Christianity.[65]

The ability to account for the teachings of Advaita Vedānta and to maintain its own integrity thus was regarded as a challenge and an opportunity for Christian faith.[66] Abhishiktānanda thus came to interpret the divinity of Jesus Christ in term, of the nonduality *Ātman* (Self) and *Brahman* (ultimate reality), the historical nature and function of Jesus in terms of the role of the guru, and the Trinity in terms of the *advaita* experience of *Saccidānanda*:

> The experience of Saccidānanda carries the soul beyond all merely intellectual knowledge to her very centre, to the source of her being. Only there is she able to hear the Word which reveals within the undivided unity and advaita of the Saccidānanda the mystery of the Three divine Persons: in *sat*, the Father, the absolute Beginning and Source of being; in *cit*, the Son, the divine word, the Father's Self-knowledge; in *ānanda*, the Spirit of love, Fullness and Bliss without end.[67]

Abhishiktānanda was fully aware that this reinterpretation also involved challenges to Christian doctrine, and in particular to the Christian belief in the uniqueness of Jesus Christ. He thus went back and forth between interpreting uniqueness in Hindu terms or abandoning the traditional Christian understanding of the ontological uniqueness of Jesus as son of God, and adjusting Hindu categories to preserve the traditional Christian meaning.[68] He believed, however, that the use of Hindu categories and experiences represented a genuine enrichment of Christian theology and "an aid in penetrating the mystery of the Spirit which, according to St. John's Gospel, relates chiefly to God's presence to men in their hearts."[69] He thus believed that it opened the tradition to a deeper experience of the mystery of God.

A close friend of Abhishiktānanda, Raimon Panikkar (1918–2010) similarly came to reinterpret Christianity in terms of the tradition of Advaita Vedānta. Throughout his later work, he uses categories to develop a cosmology and anthropology that, though still centered on Christ, came to resonate more clearly with the Hindu philosophical tradition. Thus, his understanding of Christ becomes abstracted from the historical Jesus, and representative of a universal experience of nonduality: "The figure of Christ could be described as that of a person who reduces to zero the distance between heaven and earth, God and man, transcendent and immanent, without sacrificing either pole – which is precisely the principle of *advaita*."[70] His whole theology becomes informed by the principle of nonduality, forming the basis for his interpretation of the universe, the reality of religious plurality, the notion of time, etc. Though Panikkar continues to draw extensively from Christian biblical and theological sources, they acquire radically new meaning that he believes represents a genuine enrichment for Christian theology.

Sara Grant has also turned to the tradition of Advaita Vedānta to gain a new understanding of some fundamental Christian teachings of grace, sin, Christian uniqueness, and the death and resurrection of Christ. For her, the tradition of Advaita Vedānta may serve "not to devise yet another model for theologizing, but rather to bring to the gathering of theologians that piercing intuition into the fundamental structure of existence which constitutes the essence of advaita, and which of its very nature finds itself 'contextualized' in every human situation."[71] She thus offers an alternative reading of certain elements of Christian faith, based on her own insights and experiences as a "non-dualist Christian."

Comparative theologians engaged with Buddhism have mainly focused on Mahāyāna philosophy as a basis for reinterpreting Christianity. Jan Van Bragt argues that this philosophy offers "a certain liberation of Christian theology from the captivity of Western (Greek) philosophy, whose original inspiration and fundamental notions are so very different from those of the Bible."[72] And John Keenan similarly points to the particularity, and thus also the limitations, of the Hellenistic framework through which Christian faith has traditionally been expressed:

> Greek philosophy, for all its glory, remains but one philosophical tradition in a world full of traditions. It can claim no exclusive privilege for interpreting the Christian faith, or, for that matter, anything else. The concepts of nature, substance, essence and person that determined the structure of this thinking are not present in all cultural contexts, and when they are, they are often negated as philosophical errors. A naïve claim for the universal validity of such philosophical notions ill serves either clear thinking or theological understanding.[73]

He believes that "to insist on the continuance of Greek philosophic language in a world of myriad philosophies hardly serves to communicate their original insights."[74] These theologians focus mainly on the Buddhist notions of emptiness, no-self, dependent origination, two truths, and skillful means as the basis for reinterpreting traditional Christian faith. Throughout his career,

Keenan has engaged in a systematic reinterpretation of biblical texts, from the Gospel of Mark[75] to Philippians,[76] in Mahāyāna philosophical terms. Such Mahāyāna reading of biblical narratives, he states, does not contest traditional Christian interpretations, but rather "focuses on themes which are neglected in Christian tradition and thus differs from the mainstream of that tradition."[77] On the other hand, he also acknowledges that a Mahāyāna understanding of Christianity "is deconstructive in the extreme, tearing down any fixed textual stability, maintaining that truth is empty of any fixed essence and in the final analysis beyond the grasp of discriminative thinking."[78] Applying the categories of dependent origination and emptiness to the person of Jesus Christ, for example, would mean that "He is ultimate and absolute inasmuch as he is totally empty, and human and relative inasmuch as he is totally interrelated with the world."[79] There is thus little place in this theology for the traditional Christian notion of the uniqueness of Jesus Christ and for the redemptive meaning of his suffering. Keenan also applies his critique of the essentialism of Hellenistic thought to the category of transubstantiation, thus applying his Mahāyāna reinterpretation of Christianity also to the domain of ritual or sacramental life.[80]

Joseph O'Leary applies Mahāyāna Buddhist categories of emptiness, two truths, and skillful means (*upāya*) to the interpretation and understanding of the status of doctrine itself in Christianity. While recognizing the validity and importance of doctrinal claims, the notion of *upāya* points to their provisional and conventional nature. Traditional ontological language referring to God is thus not so much rejected or reinterpreted, but rather regarded as "skillful means for pointing to the reality of God."[81] Similarly, O'Leary argues that traditional Christology "can still function as a 'skillful means' for bringing into view the truth revealed in the Christ-event … by reflecting on the intrinsically 'empty' and provisional character of these conceptions, as makeshift historical constructions marked by all the inadequacies of human language and thought in the face of the transcendent." Rather than replacing traditional Christian concepts with Buddhist ones, O'Leary thus suggests approaching traditional doctrinal language "in a modified form," and that we "use it more lightly and adroitly."[82] This interpretation of religious doctrine and religious identity may then also serve to "loosen up our thinking on the conundrums of religious pluralism."[83] In his 2018 work, *Buddhist Nonduality, Paschal Paradox: A Christian Commentary on The Teaching of Vimalakīrti*, O'Leary seeks

> to identify analogies to it in the New Testament and to see how the confrontation between the Buddhist and scriptural sources plays out, whether as mutual enrichment, correction of one by the other, or the emergence of an affinity that prompts us to look beyond both languages or to treat them as alternative conventional vehicles of an insight into or revelation of the supremely real.[84]

Though all of these different types of learning appear in the commentary, the reinterpretation of Christian texts and teachings in terms of Buddhist nonduality represents the dominant theme and refrain.

Comparative theologians are often less inclined to attempt a wholesale reinterpretation of Christianity through the lens of another tradition, but rather in discrete studies which shed new interpretive light on one tradition through the lens of the other. Tracy Tiemeier, for example, offers a reinterpretation of the relationship between the virginity and the motherhood of Mary through a reading of female Tamil saints. This, she argues, "can help Christians to rethink Mary as Virgin and Mother. Rather than Mary being the 'icon of womanhood' who unifies 'two dimensions of the female vocation,' Mary could be the one who confirms the significance of gender (in her motherhood) and undoes it at the same time (in her virginity)."[85] This, she states, may have implications for the ordination of women and for the Christian attitude toward gender in general: "The lesson here, then, is that gendered practices are indeed powerful, but not absolutely so … In this regard, women again could be seen as ritually powerful (and therefore fit for ordination) – but not because they are women, but because they, like men, have the capacity to undo their own gender through their ritually powerful bodily practices."[86]

The reinterpretation of one theological tradition through categories derived from another raises some questions and challenges. Though particular philosophical frameworks may be contingent or conventional, they do shape the faith, practice, and experience of traditions in fundamental ways. Comparative theologians often focus mainly on the theological or philosophical meaning and coherence of their systems. But the implications of all this for the life of ritual and prayer are not always taken into consideration. It also raises the question of the relationship between philosophical frameworks and faith traditions. Though philosophical frameworks may seem neutral and interchangeable, they are often themselves deeply shaped by particular religious views, or deeply engrained in the scriptures of a particular tradition.[87] This would mean that philosophical frameworks are not simply interchangeable without touching on the essence of a particular tradition, and that the interpretation of one tradition through the philosophical categories of another may amount to the interpretation of one tradition simply in terms of another. This may still lead to a source of theological enrichment and growth. But it may also at times challenge one's fundamental religious identity.

The process of reinterpretation, however, generally involves a careful negotiation of concepts or categories such that they remain faithful to the traditional self-understanding of a tradition. Just as the appropriation of Hellenistic concepts by early Christians led to their mutual adaptation and transformation, reinterpretation of Christianity through different philosophical frameworks will also involve mutual adjustment.

Some degree of reinterpretation is at work in most forms of comparative theology. The very fact of engaging another religion in one's theological reflection involves some degree of hermeneutical exchange, seeing oneself through the other and the other through one's own tradition. This involves a careful negotiation of hermeneutical horizons in which the essence of one's tradition and its social and ritual structures are not entirely compromised. The very attempt to reinterpret one's own traditional teachings through the categories and framework of another stretches the hermeneutical horizons of a tradition, while also disclosing its hermeneutical limits or edges. While religious traditions may not be restricted to particular traditions of interpretation, neither are they endlessly flexible.

It is probably not insignificant that the process of learning through reinterpretation in Christian comparative theology so often involves the Hindu and Buddhist traditions of nondualism. These traditions do have some resonances with certain traditions of mystical thought in Christianity, and they also address some of the modern or postmodern challenges of classical metaphysics.[88] The question as to whether or to what extent this type of learning through comparative theology takes a firm hold in the tradition remains to be seen. They do seem to have some appeal to Christians in search of a less hierarchical and dualistic understanding of faith and tradition.

4.5   Appropriation

One of the most challenging forms of learning in comparative theology involves the appropriation by one tradition of new elements derived from another religious tradition. As John Cobb points out, "in the course of dialogue with another tradition, partners will encounter ideas in the other tradition that seem plausible, compelling, and even true and yet unavailable within the home tradition."[89] This may involve symbols, texts, ritual elements, philosophical ideas, and types of experience that are undeveloped or underdeveloped, or untapped within one's own religious framework. Insofar as comparative theology is oriented to theological development and growth, the recognition of distinctive elements of truth and validity in other religions may lead to an attempt to integrate these into one's own religious tradition.

The process of appropriation may occur consciously or unconsciously. In the course of history, religions have spontaneously adopted elements from other religious traditions as they moved into cultural contexts dominated by particular religions. As such, early on, Indian Christians appropriated the Hindu caste system, just as Buddhism in China adopted Daoist elements to form a distinctive school of Buddhism. In the encounter between religions and cultures, elements from different religions and cultures thus naturally affect one another, leading to subtle or significant religious changes. Such appropriation may come to occur more deliberately in the process of inculturation where religions consciously adopt symbolic, ritual, or conceptual elements in order to adapt to local habits and sensibilities.[90] While inculturation is often regarded as adaptation to local cultures, it cannot but include engaging the religions that have traditionally shaped those cultures. In the process of inculturation in India, Christians thus appropriated Hindu institutional forms (*ashrams*), forms of prayer (yoga and meditation), ritual practices (*ārati*) and chants. In this regard, the appropriation that occurs in comparative theology is similar to certain forms of inculturation.

The notion of learning through appropriation requires a particular theology of religions that recognizes the possibility of truth in difference. Some theologians have based the possibility and promise of appropriation on the idea of the complementarity of religious traditions. In *The Marriage of East and West*, Bede Griffiths, for example, draws a sharp distinction between Christian and Hindu revelations, emphasizing that these differences[91] "are not opposed but complementary."[92]

> What is required is surely that we should see these two revelations in relation to one another. The danger of Hinduism is that it tends to see time and history as a passing phenomenon without any ultimate significance. The danger of Christianity is that it tends to attach too much importance to temporal events and to lose the sense of a timeless reality.[93]

As such, the process of learning through appropriating elements that are different but complementary becomes not only possible but necessary. In his approach to religious differences, Jacques Dupuis also speaks of a "mutual complementarity, by which an exchange and a sharing of saving values takes place between Christianity and the other religions and from which a mutual enrichment and transformation may ensue between the religions themselves."[94]

Whether or not comparative theologians subscribe to the idea of the complementarity between religions, the adoption of elements from another religion requires at least some degree of compatibility. Only those teachings or practices that are in continuity with established beliefs, or with certain agreed normative principles, will be eligible for learning. Often, the teachings or elements appropriated are regarded as an extension or a deepening of teachings already present in the tradition. In his comparative theological engagement of Shankara and Paul Tillich on the human predicament, John Thatamanil, for example, suggests that "conversation with Hindu nondualism challenges

Christian theologians to carry the antidualistic impulses found in Tillich further."[95] Thus, rather than introducing something new, Thatamanil argues that Shankara may help Christian theologians attain to "deeper truth."[96] While Shankara's thought is itself not without gaps or problems, Thatamanil suggests that it is "possible to absorb the virtues of Shankara and Tillich and also overcome what is inadequate in both by playing each against the other."[97] This thus also reflects some belief in complementarity of theological traditions.

In *Without Buddha I Could Not Be a Christian*, Paul Knitter also reflects on the ways in which his understanding of Christianity has come to be informed and transformed through the appropriation of elements from Buddhism.[98] While recognizing that what he came to adopt from Buddhism represent "something really new,"[99] he also argues that they "fit" Christian faith, and may even be regarded as a forgotten part of the Christian tradition: "I'm not amputating a traditional Christian belief and replacing it with a Buddhist transplant. Rather, the notion of Awakening has become for me a flashlight by which I've discovered and retrieved symbols and teachings that were on the dusty back shelves of the Christian tradition or simply not noticed and appreciated by many of us Christians."[100] Some of what he adopts from Buddhism, however, represents by his own admission "an ingredient not easily found in most Christian pantries."[101] He speaks here in particular of mindfulness meditation. Dialogue and comparative theological engagement with Hinduism and Buddhism has indeed led to the widespread adoption within Christianity of new forms of meditation, from Theravada forms of mindfulness meditation, to various forms of Zen practice, and from Tibetan Dzogchen practices to various types and schools of Hindu yoga. Though there may be traces of elements of these practices in Christian monastic disciplines (such as mantra meditation in the Hesychast tradition), it is undoubtedly true that most of these practices introduce something genuinely new to Christian prayer and practice.

In the process of appropriation, the meaning of symbols, rituals, and categories inevitably shifts in order to fit the new religious context. The task is thus, as John Cobb puts it, "to refine and hone what one has taken to be important to one's own faith and similarly to refine and hone the insight one is learning from others."[102] Paul Knitter also acknowledges that the process of "passing back," or fitting elements from the other religion into one's own, involves "repossessing but also realigning our previous beliefs."[103] While the meaning of elements appropriated thus undergoes a shift and recalibration to fit the new religious tradition, the tradition itself is also adjusted and expanded as it absorbs new religious elements. This is what might be called, with Martien Brinkman and Paul Hedges, a "double transformation."[104]

The appropriation of elements of one tradition by another may raise a series of critical theological, hermeneutical, and deontological questions (some of which have been addressed in Chapter 3). It may form a challenge for the appropriating tradition. Each religion regards itself as self-sufficient and in possession of the fullness of the means to salvation or liberation, and the very notion of borrowing from another tradition may be seen to suggest a certain lack or incompleteness. It may also lead to accusations of syncretism as elements from seemingly incompatible religions are being combined. The adoption of Hindu and Buddhist forms of meditation, for example, has been met with some resistance on the part of the hierarchy of the Roman Catholic tradition. In the "Letter to the Bishops of the Catholic Church on Some Aspects of Christian Meditation," the magisterium of the Catholic Church warns against "proposals to harmonize Christian meditation with eastern techniques" and suggests that their contents and methods need to be "ever subjected to a thorough-going examination so as to avoid the danger of falling into syncretism."[105] Though these concerns have been addressed, there is among other Christian groups considerable unease about the practice of yoga by Christians as introducing heathen forms of worship into the Christian faith.

For the tradition whose symbols, rituals, and teachings are being appropriated, this form of learning may also be unsettling and threatening, as their own cherished religious elements are absorbed into another tradition and used in ways unintended in their original context. This is a matter that calls for great sensitivity on the part of comparative theologians. Even though the desire to learn from the other religion is first of all an expression of admiration and respect, the use of one's own tradition – especially in the context of power imbalances – may be regarded as a form of expropriation. The onus is thus always on the part of the comparative theologian to pay heed to the original context and meaning of particular symbols, teachings, and practices before appropriating them within a new religious context. Rather than viewing the process of appropriation negatively, and from the perspective of domination, one may also approach it as an opportunity for reciprocal exchange, or, as Paul Hedges puts it, borrowing the expression of Musa Dube, for "liberating interdependence."[106]

4.6   Reaffirmation

A type of learning that may be somewhat unexpected or atypical involves a new appreciation or a reaffirmation of the truths of one's own tradition. This may entail a renewed recognition of the truth and value of certain teachings in light of particular alternatives in the other tradition, or else a new interpretation of certain traditional teachings in light of the other (but not in terms of the other, as was the case in the type of learning called reinterpretation). Reaffirmation is not merely a blind insistence on the truth of one's own teaching and practices regardless of the other. It involves a new focus on certain beliefs or practices one would not wish to lose or compromise in the process of engaging the religious other, or a reassessment in which one's self-understanding is somewhat changed through exposure to other religious systems and possibilities. This thus also involves a form of learning or the attainment of new insight.

To be sure, reaffirmation occurs from within a particular faith perspective. The truth of certain teachings and practices may be argued on rational or phenomenological grounds. But in the end, the affirmation of the truth of one's own tradition must be understood from within the confessional context of comparative theology, where the ultimate recourse is to some form of revealed or received truth.

This reaffirmation may seem reminiscent of traditional apologetics. Insofar as comparative theology involves the pursuit of truth, and insofar as it entails a confessional starting point and goal, some form of apologetics is inevitable. The difference with classical apologetics, however, is that while the latter is often based on an a priori denial of truth in the other religion, often misrepresenting the religious other in order to establish this point, reaffirmation seeks to grant as much veracity as possible to the other, often allowing it to color or affect one's self-understanding. Reaffirmation moreover occurs in a spirit of humility and openness to the distinctive truth of the other.

Paul Griffiths offers an example of comparative theology as apologetics in the final chapter of *An Apology for Apologetics*, where he focuses on the Buddhist and Christian notions of the self. Based on an analysis of the Buddhist teaching of no-self, and a critique of the debates and arguments advanced by Buddhist logicians, he argues for the plausibility of the Christian teaching of an eternal soul.[107] He readily recognizes that Buddhists will engage in the reverse type of apologetic, arguing that "the Christian idea of the soul is incoherent, or that there is not sufficient evidence to affirm its existence,"[108] thus reaffirming the Buddhist rejection of an unchanging and substantial self.

Though primarily a personal testimony of conversion or reconversion from Buddhism to Christianity, Paul Williams's *The Unexpected Way* may be regarded as a work of comparative theology in that it involves a confessional theological engagement with Christian and Buddhist ideas.[109] Williams focuses in particular on Christian theological positions that he came to reaffirm after a prolonged study and practice of Buddhism. He engages in both positive and negative apologetics and reaffirms the Christian belief in "a necessary Being upon whom all things depend," the communal dimension of

Christianity, and the state of "eternal life in a perfect loving relationship with God."[110] He generally affirms the optimism of Christianity, which assumes that "our lives, as the lives of the individual persons we are, are infinitely valuable, and we all have the possibility, as the persons we are, of unimaginable perfection."[111] All of these beliefs are reassumed by Williams from a new religious perspective and informed by the Buddhist teachings against which they are reaffirmed. As such, they also involve a type of learning from or through the other tradition.

In the volume *Comparing Faithfully*, a Christian and a Hindu theologian approach the question of theodicy or the meaning of unjust suffering in a comparative theological way, ultimately reaffirming the validity and truth of their own theological views. Klaus von Stosch tackles this problem in comparative theological engagement with the work of the Muslim scholar Navid Kermani.[112] While admiring Kermani's suggestion that all one can do in the face of radical evil is direct one's complaint, lamentation, and accusation against God, and that it is ultimately the irresistible beauty of God that leads one to "accept the terror of God as the shadow side of the light,"[113] von Stosch ultimately states that "I am not sure whether I can finally accept Kermani's approach to the problem of evil." Having openly and willingly considered Kermani's proposal, von Stosch reaffirms that:

> For me, it is very important that God is purely good and that God's love is always just and redemptive. God's anger – in my interpretation – is always a call for love. To me, God's nature is unambiguous. In the context of the free will defense, I argue that the practical dimension of theodicy consists of postulating this God against the ambiguity of humankind. God's love is the aim of human protest against all humiliation of humankind.[114]

Von Stosch's careful confessional statements (for me, to me, etc.) suggest a new style of apologetics in which the reaffirmation of one's own beliefs occurs in humility, and with a clear sense of one's own religious positioning.

In the same volume, Jeffery Long engages the problem of theodicy from a Hindu perspective in comparative theological engagement with Christianity.[115] Focusing on the thought of Ramakrishna and Vivekananda in dialogue with David Griffin, Long argues that the perspective of Vedānta offers a more coherent alternative to that of Christian process theology. For Vivekananda, "the suffering experienced in this world is part of the personal transformation process that leads us to our eventual right relationship, loving union or realization of identity with the ultimately real."[116] The world is thus regarded as a "moral gymnasium" that leads to ultimate liberation in the afterlife. Where Griffin and other process theologians must compromise the traditional

Christian idea of God's omnipotence in order to preserve his benevolence, Long states that "the idea of an eventual victory for good beyond this life that would not necessitate an omnipotent God is, however, quite plausible from a Vedantic framework."[117] This reaffirms his sense of the validity of the Hindu view in light of some challenges of Christian theodicy. Long thus states that his engagement with Christian thought "refines and sharpens Vedantic theodicy in a way that might not otherwise have been possible – and thus underscores the value of the comparative enterprise for thinkers inhabiting various traditions."[118]

The process of reaffirmation in comparative theology often involves a negotiation in which some elements of the other tradition are acknowledged and absorbed while insisting on preserving and affirming essential or inalienable parts of the tradition. In *Beyond Dialogue*, for example, John Cobb recognizes that Buddhist anthropology can help Christians overcome their substantialist understanding of the human person and realize the sense of interconnection and mutual responsibility that is at the core of the Christian message.[119] On the other hand, he also reaffirms the importance of the historical and social dimension of Christianity. In her careful study of the dialogue between John Cobb and Masao Abe, Annewieke Vroom notes that both theologians came to reaffirm the truth of their own religious and philosophical positions; for John Cobb, the truth of the existence of a personal transcendent God and of the historical mediation of God in Jesus Christ, and for Masao Abe, the truth of ultimate reality as emptiness, understood in dynamic terms.[120] Although the dialogue allowed both thinkers to refine their positions, she concludes that it did not lead to any fundamental change. It did, however, allow each to reaffirm their own position with greater clarity and insight. In *The Emptying God*, Jewish and Christian theologians respond to Masao Abe's use of the notion of kenosis in his own attempt at comparative theology from a Buddhist perspective.[121] While they largely reaffirm and reinforce traditional Christian understandings of the category against its Buddhist appropriation, the arguments used in fact deepen or enlarge its traditional meaning.

One of the recurring topics in Christian comparative theological engagement with other religions is the belief in the unique salvific role of Jesus Christ. This belief has been and may be subject to any of the different types of learning. It has often been subject to reinterpretation from within the context and horizon of other religious traditions.[122] However, comparative theology may also lead to a reaffirmation of its importance and value, but now based on arguments gained through engagement with other religions, and enriched with insights from those religions. This thus involves reaffirmation deeply informed by the religious other.

Learning as reaffirmation of one's own beliefs and practices in light of alternate religious views involves one of the more delicate and possibly offensive aspects of comparative theology. Despite the respect shown toward, and the knowledge demonstrated about, the other religion – indeed, sometimes even *because* of this – the process of reaffirmation in comparative theology may be regarded as particularly provocative for the tradition engaged in the comparative theological exercise since it inevitably involves some measure of rejection or critique of the other.[123] However, several factors mitigate the possible insult to the other tradition. First, reaffirmation focuses on certain particular teachings or practices and does not involve a wholesale rejection of the other tradition. Second, the process of reaffirmation may include acknowledgment of valid elements of critique deriving from the other tradition that are put in creative tension with one's own, and that lead not merely to reaffirmation, but also reformulation of one's own beliefs. David Burrell, for example, points out how the Christian belief in the Trinity and the Muslim belief in the oneness of God have shaped one another through mutual critique, and that the result of such mutual challenge is that "we will have to come to a more refined understanding of what we have long been affirming."[124] Reaffirmation itself may thus include the integration of certain elements borrowed from the other tradition. Paul Griffiths, for example, also affirms "possibilities for a broader Buddhist enrichment of my Christian understanding of the processes by which the experienced facts of self-identity come to occur."[125] In comparative theology "appropriation and creative borrowing are just as important as engagement in positive and negative apologetics; neither need exclude the other, just as long as both are taken with intellectual seriousness and argumentative passion."[126] Third, reaffirmation may also include an important dimension of self-critique, or acceptance of critique and judgment from other religious traditions. For Paul Tillich, "the judgment of Christianity against itself on the basis of the judgment it received from outside"[127] represented the main goal of the encounter with other religions. It leads not only to a reaffirmation, but also to a purification of one's self-understanding. Clooney also recognizes the importance of a "mutually critical conversation" in which theologians of one tradition take into consideration "the responses they receive from the theologians who comprehend their views to some extent and yet in part also misunderstand or disagree."[128] Though he regards this mainly as an occasion for mutual correction, it may also include some degree of self-correction, or clarification of the teachings of one's own tradition, not only for the other but also for oneself. And finally, the process of reaffirmation includes a certain humble awareness of the faith dimension of all religious affirmations.

Notes

1. I am grateful to Thierry-Marie Courau (Institut Catholique of Paris) for emphasizing this fact.
2. See, for example, Catherine Cornille, "Discipleship in Hindu-Christian Comparative Theology," *Theological Studies 77*, no. 4 (2016): 869–85. Here, I discuss different types of Christian learning from Hinduism with regard to the topic of discipleship.
3. Francis Clooney, *The Truth, the Way, the Life: Christian Commentary on the Three Holy Mantras of the Śrīvaiṣṇava Hindus* (Leuven: Peeters, 2008), 182.
4. Francis Clooney, *Beyond Compare: St. Francis de Sales and Śrī Vedānta Deśika on Loving Surrender to God* (Washington: Georgetown University Press, 2008), 183.
5. Francis Clooney, *His Hiding Place Is Darkness: A Hindu-Christian Theopoetics of Divine Absence* (Stanford: Stanford University Press, 2014), 126.
6. Clooney, *His Hiding Place Is Darkness*, 14–15.
7. Francis Clooney, *Comparative Theology: Deep Learning across Religious Borders* (Oxford: Wiley-Blackwell, 2010), 117.
8. Clooney, *His Hiding Place Is Darkness*, 46.
9. Clooney, *Comparative Theology*, 11.
10. This text represents "a compendium of the essential meaning of all the *Upanishads*" by the foremost proponent of Advaita Vedānta, the eighth-century philosopher Shankara. It is a complex text, a fairly loose compendium of what Locklin calls "scripts," dialogues between teachers and students, some in the form of poetry, some in the form of prose, on how to attain liberation or release from bondage and suffering. Underlying the text is the metaphysical notion of the nonduality (*advaita*) of the deepest self (*Ātman*) and ultimate reality (*Brahman*), and knowledge or experience of this nonduality as the means to liberation.
11. Reid Locklin, *Liturgy of Liberation: A Christian Commentary on Shankara's Upadeśasāhasrī* (Leuven: Peeters, 2011), 42.
12. Jonathan Z. Smith, "Prologue: In Comparison a Magic Dwells," in *A Magic Still Dwells*, ed. K. Patton and B. Ray (Berkeley: University of California Press, 2000), 25–26. The piece was originally published in 1982 in Smith's book *Imagining Religion: From Babylon to Jonestown* (Chicago: University of Chicago Press, 1982), 19–35.
13. Clooney, *Comparative Theology*, 11.
14. Locklin, *Liturgy of Liberation*, 43.
15. Locklin, *Liturgy of Liberation*, 175.
16. Locklin, *Liturgy of Liberation*, 177.
17. Locklin, *Liturgy of Liberation*, 309.
18. Locklin, *Liturgy of Liberation*, 42.
19. Holly Hillgardner, "Longing and Letting Go: Lessons in Being Human from Hadewijch and Mirabai," in *Comparing Faithfully*, ed. M. Voss Roberts (New York: Fordham University Press, 2016), 149–70.
20. Hillgardner, "Longing and Letting Go," 152.

21. Hillgardner, "Longing and Letting Go," 167.

22. David Burrell, *Towards a Jewish-Christian-Muslim Theology* (Oxford: Wiley-Blackwell, 2011).

23. Hugh Nicholson, *Comparative Theology and the Problem of Religious Rivalry* (Oxford: Oxford University Press 2011), 12.

24. Rudolf Otto, *Mysticism East and West* (New York: Collier Books, 1962), 225.

25. See R. C. Zaehner, *Mysticism, Sacred and Profane* (Oxford: Oxford University Press, 1957), 170–71.

26. Paul Mommaers and Jan Van Bragt, *Mysticism, Buddhist and Christian* (New York: Crossroad, 1995).

27. Nicholson, *Comparative Theology and the Problem of Religious Rivalry*.

28. Nicholson, *Comparative Theology and the Problem of Religious Rivalry*, 198.

29. Nicholson, *Comparative Theology and the Problem of Religious Rivalry*, 198.

30. Nicholson, *Comparative Theology and the Problem of Religious Rivalry*, 176.

31. Nicholson, *Comparative Theology and the Problem of Religious Rivalry*, 176.

32. Locklin, *Liturgy of Liberation*, 109–10.

33. Marianne Moyaert, "Who Is the Suffering Servant? A Comparative Theological Reading of Isaiah 53 after the Shoah," in *Comparing Faithfully*, ed. M. Voss Roberts (New York: Fordham University Press, 2016), 216.

34. Moyaert, "Who Is the Suffering Servant?" 231.

35. Daniel Joslyn-Siemiatkoski, *The More Torah, the More Life: A Christian Commentary on Mishnah Avot* (Leuven: Peeters, 2018).

36. Some of the questions Joslyn-Siemiatkoski mentions in his conclusion relate to the understanding of the uniqueness of Jesus in light of his self-understanding as a committed teacher of Torah, the relationship between Israel and the Church, and the significance of Torah for Christians.

37. Condemnations of heresy have at times been based on purely social or political rather than theological grounds.

38. Daniel Sheridan, *Loving God: Kṛṣṇa and Christ: A Christian Commentary on the Nārada Sūtras* (Leuven: Peeters, 2007), 6–7.

39. Sheridan, *Loving God*, 8.

40. Sheridan, *Loving God*, 21, 207.

41. Nicholson, *Comparative Theology and the Problem of Religious Rivalry*, 193.

42. Nicholson, *Comparative Theology and the Problem of Religious Rivalry*, 193.

43. Nicholson, *Comparative Theology and the Problem of Religious Rivalry*, 195.

44. Bede Bidlack, "What Child Is This? Jesus, Lord Lao, and Divine Identity," in *Comparing Faithfully*, ed. M. Voss Roberts (New York: Fordham University Press, 2016), 211.

45. Bidlack, "What Child Is This?" 212.

46. Paul Ingram, *The Process of Buddhist-Christian Dialogue* (Cambridge: James Clarke, 2011), 113–17.

47. Ingram, *The Process of Buddhist-Christian Dialogue*, 117.

48. Interest in Hindu and Buddhist notions of reincarnation has thus drawn renewed attention to the teachings and practices of the Cathars, as well as on the eschatological views of Origen.

49. Michelle Voss Roberts, *Dualities: A Theology of Difference* (Louisville: Westminster John Knox Press, 2010), 4.

50. Voss Roberts, *Dualities*, 20.

51. Voss Roberts, *Dualities*, 12, emphasis in the original.

52. Hillgardner, "Longing and Letting Go," 149–79.

53. Hillgardner, "Longing and Letting Go," 167.

54. Gavin Flood, "Reading Christian Detachment Through the Bhagavad Gītā," in *Song Divine: Christian Commentaries on the Bhagavad Gītā*, ed. C. Cornille (Leuven: Peeters, 2006), 9–22.

55. Flood, "Reading Christian Detachment," 21.

56. Kallistos, Bishop of Diokleia, *The Power of the Name: The Jesus Prayer in Orthodox Spirituality* (Oxford: SLG Press, 1986).

57. John Main, *Word into Silence: A Manual for Christian Meditation*, ed. L. Freeman (Norwich: Canterbury Press, 2006).

58. Christopher Conway, "Liberative Service: A Comparative Theological Reflection on Dalit Theology's Service and Swami Vivekananda's Seva," Dissertation, Boston College, 2014.

59. Conway, "Liberative Service," 372.

60. Conway, "Liberative Service," 380.

61. Conway, "Liberative Service," 386.

62. Conway, "Liberative Service," 385.

63. It is true that the title of Mechthild's book is *The Flowing Light of the Godhead*, but to move from this to the idea that "Divinity is a fluid" involves some degree of reinterpretation or metamorphization of Mechthild's thought. See Voss Roberts, *Dualities*, 150ff.

64. Hans Urs von Balthasar, *Truth Is Symphonic: Aspects of Christian Pluralism* (San Francisco: Ignatius Press, 1987), 55. He continues the quote by stating that "The Greek concepts themselves had to be widened in a way that came close to a new coining (for example *hypostasis*) in order to be made at all suitable for the new content. Nor would the Indian and Chinese concepts be able to avoid a similar transmutation."

65. Abhishiktānanda, *Saccidānanda: A Christian Approach to the Advaitic Experience* (London: ISPCK, 1974), 49.

66. Abhishiktananda, *Saccidānandaa*, 70.

67. Abhishiktananda, *Saccidānandaa*, 178.

68. See Catherine Cornille, *The Guru in Indian Catholicism: Ambiguity or Opportunity of Inculturation?* (Leuven: Peeters, 2001). In the very last entry to his journal, Abhishiktānanda writes: "the Trinity can only be understood in the experience of advaita" and that "Jesus revealed to the human person who he is, who everyone is" (journal entry for September 11, 1973; Abhishiktānanda, *La montée au fond du coeur. Le journal intime du moine chrétien-sannyasi hindou, 1948–1973* (Paris: OEIL, 1986), 471).

69. Abhishiktananda, *Saccidānandaa*, 178.

70. Raimon Panikkar, *Christophany: The Fullness of Man* (Maryknoll: Orbis Books, 2004), 181.

71. Sara Grant, *Toward an Alternative Theology: Confessions of a Non-Dualist Christian* (Notre Dame: University of Notre Dame Press, 2002), 94.

72. Jan Van Bragt, *Interreligious Affinities*, ed. J. Heisig and K. Seung Chul (Nagoya: Nanzan Institute for Religion and Culture, 2014), 260.

73. John Keenan, *The Meaning of Christ: A Mahāyāna Theology* (Maryknoll: Orbis Books, 1989), 62.

74. Keenan, *The Meaning of Christ*, 226.

75. John Keenan, *The Gospel of Mark: A Mahāyāna Reading* (Maryknoll: Orbis Books, 1995).

76. John Keenan, *The Emptied Christ of Philippians: Mahāyāna Meditations* (Eugene: Wipf & Stock, 2015).

77. Keenan, *The Emptied Christ of Philippians*, 19.

78. Keenan, *The Gospel of Mark*, 5.

79. Keenan, *The Gospel of Mark*, 237.

80. John Keenan, "A Mahāyāna Theology of the Real Presence of Christ in the Eucharist," *Buddhist-Christian Studies* 24 (2004): 89–100.

81. Joseph O'Leary, *Religious Pluralism and Christian Truth* (Edinburgh: Edinburgh University Press, 1986), 189.

82. O'Leary, *Religious Pluralism and Christian Truth*, 251.

83. Joseph O'Leary, "Skillful Means as a Hermeneutic Concept," in *Interreligious Hermeneutics*, ed. C. Cornille and C. Conway (Eugene: Wipf & Stock, 2010), 168.

84. Joseph O'Leary, *Buddhist Nonduality, Paschal Paradox: A Christian Commentary on The Teaching of Vimalakīrti (Vimalakīrtinirdeśa)* (Leuven: Peeters, 2018), 4.

85. Tracy Sayuki Tiemeier, "Women's Virtue, Church Leadership and the Problem of Gender Complementarity," in *Comparing Faithfully*, ed. M. Voss Roberts (New York: Fordham University Press, 2016), 182.

86. Tiemeier, "Women's Virtue," 182.

87. There are in Christian scripture itself many traces of Hellenistic and dualistic thought. And the future Pope Benedict XVI argued for the providential confluence of biblical and Hellenistic traditions; Joseph Cardinal Ratzinger, *Truth and Tolerance: Christian Belief and World Religions* (San Francisco: Ignatius Press, 2003), 90–95.

88. This is particularly clear in O'Leary's *Religious Pluralism and Christian Truth*, and in *Conventional and Ultimate Truth: A Key for Fundamental Theology* (South Bend: University of Notre Dame Press, 2015), which deal at length with the discussions in contemporary continental philosophy.

89. Leonard Swidler, John Cobb, Paul Knitter, and Monika Hellwig, *Death or Dialogue? From the Age of Monologue to the Age of Dialogue* (London: SCM Press, 1990), 7.

90. See Jonathan Sarna, "'God Loves an Infant's Praise': Cultural Borrowing and Cultural Resistance in Two Nineteenth-Century American Jewish Sunday-School Texts," in *Interreligious Dialogue and Cultural Change*, ed. C. Cornille and S. Corigliano (Eugene: Wipf & Stock, 2012), 59–78.

91. Between the emphasis on transcendence versus immanence, between the historical and the cosmic, between rational and intuitive ways of being.

Bede Griffiths, *The Marriage of East and West* (Springfield: Templegate, 1982), *25*, 33, 149.

92.   Griffiths, *The Marriage of East and West*, 179.

93.   Griffiths, *The Marriage of East and West*, 180.

94.   Jacques Dupuis, *Toward a Christian Theology of Religious Pluralism* (Maryknoll: Orbis Books, 1997), 326.

95.   John Thatamanil, *The Immanent Divine: God, Creation, and the Human Predicament* (Minneapolis: Fortress Press, 2006), 22.

96.   Thatamanil, *The Immanent Divine*, 25. In particular, he states that "Shankara can teach Christian theologians that a realistic and sober account of the human predicament need not curtail robust hope for sanctification so long as Christians recognize that human identity is not exhausted by finitude. Shankara can also teach Christians that the radical immanence of nonduality need not eliminate transcendence. The Advaitin can help Christians to discover how an apophatic anthropology that recognizes human beings as infinite mystery can preserve a form of transcendence that does not compete with immanence" (172).

97.   Thatamanil, *The Immanent Divine*, 186.

98.   Paul Knitter, *Without Buddha I Could Not Be a Christian* (Oxford: Oneworld, 2009).

99.   Knitter, *Without Buddha I Could Not Be a Christian*, 15.

100. Knitter, *Without Buddha I Could Not Be a Christian*, 115.

101. Knitter, *Without Buddha I Could Not Be a Christian*, 151.

102. John Cobb, "Dialogue," in *Death or Dialogue?* by L. Swidler, J. Cobb, P. Knitter, and M. Hellwig (London: SCM Press, 1990), 7.

103. Knitter, *Without Buddha I Could Not Be a Christian*, 21.

104. Paul Hedges, *Comparative Theology: A Critical and Methodological Perspective* (Leiden: Brill, 2017), 67. Hedges builds on Brinkman's notion of double transformation as developed in his book *The Non-Western Jesus: Jesus as Bodhisattva, Avatara, Guru, Prophet, Ancestor, or Healer* (London: Equinox, 2009), 26.

105. Congregation for the Doctrine of the Faith, "Letter to the Bishops of the Catholic Church on Some Aspects of Christian Meditation," October 15, 1989, article 12, http://www.vatican.va/roman_curia/congregations/cfaith/documents/rc_con_cfaith_doc_19891015_meditazione-cristiana_en.html.

106. Hedges, *Comparative Theology*, 70–73. While Musa Dube admits that the interdependence of nations has often led to exploitation, she also believes that such interdependence also has the capacity to "recognize and affirm the dignity of all things and people involved." Musa Dube, *Postcolonial Feminist Interpretations of the Bible* (St. Louis: Chalice Press, 2000), 185–86.

107. Paul Griffiths, *An Apology for Apologetics* (Maryknoll: Orbis Books, 1991), 85–108.

108. Griffiths, *An Apology for Apologetics*, 107.

109. Paul Williams, *The Unexpected Way: On Converting from Buddhism to Catholicism* (London: T&T Clarke, 2002).

110. Williams, *The Unexpected Way*, 32, 72–74, 93.

111. Williams, *The Unexpected Way*, 19.

112. Klaus von Stosch, "Developing Christian Theodicy in Conversation with Navid Kermani," in *Comparing Faithfully*, ed. M. Voss Roberts (New York: Fordham University Press, 2016), 98–108. The work of Kermani he engages is *The Terror of God: Attar, Job and the Metaphysical Revolt*.

113. von Stosch, "Developing Christian Theodicy," 97.

114. von Stosch, "Developing Christian Theodicy," 102.

115. Jeffery Long, "Like a Dog's Curly Tail: Finding Perfection in a World of Imperfection," in *Comparing Faithfully*, ed. M. Voss Roberts (New York: Fordham University Press, 2016), 107–25.

116. Long, "Like a Dog's Curly Tail," 120.

117. Long, "Like a Dog's Curly Tail," 123.

118. Long, "Like a Dog's Curly Tail," 109.

119. John Cobb, *Beyond Dialogue: Toward a Mutual Transformation of Christianity and Buddhism* (Philadelphia: Fortress Press, 1982), 109–10.

120. Annewieke Vroom, "*God of Leegte? Zenboeddhist Masao Abe in Dialoog met Christelijke Denkers*," Doctoral dissertation for the VU Amsterdam, 2014, 247–57.

121. John Cobb and Christopher Ives, eds., *The Emptying God: A Buddhist-Jewish-Christian Conversation* (Maryknoll: Orbis Books, 1990).

122. See, for example, Gregory Barker, ed., *Jesus in the World's Faiths: Leading Thinkers from Five Religions Reflect on His Meaning* (Maryknoll: Orbis Books, 2005).

123. Jose Cabezon and Perry Schmidt-Leukel thus engage in a spirited counter-argumentation against the way Williams argues for the superior truth of Christianity; in John D'Arcy May, ed., *Converging Ways?* (Sankt Ottilien: EOS, 2001), 67–154.

124. David Burrell, *Towards a Jewish-Christian-Muslim Theology* (Oxford: Wiley-Blackwell, 2011), 174.

125. Griffiths, *An Apology for Apologetics*, 107.

126. Griffiths, *An Apology for Apologetics*, 108.

127. Paul Tillich, *Christianity and the Encounter of the World Religions* (New York: Columbia University Press, 1963), 89.

128. Francis Clooney, *Hindu God, Christian God* (Oxford: Oxford University Press, 2001), 172.

5

Comparative Theology
and Confessional Theology

As comparative theology is becoming an established mode of theological thinking, the question of its relationship to confessional theology and its place in the academy has become increasingly pertinent. Does comparative theology constitute a distinct discipline with its own method and object? Or does it represent a particular approach to the classical disciplines of theology? How do comparative theologians organize themselves into research groups or scholarly organizations: by their tradition of origin, by the religions involved in their comparative theological work, or more broadly by the use of a comparative theological method?[1] If it is considered to be a distinct theological discipline or area of research, how does comparative theology relate itself to other theological disciplines or to the tradition as a whole? These questions are particularly relevant for confessional comparative theology, which is grounded in a particular faith tradition and which seeks to contribute to theological reflection within that tradition. We will here thus reflect on the importance of comparative theology for confessional theology and on the importance of confessional theology for comparative theology.

The term confessional is here used not in a narrow sectarian sense, but in descriptive terms to refer to the real, though at times permeable, boundaries between religious traditions. Critiques of the term religion, combined with a strong awareness of regional and individual differences in the life and experience of a particular religion, have led to a questioning of the very notion of distinct religious and confessional traditions. While individual experiences may differ, confessional traditions and denominations are still based on distinct religious lineages with their own sets of texts, practices, and hermeneutics, and with their own sense of community as well as historical and theological indebtedness. Each confessional tradition is thus based on

Meaning and Method in Comparative Theology, First Edition. Catherine Cornille.
© 2020 John Wiley & Sons Ltd. Published 2020 by John Wiley & Sons Ltd.

certain normative ideas and principles that establish its continuity in time and space. These normative ideas and principles also form the basis for different theological traditions. They establish a sense of theological foundation and coherence and guide the process of discernment in theological development and growth.

From a confessional perspective, comparative theology may be regarded as a challenge or a threat. Insofar as theology is traditionally conducted from within clear religious paradigms and a given set of data and normative claims, the expansion of the theological data to include other religious traditions as possible sources of truth may be unsettling. Comparative theology may be seen to introduce a massive amount of new data which are not easy to assess. Traditional confessional theologians typically do not have the training to judge the validity and relevance of the work of comparative theologians. The field is also developing rapidly and in so many different directions that it is difficult to have an overview and absorb its findings. Moreover, comparative theologians may be viewed with some suspicion, as their interest in other religions may be thought to reflect a lack of commitment to or proper grounding in their own. As such, confessional theologians may be tempted to ignore comparative theology, or to relegate it to the margins of theological reflection.

Conversely, comparative theologians may also be inclined to settle in the margins of confessional traditions, free to pursue their own work without interference or control. The study of other religious traditions leads to involvement in various scholarly communities (religious studies, area studies, as well as other scholarly groups focusing on the same two traditions), so that it becomes challenging to also remain abreast of or connected to mainstream theological developments.

However, the relationship between confessional and comparative theology is vital, both for comparative theology and for confessional theology. Comparative theology represents a new frontier of theological thinking, allowing theological reflection to develop and grow through the insights of other religious traditions, and understanding one's theological position within a broader religious and theological horizon. And confessional theology grounds comparative theology within a normative tradition which may help in directing its focus, and inform the process of discerning the truth of other religions. It also establishes the accountability of the comparative theologian to a particular community of faith and practice, allowing for a broader reception and dissemination of the fruits of comparative theology. We will here focus on areas of intersection between comparative and confessional theology and on some of the critical issues or questions that may arise.

5.1   Comparative Theology as Constructive Theology

All theology may be regarded as constructive theology insofar as it is oriented toward discovering, elaborating or advancing religious truth. When conducted within particular religious traditions, it involves further reflection on the foundational texts, teachings, and practices of that tradition. Though theology plays a more central role in some traditions than in others, most religions attach some importance to the conceptual expression and rational articulation of their faith experience and practice. And though the term theology may be seen to contain theistic connotations, it has come to be used more broadly to refer to the logical and philosophical elaboration of the basic teachings of any religious tradition. Even though theology is generally seen to be grounded in a particular tradition and transmission of faith, some may approach the term more generically as "the science of God" or "the study of ultimate reality."

Comparative theology is constructive theology in that it seeks to contribute to or advance the understanding of faith and truth. Sharing this same goal with other classical areas of theology (systematic theology, biblical theology, moral theology, practical theology), what distinguishes comparative theology is the material it brings to theological reflection. While other approaches to theology may bring theology into engagement with history, philosophy, philology, and the social sciences, comparative theology brings the data of other religious traditions to bear on theological reflection. Clooney states that:

> Comparative theology can also be thought of as truly constructive theology, distinguished by its sources and ways of proceeding, by its foundation in more than one tradition (although the comparative theologian remains rooted in one tradition), and by reflection which builds on that foundation, rather than simply on themes and methods already articulated prior to the comparative practice.[2]

Comparative theology indeed opens the door to a vast new source of religious insight and practice that may be engaged in a constructive way.

Though various religious traditions provide new material for theological reflection, comparative theology remains grounded in the normative teachings and theological insights of a particular tradition. While this is particularly the case for confessional comparative theology, meta-confessional comparative theologians also ultimately rely on the texts, teachings, and theological insights of a particular religion.

Though drawing from different religious and philosophical systems, Raimon Panikkar still used predominantly Christian scriptural references and the basic Christian symbol system to develop his thought.[3] And even while rejecting the confessional approach to comparative theology, Robert Neville states that "as a Protestant, I look to comparative theology as a way to gain perspective on my home tradition. Of course, my home tradition needs to be examined critically and in detail. Nevertheless, the perspective of other traditions helps to see what is really going on within Christianity, Protestantism, and Methodism."[4] While predicting that "theology, instead of being an essentially denominational enterprise, will become increasingly interreligious," Perry Schmidt-Leukel also speaks of the need to "reflect on one's own tradition in order to see what possible contribution might be made to the issues on the agenda of a global interreligious theological inquiry."[5] Comparative theologians are thus always consciously or unconsciously shaped by a particular religious tradition.

However, while confessional comparative theologians engage in constructive theology from within the theological bounds of a particular religion, meta-confessional comparative theology is not constrained by the given theological views of any particular tradition. "To undertake serious theology," Robert Neville thus states, "requires loosening the holds of the biases in the home tradition, not tightening them by deeper participation."[6] Whereas confessional comparative theologians approach the constructive effort as a matter of elucidating, deepening or elaborating on what might be called a given deposit of faith, meta-confessional comparative theologians approach it as a matter of discovering or determining truth in the process of comparative theological engagement. From within a Christian confessional framework, Francis Clooney thus states that:

> Comparative theology's contribution will not occur merely in the repetition of claims already familiar to non-comparativists. It does not disrespect doctrinal expressions of truth, neither does it merely repeat doctrinal statements as if nothing is learned from the comparative reflection. Rarely, if ever, will comparative theology produce new truths, but it can make possible new insights into familiar and even revered truths, and new ways of receiving those truths.[7]

For meta-confessional comparative theology, the constructive possibilities are entirely open and shaped by the personal insights of the theologian, or by criteria of truth determined in the process of engagement. John Thatamanil thus speaks of comparative theology as a way to "determine the truth of theological matters through conversation and collaboration."[8] The aim is to develop theological insights that are universally true, rather than valid only for members of a particular religious tradition. However, in divorcing theological insight from its grounding in practice, meta-confessional comparative theology risks remaining a purely speculative endeavor with little bearing on the religious life and practice of any particular community.

In engaging the data and insights of other religious traditions, comparative theology may contribute to theological reflection within any of the classical areas of theology. The study of scripture and of methods of scriptural exegesis in other traditions may contribute to biblical or scriptural theology. Deeper understanding of the historical figures and theological influences within and across religious traditions may prove fruitful in advancing historical theology. Ethical principles and modes of moral reasoning in other religions may inform moral theology in new and enriching ways. And the theological and philosophical insights of other religions may offer new categories and frameworks for both fundamental and systematic theology. Knowledge of other religions and of developments in theology of religions is essential for all pastoral and practical theology in a world of religious pluralism. Comparative theology may thus be regarded as a distinct area of theology when considering its material and method. But it may also be seen as grounded in and part of any of the classical disciplines of theology.

5.2 The Hybrid Religious Identity of the Comparative Theologian

Profound and prolonged engagement with the teachings and practices of another religious tradition often derives from, and sometimes leads to, identification with at least some of its teachings and practices. This may raise questions about the commitment of the comparative theologian to any particular tradition and about the relevance of comparative theology for theological reflection within a particular theological tradition.

There has been a growing scholarly interest in the topic of hybrid religiosity or multiple religious belonging. It has been approached from various perspectives and from various contexts and cases of hybridity. The term multiple religious belonging or hybrid religious identity may cover a wide array of different types and degrees of belonging to more than one religion.[9] It may refer to voluntary or involuntary, permanent or occasional, and symmetrical or asymmetrical belonging to more than one tradition. Involuntary multiple belonging refers to the inheritance of elements from different religions through birth in a culture or in a family defined by more than one religious tradition. Being Chinese traditionally meant identifying with elements from Confucianism, Buddhism, and Daoism, depending on the occasion or the time of the year, while Japanese religious identity was traditionally shaped by a mixture of Shinto and Buddhism. Children born from parents who each profess a different religious tradition may also be seen to acquire elements from different religions involuntarily. Voluntary hybrid religious identity, on the other hand, involves the deliberate identification with elements from more than one religion. This may represent an occasional and temporary reality. In times of crisis or need, individuals tend to spontaneously turn to any religious source which is believed to have the power to address and resolve the crisis. This type of religious hybridity tends to last only as long as the crisis persists. Voluntary religious hybridity may also cause a more permanent or enduring identification with more than one religion. For some, this takes the form of primary or predominant identification with one tradition and partial identification with another. Here, one religious tradition remains the basis and norm for selectively identifying with elements of another religion. However, others may come to identify equally with elements from different religions, without primary commitment. Here, individuals go back and forth between the teachings of different religions, identifying with one or the other depending on the question or the practice at hand.

Comparative theologians may identify with different religions to varying degrees. Some form of identification with teachings and practices of another religion may in fact be regarded as necessary or desirable for comparative theology. It is the appeal of a particular teaching or practice in another religion which forms the motivation for in-depth study of another religion and for trying to integrate it within one's own religious tradition. Francis Clooney, for example, speaks of the importance of "cultivated hybridity" in comparative theology:[10] "Comparative study leaves her, if she is successful, at the border between two worlds, in a space distinguished by a seeming multiplication of loyalties. She exists in between, no longer a sure fit in a theological world defined within one community."[11] He says, "She will be always both this and that, always finding that deference to two traditions means that she in a way belongs to both, without fully belonging to either."[12]

This may be seen to contradict Clooney's emphasis on the need for comparative theology to remain rooted in a particular tradition. It may indeed reflect a certain tension in his work, as in that of some other comparative theologians. But it may also point to the difference between process and purpose in comparative theology. Engagement with another religion often involves full immersion in that tradition, and identification with its teachings and practices, unencumbered by a sense of religious responsibility or loyalty. Rather than avoiding or escaping this liminal position between religions, Clooney insists that "this uncomfortable borderline position must not only be tolerated but it is necessary, and it must be intentionally nurtured."[13] The discomfort of this position is expressed powerfully in Abhishiktānanda's experience of being torn between Christianity and Hinduism: "You cannot be torn apart in the depth of your soul, as we are by this double summons (from advaitin India on one side and from Revelation on the other), and by this double opposition (from India and the church, in their ritualism, their formalism and their intellectualism), without being lacerated even physically."[14] Not all comparative theologians experience this state of torment. But it does reflect the difficulty or challenge, if not the impossibility, of fully identifying with more than one religious tradition.

While religious hybridity may be experienced as a source of freedom and initiative on the part of individuals, it represents a challenge for most religious traditions. Not only do the teachings of different religious traditions often directly contradict one another, but the practical demands or religious expectations set upon believers also tend to militate against equal participation in different religions.[15] Most religious traditions also presume full commitment to their teachings and practices, at least as an ideal. Any identification with another religious tradition may be seen as diminishing the ideal of full and unwavering commitment to a particular religion. While this may be regarded as an expression of religious possessiveness or jealousy, it may also be seen as related to the state of complete self-surrender required to attain the ultimate religious goal.[16] From this perspective, religious hybridity may thus be thought to compromise the spiritual life and growth of individuals.

Comparative theologians resolve the tension involved in religious hybridity in various ways. Confessional comparative theologians remain rooted in a particular religious tradition which remains the basis and norm for identifying with elements from another religious tradition. Some degree of religious hybridity may nourish, rather than diminish, spiritual life. Comparative theologians identify generally with elements that are in continuity, or not in contradiction, with one's primary religious tradition. Jacques Dupuis grounds the possibility of multiple religious belonging in what he calls an "asymmetrical complementarity," recognizing the complementarity between religions while still affirming the normativity of one's own tradition.[17] This may thus involve a strong pull toward elements of another religion that might be underdeveloped or missing in one's primary religion. But one's religious identity remains primarily – implicitly or explicitly – shaped by one particular religion. And the experience of religious hybridity is aimed at informing or enriching one particular religion.

Meta-confessional comparative theologians may develop various strategies to resolve the tensions and contradictions involved in religious hybridity. As Rose Drew has pointed out in her research on Buddhist-Christian dual belonging, most resort to a "monocentric pluralist perspective,"[18] or to a transcendent unity of religions, treating "pivotal points of disagreement between the Buddhist and Christian worldviews as 'bracketed questions' rather than siding firmly with one tradition or the other."[19] Other strategies of negotiation might involve focusing on practical efficacy, rather than doctrinal coherence, and developing a new personal synthesis of elements selected from the various traditions.[20] Rather than resist or resolve religious hybridity, Ulrich Winkler calls on comparative theology to precisely inhabit a "third space," which cannot be reduced to any existing tradition.[21]

The various types and degrees of religious hybridity are often in flux and difficult to parse or assess in any particular comparative theologian. Comparative theologians who no longer identify exclusively with any one particular religion tend to still be shaped primarily by the symbols, teachings or practices of one or the other religion. And they may still be focused on enriching one particular tradition through their own hybrid identity. Thus, Paul Knitter, who calls himself a Buddhist-Christian hybrid, still focuses on Christianity, as the ultimate target or goal of his hybrid experience:

> So, the "orthodox question" I'm asking in the chapters that follow is directed to the Christian community, not the Buddhist. My central concern is that the theological genes I'm passing on are still Christian, that my reinterpretation of Christian belief, though really different, is not *totally* different from what went before. All good theology is a matter of discontinuity in continuity, creating something new that is rooted in and nourished by the old.[22]

Even though the question of orthodoxy is directed to the Christian community, and even though for him "Christ has a certain primacy over the Buddha,"[23] Knitter also states that "not only does double belonging seem to work," for him, "It's necessary."[24]

In addition to the fluidity of the religious identity of individuals, the identifying elements or the limits of orthodoxy or orthopraxis of religious traditions themselves are not always clearly demarcated or fixed, so that it may be difficult to determine whether a particular theological view is to be regarded as theological development or as a form of hybridity that is incompatible with a certain tradition. Is the identity of a tradition determined only by its originating texts and symbols? Or does its philosophical interpretation belong integrally to its identity? This has an impact on whether the reinterpretation of Christianity in terms of Advaita Vedānta or Mādhyamika terms may be regarded as a legitimate theological development or as an expression of an unresolvable religious hybridity, identifying with the symbolic framework of one tradition and the hermeneutical framework of another.

Though full religious hybridity may be a challenge and a threat for religious traditions, partial hybridity or the exploration of and identification with elements that are continuous with one's own tradition may be regarded as a condition for religious development and growth. It points to areas of thought and practices that may be lacking in one's own tradition, and/or it introduces new forms of religious experience and expression. The creative potential of some degree of religious hybridity is evident in a figure such as Thomas Merton, whom David Tracy speaks of as a "self-transcending Christian."[25] Though he remained deeply rooted in the Christian tradition, he was also profoundly inspired by Daoist, Buddhist, Hindu, and Sufi teachings and practices, all the while becoming one of the most important and inspiring Christian authors of the twentieth century. Some degree of religious hybridity may thus be regarded as vital for religious renewal and growth.

5.3   The Problem of Choice in Comparative Theology

One of the important challenges for comparative theology itself and for its relationship to confessional theology involves the seemingly limitless possibilities provided by themes and traditions available for comparative theological engagement. One may choose among thousands of traditions, living and dead religions, old and new religions, scriptural and oral religions. While the focus of comparison is often on the so-called "World Religions" (which are some of the larger among the old, living, scriptural traditions), there are in fact a plethora of other religions that are eligible for comparison and that are not by definition less interesting or less promising. Within each religion, one may again focus on any particular school or denomination or sub-tradition. And within any sub-tradition, one may again choose among any number of texts, teachings, rituals or artifacts. In each case, the choice of tradition and text of practice may be brought into comparison with any number of teachings, texts, and practices in one's own tradition.

The act of comparison does not generally impose itself as natural or necessary, or as emerging from an evident relationship between data from different religions. This has been the subject of self-critical discussion in the comparative study of religion. In noting the absence of any rules for the production of comparisons, Jonathan Z. Smith famously likened comparison to a form of "magic."[26] Comparison is thus for Smith not a matter of discovery, but of invention, and must be regarded as "more impressionistic than methodical."[27] Though recognizing the unscientific nature of comparison, Kimberley Patton and Benjamin Ray reappropriate the term magic in a more positive sense to emphasize the creative potential of comparison:

> Recognizing that Smith used the term "magic" derogatorily, we do so, not as an act of defiance, nor even one of irony, but rather to highlight a reenvisioned potential for comparative study. We reclaim the term "magic" to endorse and to extend his claim that comparison is an indeterminate scholarly procedure that

is best undertaken as an intellectually creative enterprise, not as a science, but as an art – an imaginative and critical act of mediation and redescription in the service of knowledge.[28]

Smith, Patton and Ray thus all admit the element of randomness or arbitrariness in comparative work. Whereas Smith takes issue mainly with the (past) pretense of comparison to reflecting objective historical contiguity or diffusion, Patton and Ray focus on the way in which comparison may bring new insight to particular religious phenomena by placing them in a broader hermeneutical context.

Comparative theology also approaches the act of comparison as a source of potential theological insight, rather than evidence of any necessary or historical connection. It readily recognizes the fact that it involves a "necessarily arbitrary and intuitive practice."[29] The choice of tradition and topic for comparative theological engagement is often based on chance encounters with particular teachers or programs, and on one's personal religious background, taste, and affinities.

The abundance of choice may be regarded as a richness and an opportunity for comparative theology. It opens the door to seemingly endless possibilities for exploration and inspiration and for continuous creative theological imagination. It allows theologians to be selective and to focus on teachings, texts or practices with which they feel a personal affinity. However, it also poses certain important challenges. If theology involves not merely an individual enterprise but a communal pursuit of religious insight and truth, the choice of a particular tradition, text, teaching or topic may require some justification. Klaus von Stosch warns against the risk of comparative theology becoming "a playground for detail-loving eccentrics who meticulously compare irrelevant subjects."[30] The desire to render comparative theological insights relevant to a broader religious community thus requires continued engagement with other comparative theologians as well as with mainstream theologians.

A problem or threat endemic to comparative theology is that of fragmentation. Since comparative theologians focus on divergent traditions, texts, teachings or practices, and since this requires specialized study and expertise, it can become difficult even for comparative theologians with different specializations to speak to one another. A Buddhist-Christian comparative theologian may have little to contribute to the work of a Muslim-Christian comparative theologian, and vice versa. And even within the field of Buddhist-Christian comparative theology, Christian experts in Tibetan Buddhists may have little to say to Christian theologians focused on Japanese Buddhism. The seemingly endless proliferation of choice thus presents a challenge for collaboration and exchange among comparative theologians and with the tradition at large. This is already evident in the academy, where different scholarly groups have formed around the comparison, theological or otherwise, between specific traditions, and in the publication of journals with special comparative foci. Within the American Academy of Religion, there are groups focusing on Hindu-Jewish, Buddhist-Christian, Hindu-Christian, Muslim-Christian comparison, and there are specialized journals focusing on Muslim-Christian dialogue, Buddhist-Christian studies, and Hindu-Christian studies. There is also a Christian scholars group focusing on their common interest and expertise in Judaism. Religious scholars and theologians within each of these groups and societies may assess one another's interpretation of the other religion as well as its relevance for theological reflection within one's own tradition. But there is little exchange between the various groups.

Though much creative theological work may be done within the various communities of specialized comparative theologians, the question remains how comparative theologians specialized in different traditions may continue to speak with one another and how they might interact with traditional confessional theologians. The topics or questions addressed in comparative theology are often determined by the specific texts, teachings or practices found in the other tradition. This thus inevitably leads to a diffusion of foci in comparative theology. Comparative theologians at the very least share common methodological questions and theological presuppositions. But classical theologians generally do not have the tools to judge the accuracy and importance of comparative theological findings, let alone contribute to discussions. It is also difficult to remain abreast of the works being produced in the various areas of comparative theology and to assess their relative value. All of this points to the difficulty of generating a constructive exchange among and between comparative theologians and classical theologians.

There are various ways to address this challenge and to generate a more fruitful working relationship among various types of theologians. One way is for comparative theologians to focus on particular burning or pressing issues and questions within their respective religious traditions. While it may be possible to compare any religious idea or practice with that of another religious tradition, engaging topics that are of interest to mainstream theologians makes it more likely that they will pay attention. Comparative theologians engaged in different religious traditions might also agree among themselves on a particular topic to be addressed or engaged in dialogue with the other religion. They may first exchange thoughts on their own findings before bringing it to the broader community of theologians. Comparative theologians engaged with a particular tradition may then also collaborate in both selecting the most relevant texts and teachings in the other tradition and in verifying or vetting the insights gained from another tradition. This may expand in a broader discussion among comparative theologians engaged in different religions and finally also involve mainstream theologians. Comparative theologians might also focus on topics and traditions that have already left their mark on the tradition, and that might be revised or expanded. In his work, David Burrell, for example, builds on the theological themes of freedom and creation, grace, divine providence, abandonment, and eschatology that were already shaped by theological exchanges among medieval Christian, Jewish, and Muslim theologians.[31] All this would thus ground the work of comparative theologians in existing theological discussions and render it immediately relevant for a particular tradition.

This, of course, does not mean that comparative theologians should limit themselves only to fashionable theological topics of the day or to classical discussions. One of the promises of comparative theology is that of surprise, of introducing new insights and approaches to stultified religious ideas or practices, or of drawing renewed attention to neglected or forgotten figures and teachings. This involves a discovery in another tradition that has – as is the case in many forms of comparison – "a visionary quality."[32] The comparative theologian suddenly sees or understands something in and through the other religion that she deems important and enriching also for her own tradition, and that she cannot but attempt to integrate or reflect upon from within her own religious framework. This may not prove to be immediately relevant for other theologians within a particular tradition. But it may still come to leave its mark in time or among some fellow theologians and believers.

Comparative theology, when conducted from within a particular religion, may thus avoid the sense of randomness by directly contributing to theological discussions occurring within their respective traditions, or by attempting to awaken other theologians to the relevance of their own visionary insight. It is this focus on a particular religious and theological community that saves comparative theology from the negative implications of randomness.

5.4   Discernment in Comparative Theology

Related to the problem of choice is the question of discernment in comparative theology. Insofar as comparative theology is oriented toward advancing or deepening one's religious understanding and experience, engagement with religious others involves not only the question of which traditions, topics or texts to engage, but also how to determine which elements in the other religion might be edifying or advance one's own religious understanding. The question of discernment in comparative theology often focuses on questions of truth. This may refer in the narrow sense to the conceptual or categorical dimension of a religion, or more broadly to any element in a tradition that might be regarded as valid or valuable and that might come to enrich one's own tradition. It may thus refer to ethical principles, ritual practices, esthetic expressions, etc., or to any of what is captured within the classical notion of the transcendentals: goodness, truth, and beauty.

The idea that comparative theology is oriented to the pursuit of truth is itself not uncontested. David Burrell, for example, argues that "dialog, like any probing conversation, attends to *meaning* rather than *truth*."[33] He understands the notion of truth here, however, as a judgment of the teachings of one tradition over another. From that perspective, he states that his own approach to comparative theology "will not attempt to assess which (if any) of these traditions is *true*, but it should assist believers in each to find their way to assessing – as best they can, and must – the truth of their tradition."[34] Burrell is right to say that comparative theology is not involved in the blanket judgment of the truth of one religion over against the other. However, it is interested in deepening understanding of the truth of one's own tradition through constructive engagement of elements of truth found in other traditions. In that sense, it necessarily involves some form of discernment of truth.

The elements of goodness, beauty, and truth are intimately related in the process of discernment. The initial appeal of another religious tradition often derives from the exemplary behavior of its members or from the beauty of its symbols and rituals, as much as from the truth of its teachings. The discernment of beauty in other religions, however, often presupposes some predisposition toward recognizing truth and goodness,[35] while the recognition of goodness often leads to a further exploration of its truth. Religious traditions also tend to spontaneously evaluate the validity of other religious traditions on the basis of ethical criteria. This is evident in the volume *Criteria of Discernment in Interreligious Dialogue*, where contributors from different religious traditions focus less on the truth of particular doctrines than on their fruits, on the lifestyle, values, and ethical attitudes manifest among believers. In the introduction to this volume, I noted that:

> This emphasis on the fruits rather than the contents of religious teachings need not be regarded as a way to avoid the difficulty of judging one religion according to the highly particular belief system of another. It is also more than a turn to a highest common denominator. The ethical criteria used are themselves firmly grounded in the worldview and teachings of particular religions. And in some cases, the call to judge other religions according to their fruits is itself a scriptural injunction or an admonition of the founder.[36]

Theologians within the same religion may identify varying qualities as basic criteria of discernment. Whereas Reinhold Bernhardt mentions freedom, agape, and responsibility,[37] Dermot Lane focuses on the fruits of the Spirit as outlined in Galatians 5:27: "love, joy, peace, patience, kindness, goodness, faithfulness, generosity and self-control."[38]

The actual criteria of discernment to be used in comparative theology generally depend on the particular situation or case. In general, any teaching or practice that is not in contradiction with the basic teachings and practices of a tradition may be eligible for consideration. While this may be a simple and clear principle, its application is often more complex. Each religion represents a complex whole of doctrinal teachings, ethical principles, philosophical categories, ritual prescriptions, etc., which all form part of the normative structure of a religion. Different and at times mutually conflicting principles may be at play in any particular case of discernment. This is evident in Gavin D'Costa's application of Christian criteria of discernment to the Hindu practice of widow burning or *sati*. When applying the criterion of self-sacrificing love to this practice, D'Costa argues that it might be seen as Christ-like since "in the finely balanced system of karmic reward and punishment, which does bear interesting analogy with the medieval picture of merit and demerit and the satisfaction owing to the deity due to sin, we find an instance of a breaking of the circuit, where a single person's self-sacrifice can alleviate the karmic punishment due to another."[39] From the perspective of the image of women and the overall view of women in Hinduism, however, this practice may also be seen as radically opposed to Christian notions of the dignity of every person and the equivalence of men and women. As such, the process of discernment generally involves a detailed parsing of what aspects of a particular teaching or practice might be judged valid or true on the basis of which precise normative teaching or value in one's own tradition.

With regards to the principles of discernment, confessional comparative theologians thus remain deeply rooted in the normative teachings of their traditions. Others, however, attempt to overcome the particularity of those norms and the seeming imposition of one religion onto another by either developing neutral or common criteria, or by proposing a mutual normativity. In applying neutral criteria or criteria derived from the social sciences, religions might thus be evaluated, for example, on the basis of their support of ecological views and behaviors, according to their views on gender equality, or their consistency with certain scientific theories regarding cosmology or biology. Though this may work with regard to particular questions, it does not allow for a discernment of the ultimate claims of any particular religion. This is why J. R. Hustwit also points out that "the most difficult obstacle for the transreligious project" involves how to "hammer out or how to adjudicate competing truth claims."[40] While he suggests possible criteria such as "phronesis … coherence with widely accepted beliefs, fruitfulness, predicative value, etc." he recognizes that "no matter how many experts agree, or how elegantly a theological hypothesis coheres, in the end, truth claims can never be verified with finality."[41] In an attempt to overcome the sense of unilateral judgment of one religion by another, Roger Haight proposes the notion of "mutual normativity," in which religions judge one another and themselves according to not only their own norms but also those of the other religion. For him, "other perceptions of God can be universally normative, and thus, too, for Christians, even as Jesus Christ is universally normative."[42] This would seem to clash with the logic of faith and adherence to the normative truth of a tradition. The teachings of any particular religion will be normative only for believers, and members of one tradition will not likely recognize the teachings of another religion as equally normative. While certain norms may overlap, and while members of one tradition may respect and even learn from the norms of another, they will not have the same importance and weight as one's own religious criteria. The sense of equality between religions may be established not by adopting the norms of the other religion, but by recognizing that each religion evaluates the other according to its own particular norms.

Though a lack of objective certainty or finality also applies to the criteria used in confessional theology, it does have the particular kind of certainty or confidence that arises from a position of faith. The texts, teachings, and practices of one's own tradition then become the stable ground and criteria for discerning truth in other religious traditions. This, however, does not resolve the question of which criteria one might need to draw from in any particular instance of discernment.

When it comes to the process of discernment, comparative theology tends to involve different steps or stages. The initial recognition of elements of truth, beauty or goodness in another religion generally involves a spontaneous, rather than a systematic, process. This may involve a recognition of familiar forms and teachings or a sense of surplus or excess in the other tradition. In visiting the Buddhist images in Polonnaruwa, Thomas Merton was unexpectedly overcome by their majesty and beauty:

> Looking at these figures I was suddenly, almost forcibly, jerked clean out of the habitual, half-tied vision of things, and an inner clearness, clarity, as if exploding from the rocks themselves, became evident and obvious … I don't know when in my life I have ever had such a sense of beauty and spiritual validity running together in one aesthetic illumination.[43]

For Henri Le Saux, it was similarly the unprovoked experience of nonduality in the presence of the Hindu sage Ramana Maharshi that set him on a journey to reconcile this experience with his Christian faith. Some comparative theologians may engage in a more deliberate search for insight or inspiration in another religious tradition, based on personal interest or on the pressing questions within their own tradition. The attempt to synthesize these teachings or make sense of them from within one's own religious framework is the work of the individual theologian. Comparative theology, like all theology, thus involves a solitary process of reflection and creative theological construction, building on the theological resources of one and the other tradition.

For confessional comparative theologians, the process of discernment is ultimately a matter of communal deliberation. Here, the comparative theologian remains accountable to a normative theological tradition that may both broaden the process of discernment and integrate the fruits of comparative theology into the tradition at large. Even while comparative theologians remain grounded in a particular tradition, their sense or judgment of the relevance, validity or truth of elements of another religion may be misguided or idiosyncratic. Engagement with a broader community of theologians thus allows for greater critical vetting, and ultimately also greater credibility for the work of comparative theology. As Francis Clooney puts it, "I cannot decide on my own, or just with my friends, that I actually am a successful Catholic theologian. It is something the Church has to think about and decide, in the complex ways the Church does such things."[44] Insofar as the work of comparative theology is to nourish the religious life not only of a single theologian, but of a broader community, some type of reception and deliberation among fellow theologians within a tradition is essential. This emphasis on the necessary communal process of discernment also comes to the fore in Paul Knitter's work:

> Yet really to know, I have to hear from my fellow Christians. They'll have to tell me whether what I'm putting forth in this book makes sense to them, whether it enables them to connect (or reconnect) with their Christian identity and tradition. That's the way things work in Christianity; we're a community called church. There's got to be some kind, or degree, of community affirmation if a particular belief or practice is going to be labeled Christian. That means that the new insights of a theologian, or the teachings of a bishop or church leader, have to be, to some degree, received by the community of believers.[45]

The communal process of discernment may involve fellow theologians, teaching authority, and/or fellow believers. Since the work of comparative theology is relatively new, but already accessible to believers as well as to theologians or authority figures within a tradition, it may at times find reception among ordinary believers even before it has been officially vetted by mainstream theologians or by the official hierarchy of a tradition.[46] The Christian tradition speaks in this regard of the *sensus fidelium* which itself may play a role in the broader process of discernment. While some traditions may have an official teaching authority which represents the ultimate recourse in matters of religious orthodoxy and orthopraxis, others may rely on more informal processes of discernment and reception. While recognizing the internal diversity within Christianity and the possibility of varying assessment and reception, John Thatamanil, a Protestant comparative theologian, states that:

> Comparative theologians can go it alone, unmoored from tradition and free of accountability. Ultimately only sustained conversation between theologians and their home communities will determine whether the fruit of any particular venture in comparative theology will be received by those communities and contributing to their collective flourishing. Comparative theologians cannot afford to be solo operators. They are obliged to articulate why their proposals ought to be received by their home communities even if globally valid a priori criteria are unavailable.[47]

Hence, the process of communal discernment does not require a magisterium or even a strong notion of orthodoxy. It merely requires a theological community willing to engage, debate, and refine one's comparative theological insights so that they become part of a larger discourse. This keeps comparative theologians from developing purely idiosyncratic thoughts and lines of inquiry, and allows their insights to have a genuine bearing on the tradition as a whole.

This process of discernment requires openness, humility, and generosity both on the part of the comparative theologian and on the part of the community and its leading theologians. Not only must the comparative theologian be willing to submit her thoughts to scrutiny by other theologians, but those theologians must also be willing to engage such thought in open and constructive ways. This is still a challenge for comparative theologians, who often find themselves by necessity or by choice on the margins of their own traditions. A focus on topics that are of immediate interest to other theologians within the tradition may engender greater interest on the part of traditional theologians to critically and constructively engage the work of comparative theologians. However, it also requires on the part of the broader tradition a recognition of comparative theology as a fully legitimate form of theology and a promising source of new theological insight.

Comparative theology is often still regarded as a marginal or esoteric theological discipline. The very fact of learning from other religious traditions is frequently regarded as challenging or threatening. Theologians venturing into the area of comparative theology are thus often viewed with suspicion by mainstream theologians or the teaching authority. One of the challenges for mainstream theologians is their inability to judge the accuracy or relevance of the data or material derived from the other tradition. It is true that, as Clooney points out in the case of Hindu-Christian comparative theology, "Christian theologians who know nothing of the Hindu tradition will … be at a loss."[48] This is why it is important for comparative theologians engaged with the same tradition to first discuss their findings or insights with one another. Mainstream theologians may then focus mainly on whether these insights fit within and enrich the broader theological tradition. The insights of comparative theologians ought to be intelligible to other theologians, who may offer their own views on their coherence and pertinence. The essential process of discernment thus demands an open and constructive relationship among comparative theologians as well as between comparative theologians and their broader theological tradition.

5.5   The Target Public of Comparative Theology

Comparative theology, like all theology, is oriented toward a particular community or audience who might benefit from one's theological reflection. The question of the author's intended audience is thus at the heart of comparative theological work. While meta-confessional comparative theology may aim at a broad community of seekers who are not defined by any particular religious affiliation, confessional comparative theology is oriented toward particular religious communities, or believers sharing certain basic religious presuppositions and practices. This may be seen to either delimit or focus the work of the comparative theologian. But it provides a clear sense of accountability of the comparative theologian to a larger community.

This target community of comparative theology may vary in size and kind from one tradition to the next. Within any particular religion, theologians may be mindful of addressing their particular denomination, or else the broader religious tradition, depending on the subject at hand. Christian comparative theologians who focus on mystical thinkers and thought will thus be oriented mainly toward Catholic and Orthodox communities.

Comparative theologians may also target primarily culturally specific communities, engaging other religions that have shaped that particular culture. The Indian theologian Thomas Tangaraj states: "Thus, contextualization meant for me and other theologians in India the task of constructing a theology that was relevant and meaningful to the Indian experience: such a theology would seek neither to be guided nor to be judged by the theological enterprise in the West."[49] In *The Crucified Guru*, he engages the notion of the guru in the Tamil Saiva tradition in order to develop an understanding of Christ more in tune with South Indian religious sensibilities. The particularity of the target audience of comparative theology does not exclude its broader relevance. Tangaraj himself emphasizes the importance of a broader theological community and dialogue since "a Christology that is self-consciously local needs to take the global dimension seriously so that it does not end up as tribal and parochial."[50] And Gordon Kaufman states in the introduction that the book "is as important for the American and European theological scene as it is for India."[51] While the target community of the comparative theologian may thus be culturally specific or more global, limited to a particular denomination or to a broader religious tradition, it determines and delimits the theologian's sense of responsibility and accountability.

Since comparative theology involves at least two religious traditions and communities, there is some discussion about the extent of the theological responsibility or license of the comparative theologian. The goal of comparative theology is often expressed in terms of "mutual transformation," "mutual fecundation," or "reciprocal illumination."[52] This may have different meanings or connotations. It may involve a process of reciprocal learning in which theologians from each tradition learn from the other in the service of their own respective communities. Or it may involve one comparative theologian determining what each tradition may learn from the other. Here, the comparative theologian, while belonging to only one tradition, speaks to and for both religious traditions. In *Beyond Dialogue*, Christian theologian John Cobb elaborated not only on what Christianity might learn from Pure Land Buddhism, but also on what Pure Land Buddhism might learn from Christianity.[53] In his famous article, "Kenotic God and Dynamic Śūnyatā," Masao Abe also went beyond arguing for a less static understanding of the Buddhist notion of emptiness, to suggesting ways in which the Christian understanding of God might learn from Buddhist notions of emptiness.[54] And in *The Marriage of East and West*, Bede Griffiths suggested ways in which Christianity might learn from the more transcendental worldview of Hinduism, and Hinduism from the more historical approach of Christianity.[55]

There is a natural inclination in comparative theology to engage in a normative reflection on and for each of the traditions compared. The comparative exercise allows one to see each tradition in light of the other, and to thus assess the strengths and weaknesses of both. However, the target of the comparative theologian grounded in a particular tradition is in the first place that tradition itself. To argue or propose what another religion might learn from one's own might seem inappropriate and presumptuous. It could imply knowing better than theologians of that particular religion, and it might be construed as imposing oneself on the other. The Jewish and Christian responses to Abe's paper illustrate the difficulty of assuming one understands the intricacies of the other tradition and that one can theologize for a tradition that is not one's own.[56] Though in the ideal case, one's view of how another religion might learn from one's own may stimulate reflection among theologians belonging to that tradition, it may also be received as an imposition or an affront. One may certainly hope that theologians in the other tradition will be able to learn from one's own, just as one is able to learn from the other. However, it is for the theologians or thinkers from each of the traditions to determine whether and what they might learn from one another. Thus conceived, the notion of "mutual illumination" would here thus refer to a reciprocity to be determined from within each tradition. The aspect of mutuality can neither be presupposed nor imposed on the other. One must thus also respect the fact that one religion may be eagerly engaged in learning from the other, while the other religion remains uninterested in learning from the other.

This does not compromise the importance of apologetics in comparative theology, as we will see. But it does set bounds on the target audience of comparative theology, thereby also respecting the autonomy of the other tradition.

Though the confessional goal of comparative theology may be regarded as an unnecessary form of self-limitation, it may also be seen as a recognition of the alterity of the other. Each religion has its own theological history and training, and its own criteria for discerning truth in other religious traditions. To suggest to other religions what they might learn from one's own thus may come across as patronizing and inappropriate. Though it is of course true that comparison may shed new light on both religious traditions, and though one may hope that the process of learning is indeed reciprocal, all one may strictly account for theologically is one's own process of learning from the other.

Though comparative theologians should refrain from dictating what another religion might learn from one's own, they may reflect on elements in their own tradition they would not want to lose or compromise as a result of the comparative theological effort. While this may come close to implying what the other tradition might learn from one's own, it is not phrased as an imposition or a form of external meddling into the other tradition, and it leaves the religious other free to ignore or take up the point of resistance or reaffirmation. Thus, rather than dictating to Pure Land Buddhism or to Hinduism that they should or could learn from the Christian emphasis on the value and importance of history and of a historical incarnation, Christian comparative theologians may simply come to express a renewed appreciation of this aspect of the Christian tradition resulting from their engagement with those traditions. Theologians from the other traditions are then free to determine whether or not they also find these elements compelling.

5.6   Comparative Theology and Apologetics

Reflection on the relationship between comparative theology and apologetics inevitably raises the question of the role of apologetics in comparative theology. Apologetics is understood as the defense and argumentation of the truth and validity of particular teachings and practices against opposing views or positions. It may be practiced in a defensive or in an offensive mode. But it presupposes commitment to a clear and concrete set of beliefs and practices that are engaged in a debate over religious truth and validity.

Though confessional theology for the most part builds upon its own religious premises, without concern for alternative views, the ever growing awareness of the reality of religious plurality forces every religion to develop resources to uphold the truth of its own beliefs in light of competing beliefs. For example, while the Christian belief in the uniqueness of Jesus Christ may be taken for granted within a Christian theological framework, it is put under greater pressure through confrontation with other religious traditions and other salvific figures. Christian apologetics here thus involves a renewed attempt to establish the credibility of this belief in light of its various contenders, and in light of its general questioning. Apologetics is thus a changing discipline in which theological reflection must respond to concrete challenges, while also addressing a continuously changing religious landscape. The question is thus what role comparative theology plays in apologetics, and what role apologetics plays in comparative theology.

The goal of comparative theology is certainly not primarily arguing for the truth of one's own religion against the other. While this may be the sole purpose of exclusivist theologians, comparative theologians are generally inspired and motivated by the promise of learning from other religions, rather than by the desire to defend the superior truth of their own religion. Comparative theologians thus tend to focus on the similarities and complementarities between religions, rather than on the contrasts. However, any fair and in-depth study of religions inevitably also reveals areas of irreconcilable difference. Comparative theology may thus assist confessional theology in properly identifying and understanding those differences. Classical apologetics was often based on misunderstanding, whether innocent or deliberate, and on the projection of distorted images onto the other in order to serve one's own apologetic purposes. Comparative theology may thus help in rectifying and nuancing one's understanding of the other, and thus in rendering religious apologetics more credible.

The question is whether apologetics should also form part of comparative theology itself. Some adamantly oppose the practice of apologetics in comparative theology. Raimon Panikkar, for example, states that "apologetics has its function and its proper place, but not here in the meeting of religions."[57] For him, the encounter with other religions must be free from both specific and general apologetics, by which he means a defense of religion itself. For him, comparative theology involves letting go of any preconceived conceptions of truth and attempting to understand each religion in its own integrity. He explicitly declares that he is "not writing on behalf of one or another religious tradition" and that he is looking to take seriously and preserve the truth of all of the religions he is concerned with.[58]

Hugh Nicholson also believes that apologetics is out of place in comparative theology. He argues that: "To the extent that the comparative theologian acknowledges his or her normative religious commitments only in order to affirm and defend them, comparative theology can devolve into a form of interreligious apologetics … With this affirmation of apologetic theology, religious antagonism threatens to reappear in more or less unsublimated form."[59] For him, all apologetics is based on a misconstruing and misunderstanding of the religious other as part of the affirmation and preservation of one's own distinct religious identity. Thorough study of other religions necessarily reveals the complexity of any particular religion, which problematizes traditional apologetic arguments, and which raises "questions about the ground and plausibility of evangelical initiatives."[60] Nicholson thus regards comparative theology as a post-apologetic form of engagement with other religions, which involves redressing past distortions and "balancing willingness to revise their theological understanding in light of the teachings of other traditions with affirmations of religious commitment."[61]

However, other comparative theologians view apologetics as an integral part of the work of comparative theology. While acknowledging that "apologetic arguments will only be occasional and preliminary,"[62] James Fredericks insists that comparative theology should be open to apologetics. He even states that "dialogues that exclude argument and debate in the name of a misguided irenicism often become barren and platitudinous."[63] Francis Clooney, for his part, points to the natural connection between comparative confessional and apologetic theology:

> The deeper, more difficult, and more acute differences become, the more slender the distinction between a "confessional" theology, where one pronounces and explains the truth of one's positions, and an "apologetic" theology,

where one also asserts the error of others' positions. For this reason I speak of an interreligious theology's "confessional and even apologetic" dimension. Strong arguments in favor of one's own tradition often go along with critiques of others' theological positions, and theologies are often confessional and apologetic at the same time, testifying and criticizing, explaining and arguing, persuading and disproving. But even criticism need not be a problem if it is offered respectfully and professionally.[64]

Insofar as comparative theologians are themselves confessional theologians, or "representative intellectuals" actively engaging other religious traditions, they cannot circumvent the more confrontational or controversial questions involving competing or conflicting claims to truth.

What is distinctive about apologetics when done in the context of comparative theology is its particular focus on very specific teachings, and its immersion within a broader context of learning from the other religion. For example, John Thatamanil, while focusing mainly on what Christian anthropology as developed in the work of Paul Tillich might learn from the nondualist approach of Shankara, also argues that "Tillich's dynamic theology of ecstatic union is compelling because it attempts to overcome dualism without defining away the world of experience as Sankara is tempted to do."[65] This may be regarded as a subtle form of apologetics in which the validity and truth of one's own tradition is affirmed without entirely dismissing the position of the other.

Comparative theologians may also occasionally engage in more explicit critique of the beliefs of the other religion, or in both positive and negative apologetics, as defined by Paul Griffiths. As Christian theologians steeped in the study of Buddhism, Griffiths engages in both positive and negative apologetics with regard to the Buddhist notion of no-self,[66] while Paul Williams does the same with regard to the existence of a personal God and an immortal soul.[67] Though these forms of apologetics must also be possible in comparative theology, they are generally framed within a broader context in which engagement with the other religion also generates constructive insight. Griffiths also acknowledges that positive apologetics is "an occasional discipline, not a systematic one. That is to say, it is occasioned by a particular encounter, a particular realization on the part of the representative intellectuals of some religious community that the doctrine-expressing sentences to which they assent are challenged in an interesting way by those of some other religious community."[68] Faithfulness to one's own tradition thus presupposes an attempt to argue for the greater coherence of one's own particular teachings. This, however, does not imply a denunciation of the other tradition as a whole. Comparative theology does not engage in apologetics for the sake of apologetics, or solely for the purpose of critiquing the other religion.

While the notion of apologetics is often associated with a static and stubborn defense of the faith, it may also involve shifts in the original religious position. Paul Griffiths recognizes this when he states that: "Proper apologists will engage in their enterprise with passion; with a powerful trust in the truth and efficacy of the doctrine-expressing sentences on whose behalf they enter the lists; but also with an awareness that engaging in the enterprise may lead them to abandon the same doctrine-expressing sentences, or to modify them significantly."[69] As pointed out in Chapter 4, in the process of reaffirming the truth of one's own teachings or practices over against the other, certain shifts may occur in one's self-understanding as elements from the other tradition may shape new lines of argumentation and particular aspects of one's own tradition are granted greater importance. Though apologetics manifests predominantly in reaffirmation, other types of learning may also include an apologetic dimension as comparative theology is oriented toward the advancement of theological truth, and the affirmation or focus on certain elements of truth implicitly or explicitly involves the rejection of others.

5.7   Importance of Comparative Theology for Confessional Theology

It has become clear that comparative theology relies in various ways on traditional confessional theology. Not only does comparative theology build on the data of confessional theology, but the latter also provides the critical questions, the criteria of discernment, and the broader theological context in which comparative theological insights are vetted, digested, and disseminated. But comparative theology also represents an important new area of theological reflection which is vital to theological reflection and growth in a pluralistic world. Confessional theology depends on comparative theology to identify particular areas of promising theological development, to provide the religious data relevant for further theological reflection, and to experiment with ways in which certain teachings or practices might be integrated in one's own religious tradition.

David Tracy defines theology as "the hermeneutical attempt to establish mutually critical correlations between the claims to religious meaningfulness and truth of a religious tradition and the claims to religious meaningfulness and truth within the historical situation for which that tradition is being interpreted."[70] The reality of religious plurality forms one of the most challenging and the most promising aspects of the current and foreseeable historical situation. Just as theology has been challenged to engage with critical theory and with modern science, it cannot but focus on the reality of religious diversity as an avenue for new and creative theological insight. Comparative theology expands the theological horizon of the confessional theologian. As a result, "we come to see differently doctrines already familiar to us, we learn to extend and modify our methods of learning, we enter conversations with new colleagues from other traditions and we come to receive truth, the truth, in hitherto unexpected ways."[71] Each of the types of learning discussed in Chapter 4 pertains to confessional theology. They presuppose grounding in a particular tradition and focus on the theological development and growth of that tradition. Comparative theology offers new categories and frameworks, and a wellspring of possibilities for creative theological reflection. David Burrell thus points out that:

> Each of the twentieth-century figures who stand out as spiritual leaders in their respective traditions reflects a creative interaction with another faith-tradition, from Martin Buber and Franz Rosenzweig in Judaism, to Louis Massignon, Jules Monchanin and Bede Griffiths among Catholic Christians; and in Islam, the Pathan leader and man of God, Abdul Ghaffar Khan.[72]

One could of course add the names of Gandhi in Hinduism, or Thich Nhat Hanh or the Dalai Lama in Buddhism. Creative and innovative religious thinkers in various traditions have drawn inspiration from other religious traditions.

Comparative theology enhances the credibility of traditional theology. It operates from within its own religious presuppositions and from within its own particular frame of references. As awareness of the horizon of religious options has expanded, the particularity of every specific religious tradition has become obvious. In order to avoid the danger of relativism on the one hand, and sectarianism on the other, religions claiming universal truth thus cannot but engage the reality of religious plurality, both in general and in its particular expressions in the teachings and practices of various religions. Though the argument from faith will always play an important role in theology, the fact that theologians have considered other religious options and seriously engaged questions of truth in light of this broader religious horizon adds weight and importance to their respective conclusions.

Comparative theology may provide a more solid theological foundation for relating to those realities which have resulted in the phenomenon of many individuals defining themselves as "spiritual but not religious." This phenomenon arises from an abundance of choice in religion and from a sense of the narrowness, parochialism, and conservatism of traditional religious thought. However, as Perry Schmidt-Leukel points out, "the religious practice of people who draw for their own spirituality on sources from various religious traditions is usually highly eclectic and subjective and does not display, in most cases, the standards of academic reflection."[73] Comparative theology may then be regarded as the more reflective, systematic, and theologically grounded way of engaging the array of religious insights and options available in the pluralistic context. It demonstrates that one need not leave a particular tradition in order to accept and integrate what one perceives to be true and good in another religion. And it offers a more thoughtful synthesis of elements from different religious traditions that may still allow for communal discernment and practice. Such communal theological effort, based on a long and established tradition of theological reflection, may at least for some seem more compelling than a more personal and subjective religious synthesis.

The importance of comparative theology for confessional theology is ultimately based on the fact that theology cannot but engage truth wherever it is found. Since other religions are recognized as possible repositories of truth, Robert Neville states bluntly that "Faith seeking understanding in today's world that is not also seriously comparative cannot be serious theology, however practical it might be for organizing and nourishing the faithful."[74] Though himself not trained as a comparative theologian, Tracy also insists that "the different questions and responses of the various religions present in the contemporary pluralistic situation must be explicitly and comparatively analyzed as part of the task of any theological interpretation in any tradition," and predicts that:

> The future is likely to see the evolution of most traditional theologies into comparative theology in all non-fundamentalistic traditions. With that development, the conflict in interpretations among various models and differing conclusions among contemporary comparative theologians may eventually lead to a disciplinary consensus for all theology. Any theology in any tradition that takes religious pluralism seriously must eventually become comparative theology.[75]

There are various ways in which this may come to pass. Every theologian within a particular tradition may be expected to gain some expertise in at least one other religion. A good deal of traditional theology is in fact comparative theology. Throughout history, Christian theologians have developed their theological systems based on or in reaction to other philosophical and theological traditions, from Augustine's engagement with Neo-Platonism and Manichaeism, to Aquinas's encounter with the Greek philosophy of Aristotle, the Arabic philosophy of Avicenna and Averroes, and the Jewish philosophy of Maimonides.[76] Discussing the three ways (confirmation, transformation, and contestation) in which Aquinas engaged with and drew from these philosophies, Martin Ganeri points out that they are to a considerable degree "the material out of which theology is made" and that in that sense comparative theology may be regarded as "a legitimate and worthy successor of Aquinas' science of theology."[77]

In commenting on the work of Jesuit missionaries in India between the sixteenth and eighteenth centuries, Francis Clooney also recognizes that "their synergy of faith and inquiry in a way models the participatory learning essential to today's comparative theology."[78] Engaging other religious traditions thus forms part of the tradition of theological reflection, not only in Christianity but in most other religions.

As knowledge of other religions has increased exponentially over the past century, gaining expertise in a tradition other than one's own has become ever more challenging. This is why comparative theology has developed as a specialized theological discipline, and why confessional theologians rely on the expertise of comparative theologians. While grounded in a particular religion, the latter come to focus their theological attention entirely on deepening their understanding of another tradition and reflecting on its relevance for their own religious tradition. Theology thus requires active collaboration between traditional confessional theologians and comparative theologians in exploring theological questions and insights together. This requires humility, commitment, and trust on both sides. While comparative theologians have greater expertise in the other religion, confessional theologians are more likely to be steeped in the intricacies of their own theological tradition. Comparative theology may thus serve confessional theology by offering insights from other religious traditions in response to theological questions, while confessional theologians may draw from the deep well of resources of their own tradition in order to bring about a constructive engagement.

All this may seem intimidating for traditional theologians, whose work has been based on a more or less fixed set of texts and hermeneutical principles. The introduction of a vast new body of material to be engaged may seem intimidating or overwhelming. The reality of religious plurality challenges the very discipline of theology to expand its self-understanding and explore various ways to include new religious insights and methods that will challenge and enrich theological thinking. Marianne Moyaert refers to comparative theology as "vulnerable theology."[79] Her notion of vulnerability here refers primarily to the fact that comparative theology is "all about leaving the theological comfort zone of the centralist approach to theology"[80] in order to meet and learn from the religious other. It is true that comparative theologians are particularly able and willing to put their theological security at risk in order to encounter the religious other. But the notion of vulnerability may be seen to apply to all theology, insofar as it can only develop and grow through recognizing its imperfection or incompleteness and by accepting and embracing new theological insights and methods that present themselves.

5.8   The Place of Comparative Theology within Confessional Theology

The discipline of comparative theology is the natural and necessary outcome of the recognition of other religions as sources of truth. The discovery and discernment of elements of truth in other religions requires theologians with expertise in other religions. This raises the question of the place of comparative theology among other religious disciplines. Should comparative theology be regarded as a subfield within the classical areas of theology? Or should it be regarded as a distinct area or discipline of theology?

A discipline is defined by its particular object of study and method. Within theology, a distinction is often made between systematic theology, moral theology, historical theology, biblical theology, pastoral theology, and practical theology, each of which is based on a particular area of theology and on particular methods. Systematic theology, for example, often engages philosophical and social scientific approaches, while biblical theology variously uses philological, historical, and literary methods in exegesis. Each area of theology also ideally draws insights from any of the other areas.

Comparative theology is defined by its distinct material and method. It differs from other areas of theology in that it reflects on theological questions in relation to the data of other religious traditions, and it differs from religious studies in that it approaches this data from an explicitly normative religious perspective. For the past decades, the discussion in departments of theology has focused mostly on the relationship between theology and religious studies, and tensions between the two approaches to the study of religion continue to polarize departments. Comparative theology represents a natural or coherent way of approaching the reality of religious diversity within departments of theology and/or at educational institutions with religious affiliations. Comparative theologians are experts in two different religions and able to approach religions from a historical as well as from a normative theological perspective.

The ultimate goal of comparative theology is to inform and enrich all of the classical areas of theology. Any of these areas may come to include the data of other religions in its reflection on ethical, philosophical, historical or exegetical questions. However, there are still important theoretical as well as practical reasons for approaching comparative theology as a distinct theological area or discipline. Even though they engage different religious traditions, comparative theologians still face common theological and methodological questions. These involve the theological grounds for engaging in comparative theology, as well as the proper way to go about comparing religions from both a historical and a theological perspective. Comparative theologians engaged with one tradition may learn from the method and insights of comparative theologians engaged with other religions, and they may also engage in reflection on a common theological question, bringing together the insights from various religions. This may then serve as a preamble for broader theological reflection.

Comparative theology may of course be conducted from various religious perspectives. The area of comparative theology may thus consist of comparative theologians who approach the religious other from the same or from different religious perspectives. In order to allow for dialogue and constructive exchange between theologians, it would seem that they would need to have at least one religion in common. As such, an area of comparative theology may consist of comparative theologians from different religions focusing on the same other religion (e.g. Buddhist, Muslim, Hindu, Jewish, and Daoist comparative theologians focusing on Christianity), or else comparative theologians from the same tradition focusing on different religions (e.g. Christian comparative theologians focusing on Hinduism, Buddhism, Judaism, Islam, and Daoism). This still leaves out many other religious traditions that could be the object or subject of comparative theology. There are no obvious principles according to which one religion might be privileged over another, since any religion may contain elements of truth. But theologians will probably be most inclined to engage with religions with which they have immediate historical or geographic connections, or that have historical, geographical, and numerical importance.

Though comparative theology may thus be considered a separate area or discipline of theology, it is of great importance that it remains in direct dialogue and interaction with the other areas of theology, both in order to share the fruits of comparative theological reflection and to receive feedback in the process of discernment. The bridging between comparative theology and other disciplines of theology may happen organically. In addition to focusing on other religions as a theological resource, comparative theologians tend to also have a particular area of theological interest, whether this involves a particular ethical, doctrinal or philosophical question. This thus allows the comparative theologian to build on these other areas of theology while drawing in comparative theological insights.

5.9   Comparative Theology beyond Confessional Theology

While comparative theology is grounded in the data or the material provided by the various confessional traditions, it may also find itself wittingly or unwittingly beyond the boundaries of particular confessional traditions. This is the case for what I have called meta-confessional comparative theology, which deliberately seeks to pursue religious truth unconstrained by the doctrinal or ritual particularities of existing religious traditions. The data of different religions are here thus used to develop what is believed to be a higher and more universal truth. This may be regarded as the more systematic expression of the popular forms of religious hybridity, where individuals develop their own idiosyncratic form of religiosity or spirituality, based on the teachings and practices of any number of religions.

But engagement with the texts, teachings, and practices of another religion may also unintentionally lead to insights or conclusions that do not easily or immediately fit within traditional confessional frameworks. The outcome of comparative theology is not always predictable or controllable. Genuine dialogue with the religious other involves, as Panikkar puts it, "accepting the challenge of a change, a conversion, and the risk of upsetting my traditional patterns."[81] David Tracy also argues that dialogue requires a "willingness to risk all in the questioning and inquiry that constitutes the dialogue itself."[82] As such, comparative theologians, in following their understanding of truth, may come to find themselves in a state of greater affinity with the teachings of another religion, or else beyond the given doctrinal and ritual boundaries of any religion.

The decision whether to consider particular insights and approaches orthodox or confessionally sound lies generally not with the comparative theologian but with the broader religious tradition and/or with the religious hierarchy. While the comparative theologian may seek to merely broaden the self-understanding of a particular religion while remaining faithful to its basic tenets, fellow theologians and believers may not always be receptive to certain comparative theological insights, thus placing the comparative theologian beyond the margins of the tradition. This may lead to the development of a new tradition, as has often happened in the history of religions.[83] Or it may lead to the eventual or modified integration of certain insights within the confessional tradition. Like all new theological insights, those generated by comparative theology may be slow to digest. Of course, some comparative theological insights and proposals may never garner broader appeal, either within or beyond existing traditions, and simply remain part of the idiosyncratic views of a particular theologian.

In comparing texts, teachings or practices of particular traditions, comparative theologians may at times focus on particular aspects or ideas that are not clearly developed or defined in terms of the official teachings of particular religions, and that thus allow for a broader theological discussion beyond the boundaries of particular religions. This is the case with new social realities and challenges, such as the ecological crisis, which no single existing tradition has addressed fully as part of its official teachings, and where the resources from different religious traditions may be brought to bear to reflect on it. Certain topics addressed in comparative theology may have equal relevance for different religious traditions, and the comparative theological insights and conclusions may thus be fruitful for both traditions.[84]

The insights of comparative theologians who find themselves for various reasons and in various ways beyond the confessional boundaries of particular religions may still be a source of insight and inspiration for confessional traditions. They shed new light on the boundaries of particular religions while also pointing to ways to stretch these boundaries. Comparative theologians working from beyond the confines of particular religions may freely experiment with new religious ideas that may come to inspire confessional theologians and shake them out of a state of complacency. When traditional forms of interreligious dialogue and comparative theology become too safe and predictable, Hans Gustafson states, meta-confessional or transreligious theology "can nudge religious and interreligious theology and dialogue out of their usual secure comfort zones and possibly oversimplified view of religious identities and pull them into the liberative and imaginative growth-filled spaces of transreligious theology."[85] Any authentic search for religious truth and meaning may indeed present new insights that would not occur to individuals and theologians whose minds are shaped by a set of clear presuppositions. While emphasizing the confessional nature of comparative theology, Francis Clooney expects "important contributions to comparative theology from readers who are not committed to any formal religious tradition at the present moment, and from those who have never had such commitments."[86] They may draw attention to areas of spiritual hunger and religious need which remain submerged in established religious systems, and invite confessional theologians to think beyond established categories and to explore possibilities for stretching the boundaries of their own identity and self-understanding.

Comparative theology by its very nature straddles the boundaries between and beyond religious traditions. It is open to religious truth wherever it may be found, in other religious traditions, or in the search for truth beyond any particular religion. However, insofar as theology is grounded in a truth not of one's own making, it involves a negotiation of these sources from within a given text, tradition, and thinking and practicing community. From here, comparative theologians may engage any religious thought or practice that may stretch theological imagination and open up new frontiers for theological reflection.

Notes

1. In the first case, this would mean all Christian comparative theologians or all Muslim comparative theologians forming their own groups; in the second case, all comparative theologians focusing on Christianity and Hinduism would form a group, regardless of their religious origin; in the third case, all comparative theologians, regardless of their background and regardless of their focus traditions, would belong to one group. One might also imagine the formation of groups of comparative theologians from one tradition who have a similar expertise in one other tradition. Several of these various possibilities have in fact been realized in the formation of scholarly societies and/or journals.

2. Francis Clooney, "Comparative Theology: A Review of Recent Books (1989–1995)," *Theological Studies 26*, no. 3 (1995): 522.

3. Panikkar referred to his work not as comparative theology, but as "imparative philosophy," defining it as an "open philosophical attitude ready to learn from whatever philosophical corner of the world, but without claiming to compare philosophies from an objective, neutral, and transcendent vantage point." Raimundo (Raimon) Panikkar, "What Is Comparative Philosophy Comparing?" in *Interpreting across Boundaries*, ed. G. Larson and E. Deutsch (Princeton: Princeton University Press, 1988), 127.

4. Robert Neville, "On Comparative Theology: Theology of Religions or a Trans-Religious Discipline," Annual Comparative Theology Lecture at the Harvard Center for the Study of World Religions, March 2017 (forthcoming in the *Brill Companion to Comparative Theology*, ed. W. Valkenberg), 9.

5. Perry Schmidt-Leukel, *Religious Pluralism and Interreligious Theology* (Maryknoll: Orbis Books, 2017), 8.

6. Neville, "On Comparative Theology," 8.

7. Francis Clooney, *Comparative Theology: Deep Learning across Religious Borders* (Oxford: Wiley-Blackwell, 2010), 112.

8. John Thatamanil, *The Immanent Divine: God, Creation, and the Human Predicament* (Minneapolis: Fortress Press, 2006), 3.

9. Catherine Cornille, "Multiple Religious Belonging," in *Understanding Inter-Religious Relations*, ed. D. Thomas, D. Cheetham, and D. Pratt (Oxford: Oxford University Press, 2013), 324–40; Catherine Cornille, "Strategies of Negotiation in Buddhist-Christian Dual Belonging," in *Buddhist-Christian Dual Belonging: Affirmations, Objections, Explorations*, ed. G. D'Costa and R. Thompson (Farnham: Ashgate, 2016), 143–60.

10. Clooney, *Comparative Theology*, 160. He also states that comparative theology leads to a situation in which "we have more teachers and fewer masters"; Francis Clooney, *Beyond Compare: St. Francis de Sales and Śrī Vedānta Deśika on Loving Surrender to God* (Washington: Georgetown University Press, 2008), 209.

11. Clooney, *Comparative Theology*, 158.

12. Clooney, *Comparative Theology*, 156.

13. Clooney, *Comparative Theology*, 159.

14. This is from a letter he wrote to his friend Raimon Panikkar; in Swami Abhishiktānanda, *Essential Writings* (Maryknoll: Orbis Books, 2006), 85.

15. Paul Griffiths speaks in this regard of the "non-compossibility" of multiple religious belonging. Paul Griffiths, *Problems of Religious Diversity* (Oxford: Blackwell, 2001), 32–36.

16. See Catherine Cornille, "Double Religious Belonging: Aspects and Questions," *Buddhist-Christian Studies 23* (2003); Catherine Cornille, "Mehrere Meister? Multiple Religionszugehörigkeit in Praxis und Theorie," in *Multiple religiöse Identität*, ed. R. Bernhardt and P. Schmidt-Leukel (Zurich: Theologischer Verlag Zurich, 2008), 15–35; Cornille, "Multiple Religious Belonging"; Jeffrey Bloechl and Catherine Cornille, *Christian Identity between Secularity and Plurality* (Bangalore: Dharmaram, 2015), 107–36.

17. Jacques Dupuis, "Christianity and Religions: Complementarity and Convergence," in *Many Mansions? Multiple Religious Belonging and Christian Identity*, ed. C. Cornille (Maryknoll: Orbis Books, 2002), 61–75.

18. Rose Drew, *Buddhist and Christian? An Exploration of Dual Belonging* (London: Routledge, 2011), 53.

19. Drew, *Buddhist and Christian?* 210.

20. For a discussion of the different strategies for reconciling conflicting elements in different religions, see Cornille, "Strategies of Negotiation."

21. Ulrich Winkler, "Reasons for and Contexts of Deep Theological Engagement with Other Religious Traditions in Europe: Toward a Comparative Theology," *Religions 3* (2012): 1193–94.

22. Paul Knitter, *Without Buddha I Could Not Be a Christian* (Oxford: Oneworld, 2010), xiv, emphasis in the original.

23. Knitter, *Without Buddha I Could Not Be a Christian*, 215.

24. Knitter, *Without Buddha I Could Not Be a Christian*, 216.

25. David Tracy, *Plurality and Ambiguity* (San Francisco: Harper & Row, 1987), 94.

26. Kimberley Patton and Benjamin Ray, eds., *A Magic Still Dwells* (Berkeley: University of California Press, 2000), 26.

27. Patton and Ray, *A Magic Still Dwells*, 26.

28. Patton and Ray, *A Magic Still Dwells*, 3–4.

29. Clooney, *Comparative Theology*, 11.

30. Klaus von Stosch, "Comparative Theology as Liberal and Confessional Theology," *Religions 3* (2012): 986.

31. David Burrell, *Freedom and Creation in Three Traditions* (Notre Dame: Notre Dame University Press, 1993); David Burrell, *Towards a Jewish-Christian-Muslim Theology* (Oxford: Wiley-Blackwell, 2011).

32. Jonathan Z. Smith, *Relating Religion* (Chicago: University of Chicago Press, 2004), 80.

33. Burrell, *Towards a Jewish-Christian-Muslim Theology*, 6.

34. Burrell, *Towards a Jewish-Christian-Muslim Theology*, 7.

35. Catherine Cornille, "Beauty and Truth in Christian Theology of Religions," in *Finding Beauty in the Other: Theological Reflections across Religious Traditions*, ed. P. Casarella and S. Mun'im (New York: Crossroad, 2018). Here, I demonstrate with examples from the Christian tradition how the appreciation of beauty in other religions is closely related to the broader recognition of and positive predisposition to other religions as sources of truth.

36. Catherine Cornille, "On Discernment in Dialogue," in *Criteria of Discernment in Interreligious Dialogue*, ed. C. Cornille (Eugene: Wipf & Stock, 2009), xvii.

37. Reinhold Bernhardt, "Coordinates for Interreligious Discernment from a Protestant View: Transcendence-Freedom-Agape-Responsibility," in *Criteria of Discernment in Interreligious Dialogue*, ed. C. Cornille (Eugene: Wipf & Stock, 2009), 53–68.

38. Dermot Lane, *Stepping Stones to Other Religions: A Christian Theology of Inter-Religious Dialogue* (Maryknoll: Orbis Books, 2011), 264.

39. Gavin D'Costa, "Roman Catholic Reflections on Discerning God in Interreligious Dialogue," in *Criteria of Discernment in Interreligious Dialogue*, ed. C. Cornille (Eugene: Wipf & Stock, 2009), 84.

40. J. R. Hustwit, "Myself, Only Moreso: Conditions for the Possibility of Transreligious Theology," *Open Theology 2* (2016): 241.

41. Hustwit, "Myself, Only Moreso," 241.

42. Roger Haight, *Jesus, Symbol of God* (Maryknoll: Orbis Books, 2000), 422.

43. Thomas Merton, *The Asian Journal of Thomas Merton* (New York: New Directions, 1975), 233–34.

44. Clooney, *Comparative Theology*, 157.

45. Knitter, *Without Buddha I Could Not Be a Christian*, xiv.

46. This is the case, for example, with the ideas and teachings of Robert di Mello, or Michaël Amaladoss, or Bede Griffiths.

47. Thatamanil, *The Immanent Divine*, 173.

48. Clooney, *Comparative Theology*, 157.

49. Thomas Tangaraj, *The Crucified Guru: An Experiment in Cross-Cultural Christology* (Nashville: Abingdon Press, 1994), 21.

50. Tangaraj, *The Crucified Guru*, 25.

51. Tangaraj, *The Crucified Guru*, 16.

52. A recent volume on interreligious comparisons in religious studies and theology focuses explicitly on Arvind Sharma's notion of "reciprocal illumination" as a leitmotif for comparative theological work. Perry Schmidt-Leukel and Andreas Nehring, eds., *Interreligious Comparisons in Religious Studies and Theology* (London: Bloomsbury, 2016).

53. John Cobb, *Beyond Dialogue: Toward a Mutual Transformation of Christianity and Buddhism* (Philadelphia: Fortress Press, 1982).

54. Masao Abe, "Kenotic God and Dynamic Śūnyatā," in *The Emptying God: A Buddhist-Jewish-Christian Conversation*, ed. J. Cobb and C. Ives (Maryknoll: Orbis Books, 1990).

55. Bede Griffiths, *The Marriage of East and West* (Springfield: Templegate, 1982).

56. While they were receptive to Abe's proposal, most Jewish and Christian theologians (Thomas Altizer, Eugene Borowitz, John Cobb, Catherine Keller, Jürgen Moltmann, Schubert Ogden, and David Tracy) are also quite critical about Abe's portrayal of Christianity. Their responses are included in John Cobb and Christopher Ives, eds., *The Emptying God: A Buddhist-Jewish-Christian Conversation* (Maryknoll: Orbis Books, 1990).

57. Raimon Panikkar, *The Intra-Religious Dialogue* (New York, Paulist Press, 1999), 62.

58. Panikkar, *The Intra-Religious Dialogue*, 86–87.

59. Hugh Nicholson, *Comparative Theology and the Problem of Religious Rivalry* (Oxford: Oxford University Press, 2010), 45.

60. Nicholson, *Comparative Theology and the Problem of Religious Rivalry*, 29.

61. Nicholson, *Comparative Theology and the Problem of Religious Rivalry*, 47.

62. James Fredericks, "Introduction," in *The New Comparative Theology*, ed. F. Clooney (London: T&T Clark, 2010), xii.

63. James Fredericks, *Buddhists and Christians: Through Comparative Theology to Solidarity* (Maryknoll: Orbis Books, 2004), 109.

64. Francis Clooney, *Hindu God, Christian God* (Oxford: Oxford University Press, 2001), 11.

65. Thatamanil, *The Immanent Divine*, 173.

66. Paul Griffiths, *An Apology for Apologetics* (Maryknoll: Orbis Books, 1991), 85–108.

67. Paul Williams, *The Unexpected Way: On Converting from Buddhism to Christianity* (London: T&T Clark, 2002).

68. Griffiths, *An Apology for Apologetics*, 78.

69. Griffiths, *An Apology for Apologetics*, 82.

70. David Tracy, "Comparative Theology," in *Encyclopedia of Religion*, ed. L. Jones (Detroit: Macmillan Reference, 2005), 9132.

71. Clooney, *Comparative Theology*, 127.

72. Burrell, *Towards a Jewish-Christian-Muslim Theology*, 135–36.

73. Schmidt-Leukel, *Religious Pluralism and Interreligious Theology*, 11.

74. Neville, "On Comparative Theology," 2, 9.

75. Tracy, "Comparative Theology," 9133.

76. Burrell, *Towards a Jewish-Christian-Muslim Theology*, 12. Burrell also traces the continued theological borrowing between Muslim and Christian thinkers, evident in particular in the seventeenth-century Shi'ite theologian Mulla Sadra, whose work draws from Aquinas's "unabashed affirmation of the primacy of existing over essence" (23).

77. Martin Ganeri, "Tradition with a New Identity: Thomist Engagement with Non-Christian Thought as a Model for the New Comparative Theology in Europe," *Religions* 3 (2012): 1066–67. Ganeri also acknowledges that the Church has come to develop a more open attitude toward other religions since *Nostra aetate*, and that the thought of other religions cannot merely be likened to natural philosophy. But Aquinas still may be used as an example of constructive

engagement with other religious traditions. The three ways outlined by Ganeri may in fact loosely fit within my categories of intensification, reaffirmation, and reinterpretation.

78. Clooney, *Comparative Theology*, 28.
79. Marianne Moyaert, *In Response to the Religious Other: Ricoeur and the Fragility of Interreligious Encounters* (Lanham: Lexington Books, 2014), 183.
80. Moyaert, *In Response to the Religious Other*, 182.
81. Panikkar, *The Intra-Religious Dialogue*, 74.
82. David Tracy, *Dialogue with the Other* (Leuven: Peeters, 1990), 73.
83. The clearest example of this is the synthesis of Islam and Hinduism in Sikhism.
84. Francis Clooney's work, for example, focuses on central themes in Christianity and Hinduism, and he explicitly invites not only Christian but also Hindu theologians to respond to his work. In Clooney, *Hindu God, Christian God*, the Hindu theologian Parimal Patil offers a Hindu response (185–95).
85. Hans Gustafson, "Is Transreligious Theology Unavoidable in Interreligious Theology and Dialogue?" *Open Theology 2* (2016): 259.
86. Clooney, *Comparative Theology*, 165.

Conclusion

Comparative theology by its very nature lends itself to a diversity of approaches and methods. A theologian may be inspired by any text, teaching or practice in any other religious tradition, and the methods employed will in part depend on the particular material engaged. It may involve close textual study, historical research, philosophical analysis, and/or anthropological work, all engaging the data of at least two religious traditions. Each particular comparison may also call for its own type of justification, whether in thematic analogy, historical contingency, or structural or functional similarity. In this, comparative theology is subject to the same methodological diversity as the comparative study of religions. However, what distinguishes the comparative theological method is its varying negotiation of the validity and truth of the teachings and practices of the religions involved. This will determine the degree, and at times also the kind, of learning that might take place in comparative theology.

The process of learning in comparative theology is shaped both by religious and theological presuppositions and by the material involved. Some theological and epistemological dispositions will be more closely aligned with particular types of learning. Thus, exclusivist approaches will likely incline toward a reaffirmation of the truth of one's own tradition in light of the other, while postcolonial approaches will focus mainly on the rectification of one's understanding of the other. Intensification and recovery will tend to arise from a focus on truth in similarities or minor variations between religions, while reinterpretation and appropriation presuppose recognition of religious differences as potentially theologically meaningful and enriching. The same material may therefore lead to different kinds of learning, depending on the theological disposition of the theologian. But the type of learning may also proceed from the concrete material engaged in comparative theology. Certain teachings or practices may thus call for rectification, while others open up the

Meaning and Method in Comparative Theology, First Edition. Catherine Cornille.
© 2020 John Wiley & Sons Ltd. Published 2020 by John Wiley & Sons Ltd.

possibility of recovery or reinterpretation. The same theologian may thus engage in different types of learning, and apply varying normative judgments, depending on the material involved. And one's general theological disposition may shift and change as a result of this engagement. The purpose of mapping different approaches to comparative theology is not to label particular theologians, or to privilege a particular approach, but rather to lay out the variety of possible approaches to the discipline and to allow for a sharper identification of any particular exercise in comparative theology within the broader panoply of options.

Each of the approaches may contribute to theological development and growth. While some have associated comparative theology only with a particular theological disposition[1] or with a particular type of learning, all allow for a deepening and broadening of theological understanding. Some shed a more critical light on one's own tradition, while others may serve to confirm one's sense of its truth, and still others to enrich the tradition with new insights, interpretations, and expressions. Together, they contribute to the vitality of living theological traditions.

Engagement with the teachings and practices of different religious traditions may at times lead to a loosening of the mooring of comparative theology within a particular religious and theological tradition. Different traditions may then become normative with regard to various topics, or theologians may develop their own normative principles to discern the truth of various religious traditions. Throughout the book, I have juxtaposed confessional and meta-confessional approaches to comparative theology, partly in order to offer a comprehensive overview of the field and partly in order to delineate more clearly the challenges and possibilities particular to a confessional approach. Unbound by the truth claims of any particular religion, meta-confessional comparative theology risks becoming a highly personal and subjective theological enterprise which does not allow for much systematic theological or methodological reflection.

Each theologian may develop a synthesis of elements from different religions without reference to a particular set of teachings and practices and without accountability to any particular religious community. This allows for greater freedom to pursue theological truth and meaning wherever it is found, but it also limits the relevance of comparative theological insights. The risk of aiming for a more universal theological truth is that it becomes strictly personal. Though the meta-confessional approach may contribute to comparative theology, I have approached the discipline primarily from a confessional perspective. Insofar as theology is grounded in a set of texts, teachings, and practices, and conducted in the service of a particular religious community and tradition, it approaches questions of truth and meaning from a given normative perspective. This determines not only what might be of theological interest in another religion, but also what and how one might learn from the other. These norms may be varied and flexible, and may themselves evolve in the process of engaging other religions. But they ensure the religious or spiritual grounding of comparative theology in a norm or set of norms not of one's own making, as well as the relevance of comparative theology for a broader religious community. The difference between confessional and meta-confessional comparative theology is often a matter of degree, rather than nature. Meta-confessional comparative theologians tend to still be primarily grounded – consciously or unconsciously – in particular religious traditions, and confessional comparative theologians often tend to push the boundaries of confessional religious traditions. However, the distinction between the two approaches does shed important light on characteristics and contours of comparative theology.

The confessional approach to comparative theology puts into sharp relief the hermeneutical and epistemological questions and challenges of the discipline. It renders explicit the fact that one's understanding of the other religion is always colored by certain religious prejudices and that the process of learning from the other also involves some degree of transformation or reinterpretation of the self-understanding of the other. It also raises the question of the propriety of using the teachings and practices of another religion for one's own religious edification and theological development. While these questions and problems may seem particularly pertinent to a confessional or tradition-based approach to comparative theology, they in fact apply to all comparative theology. The engagement of teachings and practices of one tradition from within and for another religious tradition is not meant to challenge their original religious meaning and context. Characteristic of comparative theology is recognition of and respect for the alterity of the other. The process of learning here involves a humble awareness and at times a sense of guilt that one can never fully do justice to the self-understanding of the other. In spite of the fact that one's understanding of the religious other always remains approximate, even an imperfect understanding of the other religion may shed new light on one's own, and even a tainted borrowing of elements of other religions may lead to theological development and growth.

Comparative theology is based on the principle that the process of interreligious learning has and may occur in all directions or between any religions. This book has focused mainly on examples from the Christian comparative theology. But I hope and suspect that the various theological and methodological issues raised may be applicable to the practice of comparative theology from within any other religious tradition. Each religion will engage other religions from within its own particular sense of identity and normativity, whether this is defined primarily in terms of orthodoxy or orthopraxis. But every religion will have to come to terms with the question of the status of other religions in light of the truth and efficacy of one's own, with the possibility of understanding the other religion, with the various ways in which interreligious learning might occur, and with the relation between traditional and comparative forms of religious reflection and practice. While some religious dispositions toward the validity and truth of other religions and some types of learning may be more pertinent to or prevalent in some religions than in others, the typologies developed in this book are not exclusive to Christianity or any other religious tradition.

The reasons why the modern discipline of comparative theology has taken hold mainly within Christianity are complex and involve a series of factors which are both circumstantial and ideological. The systematic engagement with other religious traditions requires a developed theological and academic infrastructure and context. Theology has established itself as an integral discipline at Christian universities throughout the world, offering opportunity for theologians – both religious and lay – to immerse themselves in the academic study of various aspects of the Christian tradition. With the flourishing of the discipline of religious studies in the second half of the twentieth century, some departments of theology became religious studies departments, whether in name only or in reality, while others made room for the study of other religion in their curricula. This created the material conditions for the possibility of comparative theology. Postcolonial critique of so-called objective and neutral study of other religions has led to greater critical awareness of one's own prejudices and presuppositions, and to a more conscious affirmation of one's own religious presuppositions in approaching the religious other. In the meantime, developments in the area of Christian theology of religions also led to the recognition of elements of truth in other religions, rendering constructive engagement with other religions not only possible but necessary. Comparative theology is born naturally from the recognition of other religions as potential sources of truth or from the recognition of religious pluralism as a theological resource. Thus, the discipline came to establish itself in departments of Christian theology as the natural synthesis of theology and religious studies, consistent with the theological presuppositions of the tradition and attentive to the orientalist critiques of religious studies.

A lingering critical question for comparative theology involves the reality of power in the engagement between religions. Even though comparative theology may be done from within any religious tradition, the very fact that the majority of comparative theologians are Christians or that it is still done mainly from within the Christian tradition may raise concern. It is true that comparative theology can only be conducted from a place of theological safety and confidence. Religions that are less secure in their existence or numbers or that have a less developed tradition of theological reflection may be less inclined to render their own tradition vulnerable to engagement with other religious traditions. The reality of religious plurality remains a threat to most religious traditions, and comparative theology may be regarded as a luxury or a danger to their religious or theological integrity. There is thus a risk that comparative theology might become another expression of Christian privilege and power.

What distinguishes comparative theology from forms of hegemonic engagement with other religions is the attitude of epistemological and theological humility. It is based on a recognition of one's own particular and limited religious location and on the unfinished nature of one's understanding of the truth. It recognizes the validity and integrity of other religious traditions and it approaches the religious other as a humble apprentice, grateful for whatever it may learn. While it may hope that the process of learning might occur in both directions, it focuses not on what the other tradition might learn from one's own, but only on what one might learn from the other. As such, comparative theology accords a dignity and respect to other religions that goes far in mitigating or abating the concerns of religious hegemony in comparative theology. To be sure, the comparative theologian approaches the religious other from a commitment to truth that does not allow for a full affirmation of the truth of the other religion, or of every element of the other religion as valid or true. This, however, applies to comparative theologians from any religious tradition. It is in the reciprocal humility and generosity between comparative theologians from different religions that the domination of one particular tradition in comparative theology is overcome. And it is in integrating elements from other religious traditions that religious traditions may also draw closer to one another and to ultimate truth.

The challenge for comparative theology often involves not only accounting for its relation to other religions, but also establishing its place within established religious traditions. As a confessional theological discipline, comparative theology builds upon a particular theological tradition, contributing insights from other religious traditions to past and present theological questions. It thus requires active engagement with a particular tradition to both focus comparative theological attention on relevant questions and assist in discerning the validity and truth of elements from other religions. Conversely, religious traditions need comparative theologians in order to expand the theological horizon, deepen and enrich the theological tradition, and advance theological insight and truth. The possibilities for comparative theological learning may seem vast and daunting. Comparative theology indeed presents an inexhaustible well of theological inspiration, and the insights of comparative theologians may take time to digest. However, open and constructive engagement with the teachings and practices of other religions represents one of the most promising avenues for theological creativity, and the systematic engagement with the work of comparative theologians is thus vital for continued theological renewal and growth.

Note

1. Some have argued that only a particular type of inclusivism or pluralism allows for constructive engagement with the other. See Kristin Beise Kiblinger, "Relating Theology of Religions and Comparative Theology," in *The New Comparative Theology*, ed. F. Clooney (London: T&T Clark, 2010), 21–42. It is also reiterated in Paul Hedges, *Comparative Theology: A Critical and Methodological Perspective* (Leiden: Brill, 2017), 16, and Ulrich Winkler, "Reasons for and Context of Deep Theological Engagement with Other Religious Traditions in Europe: Toward a Comparative Theology," *Religions 3* (2012): 1190.

Bibliography

General

Almond, Gabriel, R. Scott Appleby, and Emmanuel Sivan. *Strong Religion: The Rise of Fundamentalisms around the World*. Chicago: University of Chicago Press, 2003.

Clarke, James Freeman. *Ten Great Religions: An Essay in Comparative Theology*. Boston: Houghton, Mifflin, 1889.

Cornille, Catherine, ed. *Criteria of Discernment in Interreligious Dialogue*. Eugene: Wipf & Stock, 2009.

Cornille, Catherine. "Types of Misunderstanding in Interreligious Hermeneutics." In *Antisemitism, Islamophobia and Interreligious Hermeneutics: Ways of Seeing the Other*, edited by E. O'Donnell, 11–28. Leiden: Brill, 2018.

Cornille, Catherine, ed. *The Wiley-Blackwell Companion to Inter-Religious Dialogue*. Oxford: Wiley-Blackwell, 2013.

Cornille, Catherine, and Christopher Conway, eds. *Interreligious Hermeneutics*. Eugene: Wipf & Stock, 2010.

Cornille, Catherine, and Stephanie Corigliano, eds. *Interreligious Dialogue and Cultural Change*. Eugene: Wipf & Stock, 2012.

Cornille, Catherine, and Jillian Maxey, eds. *Women and Interreligious Dialogue*. Eugene: Wipf & Stock, 2013.

Cornille, Catherine, and Glen Willis, eds. *The World Market and Interreligious Dialogue*. Eugene: Wipf & Stock, 2011.

de Lubac, Henri. *Amida*. Paris: Seuil, 1955.

Doniger, Wendy. *Splitting the Difference*. Chicago: University of Chicago Press, 1999.

Eliade, Mircea. *The Myth of the Eternal Return: Or, Cosmos and History*. Princeton: Princeton University Press, 1954.

Fitzgerald, Timothy. "A Critique of Religion as a Cross-Cultural Category." *Method and Theory in the Study of Religion 9*, no. 2 (1997): 91–110.

Huxley, Aldous. *The Perennial Philosophy*. New York: Harper & Brothers, 1945.

Jordan, Louis Henry. *Comparative Religion*. Atlanta: Scholars Press, 1905.

Kamstra, Jacques. *Synkretisme: Op de Grens tussen Theologie en Godsdienstfenomenologie*. Leiden: Brill, 1970.

Llewellyn, J. E., ed. *Defining Hinduism: A Reader*. New York: Routledge, 2005.

Masuzawa, Tomoko. *The Invention of World Religions*. Chicago: University of Chicago Press, 2005.

Muller, Friedrich Max. *Chips from a German Workshop*. New York: Scribner, Armstrong, 1874.

Panikkar, Raimundo (Raimon). *Myth, Faith and Hermeneutics*. New York: Paulist Press, 1979.

Patton, Kimberley. *Religion of the Gods: Ritual, Paradox and Reflexivity*. Oxford: Oxford University Press, 2009.

Patton, Kimberley, and Benjamin Ray, eds. *A Magic Still Dwells*. Berkeley: University of California Press, 2000.

Pye, Michael. "Syncretism and Ambiguity." *Numen 18*, no. 2 (1971): 83–93.

Said, Edward. *Orientalism*. New York: Vintage Books, 1979.

Smith, Jonathan Z. *Imagining Religion: From Babylon to Jonestown*. Chicago: University of Chicago Press, 1982.

Smith, Jonathan Z. *Relating Religion: Essays in the Study of Religion*. Chicago: University of Chicago Press, 2004.

Smith, Wilfred Cantwell. *The Meaning and End of Religion*. New York: Macmillan, 1964.

van der Leeuw, Gerardus. *Religion in Essence and Manifestation*, translated by J. E. Turner. New York: Harper & Row, 1963.

Wedemeyer, Christian, and Wendy Doniger. *Hermeneutics, Politics and the History of Religions: The Contested Legacies of Joachim Wach and Mircea Eliade*. Chicago: University of Chicago Press, 2010.

Theology of Religions

Barker, Gregory A., ed. *Jesus in the World's Faiths: Leading Thinkers from Five Religions Reflect on His Meaning*. Maryknoll: Orbis Books, 2005.

Barnes, Michael. *Theology and the Dialogue of Religions*. Cambridge: Cambridge University Press, 2002.

Barth, Karl. "Church Dogmatics." Vol. *1, The Doctrine of the Word of God, part 2*. London: T&T Clark, 1961.

Bernhardt, Reinhold. *Christianity without Absolutes*. London: SCM Press, 1994.

Bernhardt, Reinhold. *Ende des Dialogs? Die Begegnung der Religionen und ihre theologische Reflexion*. Zurich: Theologischer Verlag Zurich, 2006.

Bracken, Joseph. *The Divine Matrix: Creativity as Link between East and West*. Eugene: Wipf & Stock, 2006.

Bracken, Joseph. *The World in the Trinity: Open-Ended Systems in Science and Religion*. Minneapolis: Fortress Press, 2014.

Breton, Stanislas. *Unicité et monothéisme*. Paris: Cerf, 1981.

Cornille, Catherine. "Beauty and Truth in Christian Theology of Religions." In *Finding Beauty in the Other: Theological Reflections across Religious Traditions*, edited by P. Casarella and S. Mun'im, 33–50. Maryknoll/New York: Crossroad, 2018.

Cornille, Catherine. "Soteriological Agnosticism and the Future of Catholic Theology of Interreligious Dialogue." In *The Past, Present, and Future of Theologies of Interreligious Dialogue*, edited by T. Merrigan and J. Friday, 201–15. Oxford: Oxford University Press, 2017.

Cornille, Catherine. "Soteriological Agnosticism and Interreligious Dialogue." In *From Vatican II to Pope Francis: Charting a Catholic Future*, edited by P. Crowley, 112–26. Maryknoll: Orbis Books, 2014.

D'Costa, Gavin. *The Meeting of Religions and the Trinity*. Maryknoll: Orbis Books, 2000.

D'Costa, Gavin. "Roman Catholic Reflections on Discerning God in Interreligious Dialogue." In *Criteria of Discernment in Interreligious Dialogue*, edited by C. Cornille, 69–86. Eugene: Wipf & Stock, 2009.

D'Costa, Gavin. *Vatican II: Catholic Doctrines on Jews and Muslims*. Oxford: Oxford University Press, 2014.

Dupuis, Jacques. "Christianity and Religions: Complementarity and Convergence." In *Many Mansions? Multiple Religious Belonging and Christian Identity*, edited by C. Cornille, 61–75. Eugene: Wipf & Stock, 2010.

Dupuis, Jacques. *Toward a Christian Theology of Religious Pluralism*. Maryknoll: Orbis Books, 1997.

Ensminger, Sven. *Karl Barth's Theology as a Resource for a Christian Theology of Religions*. London: Bloomsbury, 2014.

Gilkey, Langdon. "Plurality and Its Theological Implications." In *The Myth of Christian Uniqueness*, ed J. Hick and P. Knitter, 37–52. Maryknoll: Orbis Books, 1987.

Griffiths, Paul. *Problems of Religious Diversity*. Oxford: Blackwell, 2001.

Haight, Roger. "The Case for Spirit Christology." *Theological Studies 53* (1992): 280–81.

Haight, Roger. *Jesus, Symbol of God*. Maryknoll: Orbis Books, 2000.

Heim, Mark. *The Depth of the Riches: A Trinitarian Theology of Religious Ends*. Grand Rapids: Eerdmans, 2001.

Heim, Mark. *Salvations: Truth and Difference in Religion*. Maryknoll: Orbis Books, 1995.

Hick, John. *God Has Many Names*, London: Macmillan, 1980.

Hick, John. *God and the Universe of Faiths*. New York: St. Martin's Press, 1973.

Hick, John. *The Myth of God Incarnate*. London: SCM Press, 1977.

Hick, John. "The Non-Absoluteness of Christianity." In *The Myth of Christian Uniqueness*, edited by J. Hick and P. Knitter, 16–36. Maryknoll: Orbis Books, 1987.

Hick, John. "On Grading Religions." *Religious Studies 17*, no. 4 (1981): 451–67.

Hill Fletcher, Jeannine. *Monopoly on Salvation? A Feminist Approach to Religious Pluralism*. New York: Continuum, 2005.

Hill Fletcher, Jeannine. *Motherhood as Metaphor*. New York: Fordham University Press, 2013.

Hill Fletcher, Jeannine. "What Counts as 'Catholic'? What Constitutes 'Comparative'? Embodied Practice as a Site for Comparative Catholic Theology." *Studies in Interreligious Dialogue 24*, no. 1 (2014): 78–93.

Kallistos, Bishop of Diokleia. *The Power of the Name: The Jesus Prayer in Orthodox Spirituality*. Oxford: Fairacres, 1986.

Kaufman, Gordon. *God, Mystery, Diversity: Christian Theology in a Pluralistic World.* Minneapolis: Fortress Press, 1996.

Kiblinger, Kristin Beise. "Relating Theology of Religions and Comparative Theology." In *The New Comparative Theology*, edited by F. Clooney, 21–42. New York: Continuum, 2010.

King, Ursula. "Feminism: The Missing Dimension in the Dialogue of Religions." In *Pluralism and the Religions: The Theological and Political Dimensions*, edited by J. D'Arcy May, 40–55. London: Cassell, 1998.

Knitter, Paul. *Introducing Theologies of Religions.* Maryknoll: Orbis Books, 2002.

Knitter, Paul. *Jesus and the Other Names.* Maryknoll: Orbis Books, 1996.

Knitter, Paul. *One Earth, Many Religions.* Maryknoll: Orbis Books, 1995.

Kraemer, Hendrick. *The Christian Message in a Non-Christian World.* London: Edinburgh House Press, 1938.

Küng, Hans. *Theology for the New Millennium.* New York: Doubleday, 1988.

Kwok, Pui-lan. *Hope Abundant: Third World and Indigenous Women's Theology.* Maryknoll: Orbis Books, 2010.

Kwok, Pui-lan. *Postcolonial Imagination and Feminist Theology.* Louisville: Westminster John Knox Press, 2005.

Lane, Dermot. *Stepping Stones to Other Religions: A Christian Theology of Inter-Religious Dialogue.* Maryknoll: Orbis Books, 2011.

Lindbeck, George. *The Nature of Doctrine.* Louisville: Westminster John Knox Press, 2009 (originally published 1984).

Marshall, Bruce, ed. *Theology and Dialogue: Essays in Conversation with George Lindbeck.* South Bend: University of Notre Dame Press, 1990.

Merrigan, Terrence, and John Friday, eds. *The Past, Present and Future of Theologies of Interreligious Dialogue.* Oxford: Oxford University Press, 2017.

Mibank, John. "The End of Dialogue." In *Christian Uniqueness Reconsidered*, edited by G. D'Costa, 174–91. Maryknoll: Orbis Books, 1990.

O'Leary, Joseph. *Religious Pluralism and Christian Truth.* Edinburgh: Edinburgh University Press, 1996.

Phan, Peter. *The Joy of Religious Pluralism: A Personal Journey.* Maryknoll: Orbis Books, 2017.

Rahner, Karl. "Christianity and the Non-Christian Religions." In *Theological Investigations*, vol. 5. London: Darton, Longman & Todd, 1966.

Ratzinger, Cardinal Joseph. *Truth and Tolerance: Christian Belief and World Religions.* San Francisco: Ignatius Press, 2003.

Smith, Wilfred Cantwell. *Towards a World Theology.* Philadelphia: Westminster Press, 1981.

Song, Choan-Seng. *Third-Eye Theology: Theology in Formation in Asian Settings.* Maryknoll: Orbis Books, 1991.

Starkey, Peggy. "Agape: A Christian Criterion for Truth in the Other World Religions." *International Review of Mission 74* (1985): 425–63.

Swidler, Leonard, John Cobb, Paul Knitter, and Monika Hellwig. *Death or Dialogue? From the Age of Monologue to the Age of Dialogue.* London: SCM Press, 1990.

Tillich, Paul. *Christianity and the Encounter of the World Religions.* New York: Columbia University Press, 1963.

Volf, Miroslav. *Flourishing: Why We Need Religion in a Globalized World.* New Haven: Yale University Press, 2015.

von Balthasar, Hans Urs. *Truth Is Symphonic: Aspects of Christian Pluralism.* San Francisco: Ignatius Press, 1987.

Yong, Amos. *Beyond the Impasse: Toward a Pneumatological Theology of Religions.* Eugene: Wipf & Stock, 2014.

Yong, Amos. *Hospitality and the Other.* Maryknoll: Orbis Books, 2008.

Method in Comparative Theology

Amaladoss, Michaël. "La double appartenance religieuse." In *Vivre de plusieurs religions. Promesse ou illusion?* edited by J. Scheuer and D. Gira, 44–53. Paris: l'Atelier, 2000.

Bakhtin, Mikhail. *Speech Genres and Other Late Essays*, edited by C. Emerson and M. Holquist, translated by V. McGee. Austin: University of Texas Press, 1986.

Barnes, Michael. *Interreligious Learning: Dialogue, Spirituality and the Christian Imagination.* Cambridge: Cambridge University Press, 2012.

Barnes, Michael. "Living Interreligiously: On the 'Personal Style' of Comparative Theology." In *How to Do Comparative Theology*, edited by F. Clooney and K. von Stosch, 301–23. New York: Fordham University Press, 2018.

Bernhardt, Reinhold. "Comparative Theology: Between Theology and Religious Studies." *Religions 3* (2012): 964–72.

Bernhardt, Reinhold. "Coordinates for Interreligious Discernment from a Protestant View." In *Criteria of Discernment in Interreligious Dialogue*, edited by C. Cornille, 53–68. Eugene: Wipf & Stock, 2009.

Bernhardt, Reinhold, and Perry Schmidt-Leukel, eds. *Interreligiöse Theologie: Chancen und Probleme.* Zurich: Theologischer Verlag Zurich, 2014.

Cheetham, David, Ulrich Winkler, Oddbjørn Leirvik, and Judith Gruber, eds. *Interreligious Hermeneutics in Pluralistic Europe: Between Texts and People.* Leiden: Brill, 2011.

Clooney, Francis. "Comparative Theology: A Review of Recent Books (1989–1995)." *Theological Studies 26*, no. 3 (1995): 521–50.

Clooney, Francis. *Comparative Theology: Deep Learning across Religious Borders.* Oxford: Wiley-Blackwell, 2010.

Clooney, Francis. *Learning Interreligiously: In the Text, in the World.* Minneapolis: Fortress Press, 2018.

Clooney, Francis. *The New Comparative Theology.* London: T&T Clark, 2010.

Clooney, Francis, and Klaus von Stosch. *How to Do Comparative Theology.* New York: Fordham, 2017.

Cornille, Catherine. *The Im-Possibility of Interreligious Dialogue.* New York: Crossroad, 2008.

Cornille, Catherine. "Interreligiöse Theologie und die Bescheidenheit des Ortes: Überlegungen zu den 'Christian Commentaries on Non-Christian Sacred Tests.'"

In *Interreligiöse Theologie: Chancen und Probleme*, edited by R. Bernhardt and P. Schmidt-Leukel, 161–80. Zurich: Theologischer Verlag Zurich, 2013.

Cornille, Catherine. "Interreligious Hospitality and Its Limits." In *Hosting the Stranger between Religions*, edited by R. Kearney and J. Taylor, 35–45. New York: Continuum, 2011.

Cornille, Catherine. "Multiple Religious Belonging." In *Understanding Inter-Religious Relations*, edited by D. Thomas, D. Cheetham, and D. Pratt, 324–40. Oxford: Oxford University Press, 2013.

Cornille, Catherine. "The Problem of Choice in Comparative Theology." In *How to Do Comparative Theology*, edited by F. Clooney and K. von Stosch, 19–36. New York: Fordham University Press, 2017.

Drew, Rose. "Challenging Truths: Reflections on the Theological Dimension of Comparative Theology." *Religions 3* (2012): 1041–53.

Emerson, Caryl. *The First Hundred Years of Mikhail Bakhtin*. Princeton: Princeton University Press, 1997.

Flood, Gavin. "Religious Practice and the Nature of the Human." In *Interreligious Comparisons in Religious Studies and Theology*, edited by P. Schmidt-Leukel and A. Nehring, 130–41. London: Bloomsbury, 2016.

Fredericks, James. "Introduction." In *The New Comparative Theology*, edited by F. Clooney, ix–xix. London: T&T Clark, 2010.

Fredericks, James, and Tracy Tiemeier, eds. *Interreligious Friendship after Nostra Aetate*. London: Palgrave Macmillan, 2015.

Gadamer, Hans-Georg. *Truth and Method*, translation revised by J. Weinsheimer and D. Marshall. New York: Continuum, 1995.

Ganeri, Martin. "Tradition with a New Identity: Thomist Engagement with Non-Christian Thought as a Model for the New Comparative Theology in Europe." *Religions 3* (2012): 1054–74.

Gruber, Judith. "(Un)Silencing Hybridity: A Postcolonial Critique of Comparative Theology." In *Comparative Theology in the Millennial Classroom*, edited by M. Brecht and R. Locklin, 21–35. New York: Routledge, 2016.

Gustafson, Hans. "Is Transreligious Theology Unavoidable in Interreligious Theology and Dialogue?" *Open Theology 2*, no. 1 (2016). https://doi.org/10.1515/opth-2016-0020

Gustafson, Hans. *Learning from Other Religious Traditions: Leaving Room for Holy Envy*. Berlin: Springer, 2018.

Hedges, Paul. *Comparative Theology: A Critical and Methodological Perspective*. Leiden: Brill, 2017.

Hedges, Paul. "Comparative Theology and Hermeneutics: A Gadamerian Approach to Interreligious Interpretation." *Religions 7* (2016): 1–21.

Heim, Mark. "On Doing as Others Do: Theological Perspectives on Multiple Religious Practice." In *Many Yet One? Multiple Religious Belonging*, edited by P. Jesudason, R. Rajkumar, and J. Prabhakar Dayam, 27–44. Geneva: World Council of Churches, 2016.

Holquist, Michael. *Dialogism: Bakhtin and His World*. London: Routledge, 1990.

Hustwit, J. R. *Interreligious Hermeneutics and the Pursuit of Truth*. Lanham: Lexington Books, 2014.

Hustwit, J. R. "Myself, Only Moreso: Conditions for the Possibility of Transreligious Theology." *Open Theology 2*, no. 1 (2016): 236–41. https://doi.org/10.1515/opth-2016-0018.

Jeanrond, Werner. "Toward an Interreligious Hermeneutics of Love." In *Interreligious Hermeneutics*, edited by C. Cornille and C. Conway, 44–60. Eugene: Wipf & Stock, 2010.

Jeanrond, Werner, and Aasulv Lande. *The Concept of God in Global Dialogue*. Maryknoll: Orbis Books, 2005.

Kearney, Richard. "The Wager of Carnal Hermeneutics." In *Carnal Hermeneutics*, edited by R. Kearney and B. Trainor, 15–56. New York: Fordham University Press 2015.

Leirvik, Oddbjorn. *Interreligious Studies: A Relational Approach to Religious Activism and the Study of Religion*. London: Bloomsbury, 2014.

Locklin, Reid, and Mara Brecht. *Comparative Theology in the Millennial Classroom: Hybrid Identities, Negotiated Boundaries*. New York: Routledge, 2016.

Locklin, Reid, and Hugh Nicholson. "The Return of Comparative Theology." *Journal of the American Academy of Religion 78*, no. 2 (2010): 477–514.

Maraldo, John. "A Call for an Alternative Form of Understanding." In *Interreligious Hermeneutics*, edited by C. Cornille and C. Conway, 89–115. Eugene: Wipf & Stock, 2010.

Martin, Jerry. "Is Transreligious Theology Possible?" *Open Theology 2*, no. 1 (2016).

Moyaert, Marianne. "Absorption or Hospitality." In *Interreligious Hermeneutics*, edited by C. Cornille and C. Conway, 61–88. Eugene: Wipf & Stock, 2010.

Moyaert, Marianne. *In Response to the Religious Other*. Lanham: Lexington Books, 2014.

Moyaert, Marianne. "On Vulnerability: Probing the Ethical Dimensions of Comparative Theology." *Religions 3* (2012): 1144–61.

Moyaert, Marianne. "Towards a Ritual Turn in Comparative Theology: Opportunities, Challenges, and Problems." *Harvard Theological Review 111*, no. 1 (2018): 1–23.

Moyaert, Marianne, and Joris Geldhof. *Ritual Participation and Interreligious Dialogue*. London: Bloomsbury, 2015.

Neville, Robert, ed. *The Human Condition*. Albany: SUNY Press, 2001.

Neville, Robert. "On Comparative Theology: Theology of Religions or a Trans-Religious Discipline." Annual Comparative Theology Lecture at the Harvard Center for the Study of World Religions, March 2017. To appear in the *Brill Companion to Comparative Theology*.

Neville, Robert, ed. *Religious Truth*. Albany: SUNY Press, 2001.

Neville, Robert, ed. *Ultimate Realities: A Volume in the Comparative Religious Ideas Project*. Albany: SUNY Press, 2001.

Nicholson, Hugh. *Comparative Theology and the Problem of Religious Rivalry*. Oxford: Oxford University Press, 2011.

Nicholson, Hugh. "The New Comparative Theology and the Problem of Theological Hegemonism." In *The New Comparative Theology*, edited by F. Clooney, 43–62. London: T&T Clark, 2010.

Nicholson, Hugh. "The Reunification of Theology and Comparison in the New Comparative Theology." *Journal of the American Academy of Religion 77*, no. 3 (2009): 609–46.

Panikkar, Raimon. *The Intra-Religious Dialogue*. Mahwah: Paulist Press, 1999.

Panikkar, Raimundo (Raimon). "What Is Comparative Philosophy Comparing?" In *Interpreting across Boundaries*, edited by G. Larson and E. Deutsch, 116–36. Princeton: Princeton University Press, 1988.

Ricoeur, Paul. *Figuring the Sacred*. Minneapolis: Fortress Press, 1995.

Ricoeur, Paul. *Hermeneutics and the Human Sciences*. Cambridge: Cambridge University Press, 1981.

Ricoeur, Paul. "The Metaphorical Process as Cognition, Imagination, and Feeling." In *On Metaphor*, edited by S. Sacks, 141–58. Chicago: University of Chicago Press, 1979.

Ricoeur, Paul. *Oneself and Another*. Chicago: University of Chicago Press, 1992.

Ricoeur, Paul. *Time and Narrative*, vol. 3. Translated by K. Blamey and D. Pellauer. Chicago: University of Chicago Press, 1988.

Ruparell, Tinu. "Inter-Religious Dialogue as Interstitial Theology." In *The Wiley-Blackwell Companion to Inter-Religious Dialogue*, edited by C. Cornille, 117–32. Oxford: Wiley-Blackwell, 2013.

Scheuer, Jacques. "Comparative Theology and Religious Studies in a Non-religious Environment." *Religions 3* (2012): 973–82.

Schmidt-Leukel, Perry. *Religious Pluralism and Interreligious Theology*. Maryknoll: Orbis Books, 2017.

Schmidt-Leukel, Perry, and Andreas Nehring, eds. *Interreligious Comparisons in Religious Studies and Theology*. London: Bloomsbury, 2016.

Thatamanil, John. "Eucharist Upstairs, Yoga Downstairs: On Multiple Religious Participation." In *Many Yet One? Multiple Religious Belonging*, edited by P. Jesudason, R. Rajkumar, and J. Prabhakar Dayam, 5–22. Geneva: World Council of Churches, 2016.

Thatamanil, John. "Transreligious Theology as the Quest for Interreligious Wisdom." *Open Theology 2*, no. 1 (2016): 354–62.

Todorov, Tzvetan. *Mikhail Bakhtin: The Dialogical Principle*. Minneapolis: University of Minnesota Press, 1984.

Tracy, David. "Comparative Theology." In *Encyclopedia of Religion*, edited by L. Jones. Vol. *13*. Detroit: Macmillan Reference, 2005.

Tracy, David. *Dialogue with the Other: The Inter-Religious Dialogue*. Leuven: Peeters, 1990.

Tracy, David. *Plurality and Ambiguity*. San Francisco: Harper & Row, 1987.

Tracy, David. "Western Hermeneutics and Interreligious Dialogue." In *Interreligious Hermeneutics*, edited by C. Cornille and C. Conway, 1–43. Eugene: Wipf & Stock, 2010.

Volker, Fabian. "On All-Embracing Mental Structures." In *Interreligious Comparisons in Religious Studies and Theology*, edited by P. Schmidt-Leukel and A. Nehring, 142–62. London: Bloomsbury, 2016.

von Stosch, Klaus. "Comparative Theology and Comparative Religion." In *Interreligious Comparison in Religious Studies and Theology*, edited by P. Schmidt-Leukel and A. Nehring, 163–77. London: Bloomsbury, 2016.

von Stosch, Klaus. "Comparative Theology as Liberal and Confessional Theology." *Religions 3* (2012): 83–92.

von Stosch, Klaus. "Developing Christian Theodicy in Conversation with Navid Kermani." In *Comparing Faithfully*, edited by M. Voss Roberts, 89–106. New York: Fordham University Press, 2016.

von Stosch, Klaus. *Komparative Theologie als Wegweiser in der Welt der Religionen.* Paderborn: Ferdinand Schöningh, 2017.

Ward, Keith. *Religion and Community.* Oxford: Oxford University Press, 2000.

Ward, Keith. *Religion and Creation.* Oxford: Clarendon Press, 1996.

Ward, Keith. *Religion and Human Nature.* Oxford: Oxford University Press, 1999.

Ward, Keith. *Religion and Revelation: A Theology of Revelation in the World's Religions.* Oxford: Clarendon Press, 1994.

Wildman, Wesley. "Theology without Walls: The Future of Transreligious Theology." *Open Theology 2*, no. 1 (2016): 242–47.

Willis, Glenn. "On Some Suspicions Regarding Comparative Theology." In *How to Do Comparative Theology*, edited by F. Clooney and K. von Stosch, 122–36. New York: Fordham University Press, 2018.

Winkler, Ulrich. "Reasons for and Contexts of Deep Theological Engagement with Other Religious Traditions in Europe: Toward a Comparative Theology." *Religions 3* (2012): 1180–94.

Winkler, Ulrich, and Henry Jansen. *Shifting Locations and Reshaping Methods: Methodological Challenges Arising from New Fields of Research in Intercultural Theology and Interreligious Studies.* Berlin: LIT, 2018.

Wiren, Jacob. *Hope and Otherness: Christian Eschatology and Interreligious Hospitality.* Leiden: Brill, 2017.

Jewish-Christian Comparative Theology

Boyarin, Daniel. *Border Lines: The Partition of Judeo-Christianity.* Philadelphia: University of Pennsylvania Press, 2004.

Boys, Mary. "The Salutary Experience of Pushing Religious Boundaries: Abraham Joshua Heshel in Conversation with Michael Barnes." *Modern Judaism 29*, no. 1 (2009): 16–26.

Boys, Mary, ed. *Seeing Judaism Anew: Christianity's Sacred Obligation.* Lanham: Rowman & Littlefield, 2005.

Cunningham, Philip. *Seeking Shalom: The Journey to Right Relationship between Catholics and Jews.* Michigan: Eerdmans, 2015.

Cunningham, Philip, Joseph Sievers, Mary Boys, Hans Hermann Henrix, and Jesper Svartvik, *Christ Jesus and the Jewish People Today: New Explorations of Theological Interrelationships*. Grand Rapids: Eerdmans, 2011.

Elcott, David. "Meeting the Other: Judaism, Pluralism and Truth." In *Criteria of Discernment in Interreligious Dialogue*, edited by C. Cornille, 26–52. Eugene: Wipf & Stock, 2009.

Ford, David, and C. C. Pecknold, eds. *The Promise of Scriptural Reasoning*. Oxford: Blackwell, 2006.

Frymer-Kensky, Tikva, David Novak, Peter Ochs, David Fox Sandmel, and Michael Singer, eds. *Christianity in Jewish Terms*. Boulder: Westview, 2000.

Joslyn-Siemiatkoski, Daniel. "Comparative Theology and the Status of Judaism: Hegemony and Reversals." In *The New Comparative Theology*, edited by F. Clooney, 89–108. London: T&T Clark, 2010.

Joslyn-Siemiatkoski, Daniel. *The More Torah, the More Life: A Christian Commentary on Mishnah Avot*. Leuven: Peeters, 2018.

Langer, Ruth. *Cursing the Christians? A History of Birkat MaMinim*. Oxford: Oxford University Press, 2011.

Moyaert, Marianne. "Comparative Theology After the Shoah: Risks, Pivots and Opportunities of Comparing Traditions." In *How to Do Comparative Theology*, edited by F. Clooney and K. von Stosch, 164–87. New York: Fordham University Press, 2018.

Moyaert, Marianne. "Who Is the Suffering Servant? A Comparative Theological Reading of Isaiah 53 after the Shoah." In *Comparing Faithfully*, edited by M. Voss Roberts, 216–37. New York: Fordham University Press, 2016.

Moyaert, Marianne, and Didier Pollefeyt. *Never Revoked: Nostra Aetate as Ongoing Challenge for Jewish-Christian Dialogue*. Leuven: Peeters, 2010.

O'Donnell, Emma. *Remembering the Future: Experience of Time in Jewish and Christian Liturgies*. Collegeville: Liturgical Press, 2015.

Pollefeyt, Didier, ed. *Jews and Christians: Rivals or Partners for the Kingdom of God? In Search of an Alternative for the Theology of Substitution*. Leuven: Peeters, 1998.

Rottenberg, Isaac. "Comparative Theology versus Reactive Theology: Jewish and Christian Approaches to the Presence of God." *Pro Ecclesia 3*, no. 4 (1994): 411–18.

Muslim-Christian Comparative Theology

Burrell, David. *Freedom and Creation in Three Traditions*. Notre Dame: University of Notre Dame Press, 1993.

Burrell, David. *Learning to Trust in Freedom: Signs from Jewish, Christian, and Muslim Traditions*. Scranton: University of Scranton Press, 2010.

Burrell, David. *Towards a Jewish-Christian-Muslim Theology*. Oxford: Wiley-Blackwell, 2011.

D'Costa, Gavin. "Interreligious Prayer between Christians and Muslims." *Islam and Christian-Muslim Relations 24* (2013): 1–14.

Griffiths, Sidney. *The Church in the Shadow of the Mosque: Christians and Muslims in the World of Islam*. Princeton: Princeton University Press, 2010.

Griffiths, Sidney. "Mystics and Sufi Masters: Thomas Merton and Dialogue between Christians and Muslims." *Islam and Christian-Muslim Relations* 15 (2004): 299–316.

Kaltner, John, and Younus Mirza. *The Bible and the Qur'an: Biblical Figures in the Islamic Tradition*. London: T&T Clark, 2018.

Krokus, Christian. *The Theology of Louis Massignon: Islam, Christ and the Church*. Washington: CUA Press, 2017.

Laksana, Albertus Bagus. *Muslim and Catholic Pilgrimage Practice: Explorations through Java*. Farnham: Ashgate, 2014.

Leirvik, Oddbjørn. *Human Conscience and Muslim-Christian Relations: Modern Egyptian Thinkers on Al-Damir*. London: Routledge, 2007.

Leirvik, Oddbjørn. *Images of Jesus Christ in Islam*. London: Bloomsbury, 2010.

Madigan, Daniel. "God's Word to the World: Jesus and the Qur'an, Incarnation and Recitation." In *"Godhead Here in Hiding": Incarnation and the History of Human Suffering*, edited by T. Merrigan and F. Glorieux, 143–58. Leuven: Peeters, 2012.

Madigan, Daniel. "People of the Word: Reading John's Prologue with a Muslim." *Review and Expositor 104*, no. 1 (2007): 81–95.

Marshall, David. "Mohammad in Contemporary Christian Theological Reflection." *Islam and Christian-Muslim Relations* 16 (2013): 161–72.

Renard, John. *Islam and Christianity: Theological Themes in Comparative Perspective*. Berkeley: University of California Press, 2011.

Schillinger, Jamie. "Intellectual Humility and Interreligious Dialogue between Christians and Muslims." *Islam and Christian-Muslim Relations* 23 (2012): 363–80.

Smith, Jane. *Muslims, Christians and the Challenge of Interfaith Dialogue*. Oxford: Oxford University Press, 2007.

Troll, Christian. *Dialogue and Difference: Clarity in Christian-Muslim Relations*. Maryknoll: Orbis Books, 2009.

Valkenberg, Wilhelmus. *Renewing Islam by Service: A Christian View of Fetullah Gulen and the Hizmet Movement*. Washington: CUA Press, 2015.

Valkenberg, Wilhelmus. *Sharing Lights on the Way to God: Muslim-Christian Dialogue and Theology in the Context of Abrahamic Partnership*. Amsterdam: Rodopi, 2006.

Volf, Miroslav, ed. *Do We Worship the Same God? Jews, Christians and Muslims in Dialogue*. Grand Rapids: Eerdmans, 2012.

von Stosch, Klaus. *Herausforderung Islam: Christliche Annäherungen*. Paderborn: Ferdinand Schöningh, 2016.

von Stosch, Klaus. "Reflecting on Approaches to Jesus in the Qur'an from the Perspective of Comparative Theology." In *How to Do Comparative Theology*, edited by F. Clooney and K. von Stosch, 37–58. New York: Fordham University Press, 2018.

Winkler, Ulrich, ed. *Comparative Theology: Special Issue of Frankfurter Zeitschrift für Islamisch-Theologische Studien*. Berlin: EB-Verlag, 2017.

Wright, Thomas. *No Peace without Prayer: Encouraging Muslims and Christians to Pray Together.* Collegeville: Liturgical Press, 2013.

Hindu-Christian Comparative Theology

Abhishiktānanda. *La montée au fond du coeur. Le journal intime du moine chrétien-sannyasi hindou, 1948–1973.* Paris: OEIL, 1986.

Abhishiktānanda. *Saccidānanda.* London: ISPCK, 1974.

Bloechl, Jeffrey, and Catherine Cornille. *Christian Identity between Secularity and Plurality.* Bangalore: Dharmaram, 2015.

Clooney, Francis. *Beyond Compare: St. Francis de Sales and Śrī Vedānta Deśika on Loving Surrender to God.* Washington: Georgetown University Press, 2008.

Clooney, Francis. *Divine Mother, Blessed Mother: Hindu Goddesses and the Virgin Mary.* Oxford: Oxford University Press, 2005.

Clooney, Francis. *The Future of Hindu-Christian Studies: A Theological Inquiry.* London: Routledge, 2017.

Clooney, Francis. *Hindu God, Christian God: How Reason Helps Break Down the Boundaries between Religions.* Oxford: Oxford University Press, 2001.

Clooney, Francis. *His Hiding Place Is Darkness: A Hindu-Catholic Theopoetics of Divine Absence.* Stanford: Stanford University Press, 2014.

Clooney, Francis. *Seeing through Texts: Doing Theology among the Śrīvaiṣṇavas of South India.* Albany: SUNY Press, 1996.

Clooney, Francis. *Theology after Vedānta: An Experiment in Comparative Theology.* Albany: SUNY Press, 1993.

Clooney, Francis. *The Truth, the Way, the Life: Christian Commentary on the Three Holy Mantras of the Śrīvaiṣṇava Hindus.* Leuven: Peeters, 2008.

Conway, Christopher. "Liberative Service: A Comparative Theological Reflection on Dalit Theology's Service and Swami Vivekananda's Seva." Dissertation, Boston College, 2014.

Cornille, Catherine. "Discipleship in Hindu-Christian Comparative Theology." *Theological Studies 77*, no. 4 (2016): 869–85.

Cornille, Catherine. *The Guru in Indian Catholicism: Ambiguity or Opportunity of Inculturation?* Leuven: Peeters, 1991.

Cornille, Catherine, ed. *Song Divine: Christian Commentaries on the Bhagavad Gītā.* Leuven: Peeters, 2006.

D'Costa, Gavin. "Roman Catholic Reflections on Discerning God in Interreligious Dialogue: Challenges and Promising Avenues." In *Criteria of Discernment in Interreligious Dialogue,* edited by C. Cornille, 69–86. Eugene: Wipf & Stock, 2009.

Dubois, J. A. *Hindu Manners, Customs and Ceremonies.* Oxford: Clarendon Press, 1906.

Flood, Gavin. "Reading Christian Detachment through the Bhagavad Gītā." In *Song Divine: Christian Commentaries on the Bhagavad Gītā,* edited by C. Cornille, 9–22. Leuven: Peeters, 2007.

Ganeri, Martin. *Indian Thought and Western Theism: The Vedānta of Rāmānuja.* London: Routledge, 2015.

Grant, Sara. *Toward an Alternative Theology: Confessions of a Non-Dualist Christian.* Notre Dame: University of Notre Dame Press, 2002.

Griffiths, Bede. *The Marriage of East and West.* Springfield: Templegate, 1982.

Henri Le Saux, swami Abhishiktananda, Souvenirs d'Arunachala. Recit d'un ermite chretien en terre hindoue. Paris: Epi, 1978.

Hillgardner, Holly. "Longing and Letting Go: Lessons in Being Human from Hadewijch and Mirabai." In *Comparing Faithfully,* edited by M. Voss Roberts, 149–70. New York: Fordham University Press, 2016.

Johanns, Pierre. *To Christ through Vedānta.* Bangalore: United Theological College, 1996 (originally published 1929).

Locklin, Reid. *Liturgy of Liberation: A Christian Commentary on Shankara's Upadeśasāhasrī.* Leuven: Peeters, 2011.

Long, Jeffery. "Like a Dog's Curly Tail: Finding Perfection in a World of Imperfection." In *Comparing Faithfully,* edited by M. Voss Roberts, 107–25. New York: Fordham University Press, 2016.

Otto, Rudolf. *Mysticism East and West.* New York: Collier Books, 1962.

Panikkar, Raimon. *Christophany: The Fullness of Man.* Maryknoll: Orbis Books, 2004.

Panikkar, Raimon. *The Cosmotheandric Experience.* Maryknoll: Orbis Books, 1993.

Panikkar, Raimon. *The Rhythm of Being.* Maryknoll: Orbis Books, 2013.

Panikkar, Raimundo (Raimon). *The Unknown Christ of Hinduism.* Maryknoll: Orbis Books, 1981.

Ranstrom, Erik, and Bob Robinson. *"Without Ceasing to Be a Christian": A Catholic and Protestant Assess the Christological Contribution of Raimon Panikkar.* Minneapolis: Fortress Press, 2017.

Sahi, Jyoti. "Yoga and the Wounded Heart." In *Traversing the Heart: Journeys in the Interreligious Imagination,* edited by R. Kearney and E. Rizo-Patron, 43–80. Leiden: Brill, 2010.

Sheridan, Daniel. *Loving God: Kṛṣṇa and Christ: A Christian Commentary on the Nārada Sūtras.* Leuven: Peeters, 2007.

Sydnor, Jon Paul. *Rāmānuja and Schleiermacher: Toward a Constructive Comparative Theology.* Eugene: Wipf & Stock, 2011.

Tangaraj, Thomas. *The Crucified Guru: An Experiment in Cross-Cultural Christology.* Nashville: Abingdon Press, 1994.

Thatamanil, John. *The Immanent Divine: God, Creation, and the Human Predicament.* Minneapolis: Fortress Press, 2006.

Tiemeier, Tracy. "Women's Virtue, Church Leadership and the Problem of Gender Complementarity." In *Comparing Faithfully,* edited by M. Voss Roberts, 171–84. New York: Fordham University Press, 2016.

Voss Roberts, Michelle. *Body Parts: A Theological Anthropology.* Minneapolis: Fortress Press, 2017.

Voss Roberts, Michelle. *Dualities: A Theology of Difference.* Louisville: Westminster John Knox Press, 2010.

Voss Roberts, Michelle. *Tastes of the Divine: Hindu and Christian Theologies of Emotion*. New York: Fordham University Press, 2014.

Zaehner, R. C. *Mysticism, Sacred and Profane*. Oxford: Oxford University Press, 1957.

Buddhist-Christian Comparative Theology

Abe, Masao. "Buddhism and Christianity as a Problem of Today," parts 1 and 2. *Japanese Religions 3*, nos. 2 and 3 (1963): 11–22, 8–31.

Abe, Masao. "Kenotic God and Dynamic Śūnyatā." In *The Emptying God: A Buddhist-Jewish-Christian Conversation*, edited by J. Cobb and C. Ives, 3–68. Maryknoll: Orbis Books, 1990.

Clairmont, David. *Moral Struggle and Religious Ethics: On the Person as Classic in Comparative Theological Contexts*. Oxford: Wiley-Blackwell, 2011.

Cobb, John. *Beyond Dialogue: Toward a Mutual Transformation of Christianity and Buddhism*. Philadelphia: Fortress Press, 1982.

Cobb, John, and Ives Christopher, eds. *The Emptying God: A Buddhist-Jewish-Christian Conversation*. Maryknoll: Orbis Books, 1990.

Cornille, Catherine. "Strategies of Negotiation in Buddhist-Christian Dual Belonging." In *Buddhist-Christian Dual Belonging: Affirmations, Objections, Explorations*, edited by G. D'Costa and R. Thompson, 143–60. Farnham: Ashgate, 2016.

D'Arcy May, John, ed. *Converging Ways? Conversion and Belonging in Buddhism and Christianity*. Sankt Ottilien: EOS, 2007.

Drew, Rose. *Buddhist and Christian? An Exploration of Dual Belonging*. London: Routledge, 2011.

Fredericks, James. *Buddhist and Christians: Through Comparative Theology to Solidarity*. Maryknoll: Orbis Books, 2004.

Fredericks, James. *Faith among Faiths: Christian Theology and Non-Christian Religions*. New York: Paulist Press, 1999.

Griffiths, Paul. *An Apology for Apologetics: A Study in the Logic of Interreligious Dialogue*. Maryknoll: Orbis Books, 1991

Heim, Mark. *Crucified Wisdom: Theological Reflection on Christ and the Bodhisattva*. New York: Fordham University Press, 2018.

Heisig, James. *Nothingness and Desire: An East-West Philosophical Antiphony*. Honolulu: University of Hawai'i Press, 2013.

Ingram, Paul. *The Process of Buddhist-Christian Dialogue*. Cambridge: James Clarke, 2011.

Keenan, John. *The Emptied Christ of Philippians*. Eugene: Wipf & Stock, 2015.

Keenan, John. *The Gospel of Mark: A Mahāyāna Reading*. Maryknoll: Orbis Books, 1995.

Keenan, John. "A Mahayana Theology of the Real Presence of Christ in the Eucharist." *Buddhist-Christian Studies 24* (2004): 89–100.

Keenan, John. *The Meaning of Christ*. Maryknoll: Orbis Books, 1989.

Keenan, John, and Linda Keenan. *I Am / No Self: A Christian Commentary on the Heart Sutra*. Leuven: Peeters, 2012.

Knitter, Paul. "Comparative Theology Is Not 'Business-as-Usual Theology': Personal Witness from a Buddhist Christian." *Buddhist-Christian Studies 35* (2015): 185–91.

Knitter, Paul. *Without Buddha I Could Not Be a Christian*. Oxford: Oneworld, 2009.

Lefebure, Leo. *True and Holy: Christian Scripture and Other Religions*. Maryknoll: Orbis Books, 2014.

Lefebure, Leo, and Peter Feldmeier. *The Path of Wisdom: A Christian Commentary on the Dhammapada*. Leuven: Peeters, 2011.

Main, John. *Word into Silence: A Manual for Christian Meditation*, edited by L. Freeman. Norwich: Canterbury Press, 2006.

Makransky, John. "A Buddhist Critique of, and Learning from Christian Liberation Theology." *Theological Studies 75* (2014): 635–57.

Makransky, John. "Thoughts on Why, How, and What Buddhists Can Learn from Christian Theologians." *Journal of Buddhist-Christian Studies 31* (2011): 119–33.

Merton, Thomas. *The Asian Journals of Thomas Merton*. New York: New Directions, 1975.

Mommaers, Paul, and Jan Van Bragt. *Mysticism, Buddhist and Christian*. New York: Crossroad, 1995.

O'Leary, Joseph. *Buddhist Nonduality, Paschal Paradox: A Christian Commentary on The Teaching of Vimalakīrti (Vimalakīrtinirdeśa)*. Leuven: Peeters, 2018.

O'Leary, Joseph. *Conventional and Ultimate Truth: A Key for Fundamental Theology*. South Bend: Universityof Notre Dame Press, 2015.

O'Leary, Joseph. "Skillful Means as a Hermeneutic Concept." In *Interreligious Hermeneutics*, edited by C. Cornille and C. Conway, 163–83. Eugene: Wipf & Stock, 2010.

Pieris, Aloysius. *Love Meets Wisdom: A Christian Experience of Buddhism*. Maryknoll: Orbis Books, 1988.

Pomplun, Trent. *Jesuit on the Roof of the World: Ippolito Desideri's Mission to Eighteenth-Century Tibet*. New York: Oxford University Press, 2010.

Schmidt-Leukel, Perry. "Christ as Bodhisattva: A Case of Reciprocal Illumination." In *Interreligious Comparisons in Religious Studies and Theology*, edited by P. Schmidt-Leukel and A. Nehring, 204–19. London: Bloomsbury, 2016.

Schmidt-Leukel, Perry. *Transformation by Integration: How Inter-Faith Encounter Changes Christianity*. London: SCM Press, 2009.

Senécal, Bernard. *Jésus le Christ à la rencontre de Gautama le Bouddha*. Paris: Cerf, 1998.

Simmer-Brown, Judith. "'Without Bias' – The Dalai Lama in Dialogue." In *Criteria of Discernment in Interreligious Dialogue*, edited by C. Cornille, 231–54. Eugene: Wipf & Stock, 2009.

Van Bragt, Jan. *Interreligious Affinities*, edited by J. Heisig and K. Seung Chul. Nagoya: Nanzan Institute for Religion and Culture, 2014.

Vroom, Annewieke. "God of Leegte? Zenboeddhist Masao Abe in Dialoog met Christelijke Denkers." Doctoral dissertation for the VU Amsterdam, 2014.

Williams, Paul. *The Unexpected Way: On Converting from Buddhism to Catholicism*. London: T&T Clark, 2002.

Index

Meaning and Method in Comparative Theology, First Edition. Catherine Cornille.
© 2020 John Wiley & Sons Ltd. Published 2020 by John Wiley & Sons Ltd.